D1473995

●

CONVERSATIONS

VOLUME 1

Jorge Luis Borges
Osvaldo Ferrari

●

CONVERSATIONS

VOLUME 1

Translated by Jason Wilson

LONDON NEW YORK CALCUTTA

Seagull Books, 2014

First published as *En Dialogo I* by Editorial Sudamericana in 1998/1999
© Osvaldo Ferrari, 1986 (for *En Dialogo I*)
by arrangement with Paterson Marsh Ltd.

English translation © Jason Wilson, 2014

ISBN 978 0 8574 2 188 3

British Library Cataloguing-in-Publication Data

A catalogue record for this book is available from the British Library

Typeset by Seagull Books, Calcutta, India

Printed and bound by Maple Press, York, Pennsylvania, USA

CONTENTS

Jorge Luis Borges

The best event recorded in universal history happened in Ancient Greece some 500 years before the Christian era, namely, the discovery of dialogue. Faith, certainty, dogmas, anathemas, prayers, prohibitions, orders, taboos, tyrannies, wars and glory overwhelmed the world while some Greeks acquired the peculiar habit of conversation—how, we'll never know. They doubted, persuaded, dissented, changed their minds, postponed. Perhaps their mythology helped them, which was, as with Shinto, an accumulation of vague fables and variable cosmogonies. These scattered conjectures were the first root of what we call today, perhaps pretentiously, metaphysics. Western culture is inconceivable without these few conversing Greeks. Remote in space and time, this volume is a muffled echo of those ancient conversations.

As with all my books, perhaps with all books, this one wrote itself. Ferrari and I tried to let our words flow through us, perhaps despite ourselves. We never talked with any end in view. Those who have read the manuscript assure us that the experience was pleasing. I hope our readers will not refute that generous opinion. In the prologue to one of his 'dreams' Francisco de Quevedo wrote: 'May God free you, reader, from long prologues and weak adjectives.'

12 October 1985

PROLOGUE

Osvaldo Ferrari

In this edition I will try to reflect on what stimulated our dialogues and gave them direction.

Our first public dialogue was held in March 1984. On listening to it on Radio Municipal, the radio station memorably run by our common friend Ricardo Costantino, a door seemed to open onto immensity, for me and for our listeners. Borges' spoken words contained the same extraordinary tone of his writing as well as the surprising and constantly marvellous nature of his originality.

In an attempt to explain this I came up with the notion, then, of a new dimension. A dialogue with Borges was an incursion into literature itself, a connection with the spirit of literariness that had so permeated him that it became the key to his fascinating intelligence—that literary intelligence that discovers a world and describes a new reality.

Borges' exquisite and unique reading of reality was completely spontaneous. We would observe its diversity through his eyes as, at the age of 84, he conveyed his universe. The dialogues, prompted by any topic, recorded that universe with Borges instantly combining memory, lucidity and verbal concision.

It was enough to name a favourite writer or work and he would expand on it immediately, proposing a novel understanding, a new interpretation of the man and the book. It was enough to cite a philosophy that he was attuned to or a religion he was interested in and he would elaborate upon an entirely unique and extremely personal vision. It was enough to remind him of journeys that he had undertaken or countries that he had known and he would offer us a detailed account of its literature and his impressions of its culture.

In this way, Borges, who had once pointed out to me that a dialogue was an indirect way of writing, continued to write through these conversations. When they were transcribed for publication, it was self-evident that Borges, through our talks, was prolonging his life as a writer. Thus, the magic of listening to him corresponded with the magic of reading him.

In this way we come to recognize, and perhaps understand, the man, the writer and the literary spirit. Those who had known his written work could now get to know their author and his thoughts during that act of creation. For Borges, reality was literature. And who better than he to convey his literary record of reality. It should also be noted that because he only recognized fantastic literature, and not realist writing, so too reality only revealed its coherence through his literary perspective. In other words, Borges explains literature and literature explains Borges.

From his literary universe, he launched into trying to answer the questions I put to him. If he touched on philosophy, mysticism or politics, it was always through literature, because that's where his genius lay and that's what he had been born to do. That was his destiny.

Unlike those writers who, in Borges' opinion, shone through their dialogues even more than through their writing, such as Pedro Henríquez Ureña, Cansinos Assens or Macedonio Fernández, Borges himself spoke as beautifully as he wrote and constantly revealed his astounding literary dimension through his conversations. In his own words, 'What we say is being recorded, so in that sense it's oral and written at the same time. While we speak, we are writing.' And he added, 'I do not know if I will ever write an essay again in my life, surely not, or I would do so in an indirect manner, like the two of us are doing now.'

Hence the dialogue became the best medium through which the older Borges, speaking to a man 50 years younger, could express himself, could share his literary thinking—and, at that stage of his life, his mystical thinking—with his listeners.

In these conversations, he switched from humour to scepticism, and its opposite, hope. We'll see that 'he laughs' or that 'both laugh' are inserted in the text in the ensuing conversations.

'Conrad, Melville and the Sea' is the title of one of these conversations. 'The East, *I Ching* and Buddhism' is another. 'The Geographic and Intimate South', a third. 'Scandinavian Mythology and

Anglo-Saxon Epic', 'On Love', 'On Conjecture' are the titles of others, those which form a part of the 45 conversations collected in this volume. In each of them we sense Borges' mind. They allow us a deep encounter with him and with literature, for that is what he dedicated his life to.

April 1998

1

Argentinian Identity

●

OSVALDO FERRARI. For a while now, your idea of a possible Argentinian identity has interested me greatly because, according to this idea, our identity is still developing. You have said that we Argentines, having a limited history but hailing from a vast European history, embody a new possibility of being. That we are both what we want to be and what we can be.

JORGE LUIS BORGES. Yes, indeed. I believe that our being Europeans in exile is an advantage—it means that we are not tied to any local tradition. It means that we can inherit, in fact we do inherit, the Western tradition. And by Western I mean the Eastern too, for what we call Western culture is, simply, one half Greece and the other half Israel. So we are Easterners too. Indeed, we should try to be all that we can. Free of the ties of tradition, we receive a vast inheritance. And we must try and enrich it and continue it in our own way. In my case, I have tried to know all the possibilities. But, of course, given that the world is infinite, what an individual can know is only a particle. I sometimes think that literature is like an infinite library, like the library of Babel in one of my stories, and from that vast library each individual can read only a few pages. But perhaps in those pages they can discover what's essential. Perhaps literature is always repeating the same things in a slightly different tone. In any case, I think that my duty as a writer is not to discover new themes nor to invent anything—as a writer my duty is to repeat, in the dialect of my country and my era, certain poems that are always being repeated, with slight variations that might or might not be lovely.

FERRARI. I see. Now, I must not forget to ask you this. Octavio Paz has said that your Europeanism is very American, that it is one of the ways we Spanish Americans have of being ourselves or of inventing ourselves. What do you think of that?

BORGES. It's a witty remark and it could be true, given that, on this continent especially, our destiny is more our future destiny than our past one. I'd say the same applies to the North Americans. The fact is that spoken languages are also traditions. What are they? Spanish, Portuguese, English—these were obviously not invented by the redskins or the Incas or the Pampas Indians.

FERRARI. Naturally. Paz adds that our Europeanism is neither rootlessness nor a return to the past but an attempt to create a temporal space in conflict with a timeless one, and thus, he says, an attempt to embody it.

BORGES. It's an attractive idea and I think it's true. I certainly feel so. I feel that I am a European in exile but I also feel that exile allows me to be more European than those born in Europe. I don't even know if anyone is born in Europe—rather, people are born in England, in Italy, in Spain, in Norway, in Iceland. But in Europe? Europe is a vast concept. We, on the other hand, can feel all the diverse inheritances, we can forget political limits, the frontiers between one country and another. Which is why we should try to be deserving of that vast and extremely rich continent inherited in some way or other. Precisely because we have not been born in it but in another one.

FERRARI. Amazing! So it really is an enriching possibility of being?

BORGES. Yes, I think it is and I think that Emerson thought the same way. In the piece he wrote in *American Scholar*, he was certainly not alluding to the redskins but to the whole tradition that is today called Western.

FERRARI. There was a literary movement called Modernismo in America that was perhaps the first to recognize European components in our formation.

BORGES. Well, that movement arose—and this is very significant—on this side of the Atlantic, not on that. That is, Rubén Darío, Ricrado Jaimes Freyre and Leopoldo Lugones came before the great Spanish poets and inspired them from across the sea. I recall Juan Ramón Jiménez, the great Andalusian poet, telling me about his excitement at holding the first edition of Lugones' *Las montañas de oro* (Mountains of Gold) in his hands. In 1897, two years before my birth. He received that book . . . he was dazzled by that book that came from a city he only knew by name—Buenos Aires. Well, we know how much was done with Modernismo in Spain. Everything was renovated—themes, metrics, everything. Obviously, in the shadows of Victor Hugo and Paul Verlaine. It's odd—the Spaniards were further away from France than we were for historical reasons I need not go into but the French poetry of the nineteenth century was revealed to them through America. And, above all, by Darío.

FERRARI. That time, America renewed Europe.

BORGES. Yes. I have talked to Lugones five or six times—he was a rather sad man who found conversation difficult. Or, rather, conversation was impossible with him—and each of those times he changed the conversation to talk, in the Cordoba lilt he retained, of 'my friend and master Rubén Darío'. Of course, Darío was well loved by all whereas Lugones was admired and respected but not loved which must have made him sad.

FERRARI. I think that while your memory and imagination transcend Argentina and soar to different latitudes—the history and mythology of other countries and races—the style in which you narrate your stories is a particularly sober one, peculiar to the Argentinian spirit.

BORGES. Yes, I'd say that the difference, or one of the differences, between the Spanish of Spain and the Spanish of Buenos Aires or Montevideo is that Spaniards tend to use interjections, exclamations. We speak, say things, explain, but we do not agree or disagree like the Spaniards. Spanish conversation is full of interjections. Ours is not—ours is a conversation in a more lowered voice.

FERRARI. Adolfo Bioy Casares said that the plain way in which the people of our country speak had taught him to respect language far more. He had found . . .

BORGES. I didn't know that but it must be right, yes. Another thing I've observed is that a citizen of this country is able to use irony. This, to my knowledge, is not common elsewhere. A citizen of this country is quite capable of using irony and what is referred to in English as understatement, the opposite of Spanish hyperbole.

FERRARI. To infer?

BORGES. Yes, to infer.

FERRARI. Taking this thought further, it seems important to me to speak about the Argentinian tendency towards universality that I think exists in the mind.

BORGES. Well, in Buenos Aires, it is natural for this to exist—one half of our population is Italian and the other half Spanish. In any case, this country, without a doubt, has the great advantage of being both middle class and cosmopolitan.

FERRARI. I would like you to recall another person who participated in the Modernismo movement.

BORGES. Yes, the great Bolivian poet Freyre, a teacher in Tucumán. Freyre has left us one poem that means absolutely nothing and that set out to propose absolutely nothing—something quite unforgettable. I can reconstruct the first stanza:

> Wandering imaginary dove
> Which lights up the last lovers,
> Soul of light, music and flowers,
> Wandering imaginary dove.

It means nothing. I don't know if it suggests anything but it is still perfect to me.

FERRARI. It sounds lovely to me too.

BORGES. Yes, it is lovely, his best poem. He also wrote a history of Spanish versification, quoted by Lugones in the prologue to his memorable *Lunario sentimental*. There, Freyre observes that the octosyllabic line, seeming to be so natural, hesitates and trips up in the first ballads, an almost scandalous novelty for Spanish men of letters— for Cristóbal del Castillejo, for example. The hendecasyllable, however, now seems natural, it flows and everyone hears it flow. Except, I get the feeling that we are losing this sense of hearing, that we do not hear lines, not even the octosyllables, in our local ballads.

FERRARI. I would answer you with a yes and a no. There is a slight loss of hearing but it's not complete.

BORGES. Well, that's good news you have just given me (*both laugh*).

FERRARI. We have to stop, Borges, until next week.

BORGES. Well, it was nice that you gave me the chance to recall Freyre, so unjustly forgotten, as you have discovered yourself with those four incomparable lines of his poem.

FERRARI. Yes, unjustly forgotten.

2

The Eternal Traveller

●

OSVALDO FERRARI. Borges, I would like you to explain to me, I'm sure our listeners would too, before your second journey to Japan and Italy and Greece, what it is that determines that excellent facility of yours for travel, which, by the way, seems to have grown lately.

JORGE LUIS BORGES. One reason would be my blindness, my feeling countries without being able to see them. If I stay in Buenos Aires, my life will be . . . insignificant. I will always be inventing fables, dictating. On the other hand, if I travel, I will be acquiring new impressions. Impressions which will, in the end, turn into literature. Though I'm not sure if it's an advantage, I persevere, accepting and giving thanks for what happens. I think that if I really were a poet—obviously, I'm not one—I would feel every instant of life as poetic. It's a mistake to suppose that there are, for example, poetic themes or poetic moments. Any theme can be poetic. Walt Whitman already proved, as did Gómez de la Serna in his own way, that everyday life can be poetic. There's a saying: 'Reality is stranger than fiction.' G. K. Chesterton comments on this justly and wittily when he says, 'For we have made fiction to suit ourselves, on the other hand reality is far stranger because another has made it, the Other, God.' Thus, reality must be stranger . . .

And now that I've said that bit about the Other, I recall the first section of *La Divina Commedia* . . . obviously, the first part is 'Inferno' where God's name is not allowed and so they call him the Other. 'As the Other wanted,' says Ulysses. Because God's name cannot be pronounced in Hell, Dante invented that delightful synonym—'the Other', which is terrible, isn't it? because it means that we are very far from the Other, that we are not the Other. That's why, in *La Divina Commedia*, God's name occurs . . . well, perhaps in Purgatory because there they are in the fire that purifies them, and in Heaven, but not in Hell. There, the Other is used, usually printed with a capital 'O' to leave no room for doubt.

FERRARI. That's true! Now, returning to this particular trip, what are your intentions, your plans?

BORGES. Well, one of the good excuses is the generous, undeserved doctorate that I will be awarded by Palermo University in Sicily which I hope will help me to know the south of Italy. I know the admirable north, I know Rome clearly, I could even say, like all Westerners, 'civis romanus sum'—I am a citizen of Rome. But now I will know the South, Greater Greece. You could say that the West began to think in Greater Greece—in part of Asia Minor and the south of Italy. Philosophy began in the outskirts of Greece, and we have tried to continue thinking since. And then the south of Italy which means more great names. It means Giambattista Vico, for example, so quoted by James Joyce for his theory of historical cycles. And the person who has best written on aesthetics—Benedetto Croce. And Giambattista Marino, perhaps the greatest baroque poet, Luis de Gongóra's master.

You see, I have so many memories about the south of Italy. I have always wanted to get to know it but haven't been able to, like so many other things . . . I won't say that the universe is vast but that the planet certainly is, and what a man can see is very limited. Whenever people tell me that I have read so much, I think to myself, 'No, I haven't.' If you imagine all the libraries in the world, or even one—let's say the National Library on México Street. What has one read? A few pages. Of all that's written, one has read a few pages and no more. So also concerning the world—one has had only a few visions. But perhaps it's worth a thought that in these are all the others—that, platonically, one has seen everything, read every book. Even those written in unknown languages. That's why it is said that all books are but one. So many times I have thought to myself that the themes of literature are few and all that each generation does is search for slight variations in order to rewrite in the dialect of its time that which has already been written. There are, ultimately, only small differences. Though these small differences are very, very important, as is natural, for us.

So, I am going to receive this very honourable doctorate in Palermo and, later, a no less honourable and perhaps rarer one from a new Greek university—the University of Crete. I know Crete but

I never thought that I'd be awarded a Cretan doctorate which will draw me closer in some way—well, I needn't spell it out—to the labyrinth (*laughs*). I think Doménikos Theotokópoulos, El Greco, was Cretan too, wasn't he?

Then I have to attend a congress in Japan and, in June, I think I am to be awarded a doctorate from one of the oldest universities in the world and one of the most famous—Cambridge. I am already a doctor honoris causa from Oxford, its rival. Now I will have doctorates from both.

If we recall, the first universities in Europe were Italian. The first, I think, was Bologna, then the English ones, then the French ones and finally the German, in Heidelberg.

FERRARI. It seems that the Italians, in particular, have absorbed your work for quite some time now.

BORGES. Yes, though to say that it has so pleased them could indicate that they haven't read any of it (*laughs*). I do think that they appreciate me despite having read my work and that continues to astound me. Yes, Italy has been very generous with me. I do not consider that I have personal enemies . . . Perhaps when one is 84, one is, in some ways, already posthumous . . . One can be liked without greater risks, without irritations—don't you think? That could possibly be one of the ways of being old.

FERRARI. The Japanese also seem to have a certain liking for our cultural expressions. Our music, for example.

BORGES. Yes, for tango. When I told them that tango was almost forgotten in Buenos Aires, that people listened more to rock, they felt outraged, although they like rock too, of course. The Japanese mind is very hospitable and you can see how admirably they have adopted Western culture without renouncing their own. And I think that the United States, England and Germany are quite alarmed by how Japanese industry has progressed. They make everything better, and have an aesthetic sense too. A Japanese tape-recorder, a Japanese telescope, a Japanese shaver are certainly lighter and more elegant . . . and I haven't even mentioned cameras or cars. They even make computers better.

FERRARI. Casares gave me an attractive Japanese book as a present—your *Cuentos breves y extraordinarios* (Brief and Extraordinary Tales), co-authored with him and published in Japan in 1976.

BORGES. I didn't know that—I have heard nothing about it. Yes, we did compile that book around that time but my dates are very vague. The fact is that I am losing my memory. I try and hold on to what's best—the experiences of the books that I have read but not the ones I have written. My memory is packed with lines from poems in many languages. I have never tried to learn a poem by heart but those I love have remained, still remain. I could recite lines in many languages, even Anglo-Saxon. I retain many lines from Latin too though I don't know if I scan them properly—perhaps I mistake the number of syllables.

In the end, I remember more of what I have read than what has happened to me. But, of course, one of the most important things that can happen to a man is to read a page that moves him, a very intense experience. Michel de Montaigne described reading as a languid pleasure but I think he was wrong. In my case, it isn't languid but intense. I guess that was his implication too. If one reads Montaigne's essays, one finds the pages full of Latin quotations, quotations that have to be translated now because Latin, sadly, is a dead language. At one time, though, it was the language of educated Europe. One of my grandfathers, Dr Haslam, couldn't afford to go to Oxford or Cambridge so he went to Heidelberg. Five years later he returned with a degree in Philosophy and Literature but without a word of German—he'd passed all his exams in Latin! A very British Latin, no doubt, but sufficient for those exams. Today, I doubt you'd find a teacher able to sit for those exams; in those days, that wasn't the case. My friend Néstor Ibarra told me that in his house he was forced to speak Latin at lunch and dinner. All the conversation had to be in Latin which I think was a good thing.

FERRARI. In Buenos Aires?

BORGES. Yes, in Buenos Aires. And Montaigne, I think, had a German tutor who taught him Greek and Latin but not German. It was considered a barbarian's idiom then. So he got used to speaking those languages.

FERRARI. You know that there are writers who claim that travel is a great distraction, something that leads to a lack of concentration, a violent irruption in their lives and in their writing which they must then struggle to repair through their work?

BORGES. Not for me. I return enriched by my travels—not impoverished and even less distorted.

FERRARI. They affect you positively?

BORGES. I am so chaotic that I cannot be any more disordered. I begin by being disordered, that's chaos. How amazing that the word 'cosmetic' has its origin in cosmos. The cosmos is the great order of the world and cosmetic the lesser order that a person imposes on his face. It's the same root—cosmos, order.

FERRARI. In that case, there may be a cosmic or ordered possibility to your travels?

BORGES. I hope so . . . it would be very sad to travel in vain. It's most attractive when you wake up. When you wake up and don't know where you are. Then you think, 'I am in Nara, Japan's ancient capital, nearby is the great image of Buddha . . .' That is very pleasing, even if I cannot *see* it for obvious reasons. Being able to say such a thing to oneself in such a place, in a romantic place full of suggestions, as Japan is to me . . . that to me is the most important thing. I know the two Eastern extremes, I know Egypt and I know Japan. I would love to know China and India (and hope to do so one day) as well as Persia though today Iran is more difficult. I think I would like to know the whole world.

3

Order and Time

●

OSVALDO FERRARI. Borges, after having placed the foundation stone, after having inaugurated, as you said, our series of radio talks, we are now being irreversibly circulated along mysterious radio waves. What's your opinion?

JORGE LUIS BORGES. Dialogue is one of man's best habits, invented, like almost everything else, by the Greeks. The Greeks began to hold conversations and we have been following them since.

FERRARI. This week I noticed that if you have started a journey through literature towards a vast knowledge of the world, or perhaps if literature has started a journey through you, then I too have embarked on a journey towards an equally vast world in my attempt to get to know Borges in a way that everyone may better know him.

BORGES. Well, 'Know thyself', et cetera, et cetera, as Socrates said, countering Pythagoras who was boasting about his travels. Socrates said, 'Know thyself', that is, it's the idea of an inner journey, not a touristic one which I also undertake, of course. You must not scorn geography—perhaps it's no less important than psychology.

FERRARI. Of course. One of my impressions as I get to know your work and you is that there is an order to which you remain rigorously faithful.

BORGES. I would like to know what it is (*laughs*).

FERRARI. An order that rules your writing and your actions.

BORGES. My actions? I don't know. The truth is that I have acted irresponsibly. You may say that what I write is no less irresponsible but I want it to be that way. In life, I try to be an ethical person though I may give the impression of living in almost any old way. My life is casual enough but I try to ensure that my writing is not. I try to express something from the cosmos, even if it is essentially chaotic. As may be the case with the universe, of course, for we do not know if it is cosmos or chaos. Though many things point to it being a cosmos—we have the diverse ages of man, the habits of the stars, the growth of plants, the seasons, the diverse generations. There is a certain kind of order but an order somewhat shy, somewhat secretive.

FERRARI. Certainly. But to somehow identify with a semblance of your order, it seems to me to be what Eduardo Mallea described as severe meaning or 'a severe exaltation of life' that is characteristic of the Argentinian man.

BORGES. I wish it were.

FERRARI. We could even say the Argentinian's archetype.

BORGES. Yes, because it was preached by Mallea when he spoke of the 'invisible Church', certainly not when he spoke of the various characters of the ecclesiastical hierarchy. He spoke of the 'invisible Argentine' in the same way as one speaks of the invisible Church.

The invisible Argentinian would be, then, those who are just. And those who think impartially, beyond official positions.

FERRARI. You once told me that you had been thinking about this 'severe exaltation of life' at the same time as Mallea or perhaps even before.

BORGES. Yes, perhaps it's my Protestant blood. I think that ethics is stronger in Protestant countries. In Catholic countries, it's taken for granted that sin matters less. You confess, you are absolved and you can commit the same sin again. I think that there's a stronger ethical sense among Protestants. But perhaps the knowledge of ethics has vanished from the whole world. We will have to reinvent it.

FERRARI. But Protestant ethics seems to have more to do with economics and . . .

BORGES. And sexual questions—

FERRARI. And sexual questions. Although not recently.

BORGES. No, not recently, goodness me (*laughs*). I'd say the exact opposite, don't you agree?

FERRARI. I feel that this fidelity to a personal order—not to a method but to a rhythm, at times an efficient monotony—began in your childhood and that it continues even today.

BORGES. Well, I try to make sure of that. I have great difficulties when I write. I write very slowly. But that actually helps me, for each page, however careless it may seem, presupposes many drafts.

FERRARI. That's exactly what I was talking about, that meticulousness—

BORGES. The other day I was dictating something . . . you must have seen how I lingered over every verb, every adjective, every word. And over rhythm, over cadence which for me is the essence of poetry.

FERRARI. In that case, you must be thinking of the reader . . .

BORGES. Yes, I think so (*laughs*).

FERRARI. Well, as I said before, there is order in your poems, in your stories and in your conversations.

BORGES. Many thanks.

FERRARI. Today, I would like to talk about what seems to be your greatest concern—time. You have said that 'eternity is inconceivable'.

BORGES. I believe that one of man's ambitions is the idea of living outside time. I do not know if it is possible, although twice in my life I have felt myself outside time. Although they could have been illusions. Twice in my long life I have felt myself outside time or, in other words, eternal. Of course, I have no idea how long each experience lasted because I was outside time. I cannot communicate the feeling either—it was something very beautiful.

FERRARI. If eternity is not conceivable, perhaps infinity is not either, although we can conceive of immensity . . .

BORGES. As for infinity, it's best how Immanuel Kant dealt with it. We cannot imagine that time began in one moment, for if we imagine that second when time began, that second presupposes one before it and so on till infinity. Now, take Buddhism. It holds that each life is determined by a karma woven by a soul in its previous life. But with that we are obliged to believe in infinite time, for each life presupposes an earlier life, that life presupposes an even earlier one and so on till infinity. That is, there never was a first life nor a first second of time.

FERRARI. In that case, there would be a suspicious form of eternity.

BORGES. No, not of eternity—of an infinite prolongation of time. Eternity, I believe, is something else. Eternity—I have written about this in 'The Aleph'—is that very audacious hypothesis that there is an instant and in that instant converges the past—all our yesterdays, as Shakespeare put it—the present and the future. But that would be a divine attribute.

FERRARI. What has been referred to as the temporal triad.

BORGES. Yes.

FERRARI. I have noticed your painful familiarity with time, your preoccupation with time. And I feel that when you speak of time, it seems to take on a physical shape . . . you seem to perceive it as something corporeal.

BORGES. Time is more real than we are. Now, you could also say, as I have said often, that our substance is time, that we are made up of time and not of flesh and bone. For example, when we dream, our physical body does not matter—what counts is our memory and the imaginative worlds we weave with that memory. And that is obviously temporal—not spatial.

FERRARI. That's right. Murena said that the writer has to become anachronistic—in other words, go against time.

BORGES. That's a splendid idea, isn't it? Nearly all writers try to be contemporary, try to be modern. But that is superfluous. I am inevitably immersed in this century, in the preoccupations of this century and I do not need to try to be contemporary—I already am. In the same way, I do not need to try to be Argentinian—I already am. I do not need to try to be blind—sadly or, perhaps, fortunately, I already am. Murena was right.

FERRARI. It is interesting because he didn't say metachronic or beyond time but anachronistic, against time. That is different, perhaps, to a journalist or a historian.

BORGES. Casares and I started a magazine which lasted—and I am not exaggerating—for all of three volumes and it was called *Destiempo* (A Wrong Time). And that was the idea.

FERRARI. It's the same notion.

BORGES. We did not know Murena's assertion but in the end we agreed with him. The magazine was called *Destiempo*, which led, inevitably, to a predictable joke. Néstor Ibarra said, 'A wrong time, better the French *contretemps*!' (*both laugh*), referring to the magazine's contents. Yes, it was a *contretemps*.

FERRARI. Murena referred to the artist's time, to the writer's eternal soul, opposing it to what he called 'the fallen time of history'.

BORGES. Yes, perhaps one of our greatest errors, one of the worst sins of our century, is the importance given to history. This was not the case in earlier epochs. Today it seems that we live according to history. For example, in France—where clearly the French are very intelligent, very lucid—they like synoptic pictures. The writer writes according to history and defines himself, let's say, as traditionally Catholic, born in Brittany, writing after Ernest Renan and against Renan. The writer is creating his work for history, according to history. On the other hand, in England, that task is left to the historians of literature. It was Novalis who said, 'Every Englishman is an island,' that is, every Englishman is isolated (the exact etymology of 'island') and so writes according to his imagination or his memories or whatever, without thinking about future classifications in literary-history manuals.

FERRARI. Everything coincides with what you say. Murena asserted that man's slavery to time is the worst ever at this moment of history.

BORGES. Doubtless, I am being historical too for I am speaking of our epoch's history.

FERRARI. Of course, but what place would art and literature occupy in such an epoch?

BORGES. Art and literature . . . they should try to free themselves from time. Many times I have been told that art depends on politics or on history. I believe that is untrue. James Whistler, the famous American painter, was at a meeting where the conditions of a work of art were being argued in terms of the influence of biology, of the environment, of contemporary history. Then Whistler said, 'Art happens,' that is, art is a tiny miracle.

FERRARI. It truly is.

BORGES. It escapes in some way from history's organized causality. Yes, art does or does not happen. In neither case does that depend on the artist.

FERRARI. In spite of what we have said, we cannot free ourselves from time because this broadcast must end.

BORGES. Well, we'll continue next week.

FERRARI. Yes, each time is more delightful.

BORGES. Many thanks.

FERRARI. Thanks to you, Borges.

4

Borges and the Public

●

OSVALDO FERRARI. Borges, one of the things that surprised you about your destiny was when, in the 1940s, someone predicted that you would become a lecturer.

JORGE LUIS BORGES. No, it wasn't like that. Adela Grondona took me to a ladies' club for young Englishwomen where a woman who read tea leaves predicted that I would travel a lot and earn money by talking. I found that odd. When I got home I even told my mother about it. Never in my life had I talked in public. I was very shy, and the idea that I would earn money travelling and talking seemed unbelievable, even impossible. I had a minor position as first assistant— before I became second assistant—in a library in south Almagro. You know very well who came to power at the time and I was mockingly named Inspector for the Sale of Poultry and Eggs. It was a way of insinuating that I should resign. So I resigned. Of course I knew absolutely nothing about poultry and eggs.

FERRARI. That appointment was a historical mistake.

BORGES. Yes, their joke amused me, of course. I remember the relief I felt when I went for a walk in Plaza San Martín at two in the afternoon. I thought: I am not in that least likeable library in the suburb of Almagro. And I asked myself: What's going to happen now? Well, they called me from the Colegio Libre de Estudios Superiores and suggested that I give some talks. I had never talked in public but I accepted the offer because they'd mentioned it would be the following year. So I would get two months of respite. Those, of course, ended up being two months of panic. I remember, I was in Montevideo, in the Cervantes Hotel. Sometimes I would wake up at three in the morning and think: In thirty-something days (I was counting them) I will have to speak in public. And then I wouldn't be able to sleep. I would see the sunrise through the window. I would be terrified.

FERRARI. Your shyness accompanied you?

BORGES. Yes, it accompanied me (*both laugh*). On the eve of my first lecture, I was in Adrogué. Standing on one of the platforms at Constitución Station, I thought: Tomorrow, at this very hour, it will all be over. I will probably become mute and not be able to speak a single word. Or I will speak so quietly and confusedly that I will not be heard. Which would have been a blessing for I had not written out my lecture. I was sure that I would not be able to say anything. The day arrived and I went to lunch with a friend, Sara D. de Moreno Hueyo. I asked her if she found me to be nervous. She said that I seemed more or less the usual. I told her nothing about the lecture. That afternoon I gave my first lecture at the Colegio Libre de Estudios Superiores on Santa Fe Avenue. The lectures were on classical American literature, I think, on Hawthorne, Melville, Poe, Emerson, Thoreau and Dickinson. And then some more, on the mystics.

FERRARI. At the same place?

BORGES. Yes, as well as a talk on Buddhism. Thereafter, they asked for more talks on Buddhism. Alicia Jurado and I wrote a book based on my notes for those lectures, a book unexpectedly though amazingly translated into Japanese for an audience that knows more about Buddhism than I do—it is, after all, one of Japan's official religions. Well, that's the reason for the country's tolerance, isn't it?

Later I explored our country's interior. I also gave several lectures in Montevideo and across the continent. And now, without realizing it, I have reached my 85th year. Soon I will be 86. I'm aware that everyone feels what I've felt before—that I am not good at giving lectures, that I prefer dialogue which is, in fact, more entertaining for me though I am unaware if others share this view. Dialogue, because people can participate. Recently there were two events: one lasted an hour and twenty-one minutes, the other more than two hours with questions and answers. I have discovered that asking questions, or catechism, is the best form. And it is like a game—it begins in a solemn, even timid mood but then everyone enters the game and it is hard to stop. And I always favour the same trick—I propose three final questions. But three seems too few and, as I was taught in Japan, a fourth is ominous. So there are usually five—five last questions and five last answers. At the end, everything takes place in a spirit of jest; what starts a bit forcedly and solemnly ends as a game. Everyone wants to speak. I feel rather happy, I crack jokes for I agree with what

George Moore said, 'Better a bad joke than no joke.' I always answer with a joke and people indulge this blind man by being amused by his jokes even though the jokes are really rather weak. But perhaps the words in a joke do not matter as much as the intention with which it is said. And as I am always smiling, my jokes are always accepted. I have spoken in this way in many parts of the world. In France, I've even spoken in French, an inaccurate but fluent French. In America, I gave four four-month courses at the universities of Texas, Harvard, Michigan and Bloomington, Indiana, a few others here and there. And I gave these in English, again inaccurately but fluently.

FERRARI. You never expected that the lecture form could become a genre for you or that you would turn it into a dialogue that differs from a lecture? Neither did you think of humour as a genre meant personally for you?

BORGES. No, never. I have always been a serious person. But I don't know—destiny is what happens to you, isn't it? and it has nothing to do with what you had predetermined.

FERRARI. These are genres that have sought you out.

BORGES. That's true. Now I recall when people talked about the environment, about ideology, about the state of society, why Whistler said, 'Art happens.' Art is unpredictable.

FERRARI. It is also a paradox that the most shy men end up talking to hundreds of people in different places. As you have recently.

BORGES. Yes, a few months ago, I spoke in front of about a thousand people. Or so I was told. Perhaps there were 999 (*both laugh*) or 900! Whatever it may have been, the number shocked me. But no, a thousand people with good intentions need not be frightening. To give myself courage, I invented a kind of metaphysical argument—that the crowd is a fictitious entity, that what really exists is the individual.

FERRARI. Of course.

BORGES. The fact is you could count them all. You could add them up. You can also count people who follow one another, people who are not my contemporaries. Then I think: I am not talking to 300 people, I am talking to each of the 300. That is, there really are just two—the rest are fictitious.

I do not know if this is logically right but it helped me and continues to help me at every lecture or dialogue which is attended by so many people. Thus I think: What I say is heard by one person but that person is never the same one, that it makes no difference whether 300 people or 30 people are listening to me at the time. I speak to each of them, not the whole crowd. If I could speak to all of them it would be easy. There's a book on crowd psychology which claims that crowds are simpler than individuals. This is proved in the cinema or in the theatre. A joke you wouldn't dare say in an interview is accepted at a public forum, is even found to be amusing.

FERRARI. That's true.

BORGES. Thus crowds are more straightforward. And politicians know this and they take advantage of the fact that they are not talking to an individual but to a multitude, to a simplified group. And that it is enough to use the most elemental or most awkward means of communication. In those situations, they work.

FERRARI. So you prefer Greek dialogue to Roman oratory? A transition from lecture to dialogue.

BORGES. Yes, Greek dialogue. Of course, the Greeks were also orators. Demosthenes . . . But I find it easier now, I am accustomed to it because now it's a game. And if someone thinks that something is a game, then in fact it is a game and everyone else senses that it is a game. Moreover, I warn them at the start, 'This is going to be a game. I hope that it will be as amusing for you as for me. Let's start playing. It doesn't matter who begins.' This works out well with my classes. I try to be as less of a teacher, as less of a doctor, as possible, when I give a class. That's why the best classes are seminars. The ideal would be five or six students and a couple of hours. One year I gave a course in English Literature at the Catholic University where people were well disposed towards me. But I could do nothing with 90 people and 40 minutes. It was impossible. Between arriving and leaving, 40 minutes would pass. That lasted for a few courses, and then I quit. I felt that my task there was futile.

FERRARI. What's special in what you call a game is . . .

BORGES. I hope that the game I started or invented . . .

FERRARI. That it began some 2,000 years ago.

BORGES. Preceded by questions, by an inquisition, in the end. Those are rather sad memories. But I try to turn it all into a joke, for that is the sole way of seeing things seriously.

FERRARI. Of course. But this game of dialogues perhaps gets close to the truth.

BORGES. It can get close to the truth and I hope that others imitate it. Because one of the reasons I suggested, and finally imposed, this game was my timidity. Answering a question is easy, given that every question is a stimulant. The difficult thing is to ensure that there are questions! Knowing there will be answers, people prepare speeches that last up to 10 minutes and then there is nothing to answer!

FERRARI. Because then there are several ideas.

BORGES. Yes, many ideas or . . .

FERRARI. Or none at all.

BORGES. Yes, that's why I ask for concrete questions and promise concrete answers. It's a fact that it is very hard to get people to ask something because they would rather show off or bore the rest—it's the same thing—with long, prepared speeches.

FERRARI. Instead of a conversation?

BORGES. That's right.

FERRARI. Well, Borges, we'll go on playing this game and continuing this conversation and always seeking possible truths.

BORGES. Of course.

5

How a Borges Text Is Conceived and Written

●

OSVALDO FERRARI. Borges, I have the impression that we are begin-ning to get used to the silent company of our listeners and that we are less nervous now than when we recorded the first session. What do you think?

JORGE LUIS BORGES. It's so long ago but it's true.

FERRARI. Yes, weeks back. Now, it's strange that shyness—even if often overcome with time—seems to be an unavoidable constant for those who write.

BORGES. Every lecture I give is the first. When I am addressing the public, I feel the same fear as the first time, so many years back. I am a veteran of panic . . . Perfecting the meaning though I am aware that this doesn't count. I know that I am shy, that I am scared, but it doesn't matter.

FERRARI. Today I would like to talk about something that many will want to know, that is, how do you begin the process of writing? I mean, how does a poem or a story begin in your mind? And from that initial moment, how does the process continue, the crafting, one could say, of a poem or story?

BORGES. It begins as a kind of revelation. I employ that word in a modest and not ambitious way. Suddenly I know that something is about to happen and that this something could be, in a story, for instance, the beginning and the end. It's not so with a poem. With a poem, it's the general idea; at times, a first line. Something is gifted to me and then I intervene . . . and perhaps lose it (*laughs*). With a story, for example, I know the opening, the starting point, and I know the end, the finishing line. But then I must discover, through my very limited means, what takes place between the beginning and the end. Then there are other problems to resolve: whether the story should be told in the first or the third person. Which historical period to set it in. For me, it is now—this is my personal solution for I find the last decade of the nineteenth century to be the most comfortable period. If I am dealing with a story, I pick places in the outskirts of, say, Palermo or Barracas or Turdera. And the date as, let's say, 1899, the year I was born. Because who can know exactly how dead people spoke in the outskirts? No one. I can, then, comfortably proceed. On the other hand, if a writer picks a contemporary theme then a reader scrutinizes and thinks, 'No, in that suburb no one talked like that, people of such-and-such a class did not use that expression.'

The writer foresees all this and feels shackled. So I pick a period and place that is somewhat distant and that thus gives me the freedom to fantasize or fabricate. I can lie without anyone realizing it, without realizing it myself, for it is vital that a writer who writes a fable, however fantastic it may be, believes, for a moment, in the reality of his fable.

FERRARI. That's true. Now I must tell you that I have felt attracted to and very curious about your story 'Everything and Nothing', which tells us . . .

BORGES. I do not know if it is really a story though it does have a narrative element. It could be . . . yes, a fantastic story.

FERRARI. You picked it for your *Personal Anthology*.

BORGES. Yes, but I don't know if I chose it as a story or as a prose poem. Well, who cares about classifications?

FERRARI. It seems to be like a prose poem.

BORGES. Yes, Croce said that classifications were . . . not essential. For example, to say a book is a novel or an epic is the same as saying that a book is bound in red and that it's on the top shelf, on the left. Simply this—every book is unique and its classification is up to the critics or for their convenience, nothing more.

FERRARI. 'Everything and Nothing' refers to the life of an actor. If you permit, I would like to read some fragments and then perhaps we could comment on them.

BORGES. Yes, I remember it.

FERRARI. It opens this way: 'There was nobody inside him; behind his face (which even in the bad paintings of those days resembles no other) and his words (which were copious, fantastic and flustered) there was nothing but a chill, a dream not dreamt by anybody.'

BORGES. Of course I am referring to Shakespeare.

FERRARI. In the beginning, it is hard for the reader to notice this but then it becomes clearer.

31

BORGES. By the end I think it is obvious.

FERRARI. It is.

BORGES. Moreover, his name is mentioned.

FERRARI. Yes, towards the end.

BORGES. Even before that there are so many details that let one guess.

FERRARI. Then it reads: 'At first he believed everybody was like him, but the oddity of a companion with whom he had started to comment on that emptiness, revealed his error to him and made him feel, for ever, that an individual should not differ from its species.'

BORGES. Yes, it should be 'from the species'.

FERRARI. In this edition, it appears as 'from its species'.

BORGES. Well, it's an errata and there are more. Perhaps the whole story is an errata (*both laugh*) or an error which is more serious. If there was one error that would be enough. We should thank the typesetter, shouldn't we?

FERRARI. This fear on the part of an individual of being different from the species is peculiar. I would like to ask you how you got this idea, because it's the first that strikes me as exceptional in the story.

BORGES. I think the idea that what is normal is worthy is a common notion. Andrew Lang said that we are all geniuses until we reach seven or eight years of age. That is, all children are geniuses. But then a child tries to be like others, he seeks mediocrity and nearly always achieves it. I think that's true.

FERRARI. Later, we read: 'The tasks he set himself as an actor taught him a special happiness, perhaps the first he ever knew. But once the last lines had been recited and the last corpse taken from the stage . . .'

BORGES. 'Taken from the stage' because Elizabethan theatre had no curtains. So 'the dead' had to be dragged from the stage.

FERRARI. '. . . the odious sense of unreality befell him. He ceased to be Ferrex or Tamburlaine and became nobody again.'

BORGES. That 'nobody' is Shakespeare. Ferrex and Porrex are from an English play and Tamburlaine is, of course, from Marlowe.

FERRARI. 'Nobody was so many men as that man, who like the Egyptian Proteus could exhaust being's many appearances.'

BORGES. I like that evocation of Proteus. It's a fantastic story—why not be fantastic by changing forms like the Egyptian Proteus?

FERRARI. It seems to me, somehow, to also be the story of all actors and playwrights.

BORGES. I hadn't thought of that. I was thinking of Shakespeare and that for us (and perhaps for him too) Macbeth or Hamlet or the three Parcae seem to be more alive than he.

FERRARI. 'For twenty years he persisted in that guided hallucination, but one morning he was startled by the weariness and horror of being so many kings killed by the sword and so many ill-fated lovers who get together, disperse and melodiously die.'

BORGES. I am referring to the tragedies of those times.

FERRARI. It seems to me to be one of the most successful paragraphs. It continues: 'That very day he decided to sell his theatre.' That is, he ceased to be an actor. And you comment later that, towards the end of his life, when friends from London visited his retreat he played the poet for them.

33

BORGES. Yes. Meanwhile, he was a gentleman dedicated to court cases, to lending money and charging high interests. Things could not be more mundane, could they?

FERRARI. But towards the end, it says: 'God's voice answered him from a whirlwind . . .'

BORGES. That comes from the last chapters in the Book of Job where God speaks from a whirlwind.

FERRARI. 'From a whirlwind: "I also am not. I dreamt the world as you dreamt your work, my Shakespeare, and you were there in the forms of my dreams. Like me, you are many and nobody."'

BORGES. What a terrible idea—that God too does not know who he is! Though it can be accepted from a literary angle.

FERRARI. It is terrible but the story closes like a circle with that idea.

BORGES. Yes, it is a fine story even though I wrote it.

FERRARI. You also selected it for your anthology. I think it is one of the works that will accompany you for ever.

BORGES. Let's say it is the last page that I've written . . . perhaps there are one or two more, like 'Borges and I' which is somehow similar to theses pages.

FERRARI. That's right.

BORGES. No, this one seems better.

FERRARI. Perhaps not better but just as good.

BORGES. Well, when God says 'my Shakespeare', you do feel the emotion, don't you?

FERRARI. Yes. The story is a little longer than a page but it is extremely concise. You have cultivated synthesis in your stories.

BORGES. No, it's just that I'm very idle and I can't write longer pieces. I tire quickly and that's praised as concision (*both laugh*). I really do get worn out.

FERRARI. Hopefully, it will always help create this kind of 'concision'.

BORGES. Well, I will go on wearing myself out for all of you. Many thanks, Ferrari.

6

A Geographic and Intimate South

●

OSVALDO FERRARI. Borges, I would like to touch upon some topics explored by you and try to discover new aspects that will allow us not only to recreate them but to breathe new life into them for they are intrinsic to your work. I would thus like to talk about the South which appears so often in your thought and your work. It seems to me to be less a literary idea than an ontological one—perhaps a way of knowing ourselves as we get to know the South.

JORGE LUIS BORGES. Well, the South can be understood in several ways. Thinking of the plains could be one way, as in my story 'The South'. I had been reading Henry James who wrote deliberately ambiguous stories. 'The Turn of the Screw', for example, can be read in many ways. I thought I would imitate James but against a completely different background. So I wrote 'The South' and it can be read, as far as I know, in three ways. One, as factual or real. Well, all facts are real but, in short, it can be read as it is narrated. That's a possible reading. Then we could suppose that the second half of the story is a hallucination, a dream of the protagonist under the influence of a general anaesthetic. And then we could suppose, even if I prefer the second interpretation, that the story is a kind of fable, contrary to what Oscar Wilde said, 'Each man kills the thing he loves.' Inversely, it can be said that each man is killed by what he loves, that is, killed physically or wounded but nothing more.

If you love a person and that person fails you, you feel it. So we could suppose that the protagonist loves the South though he scarcely knows it. When he reaches the South, it kills him as indicated in various passages in the story. I think this explanation is rather far-fetched. I think it is better to suppose that in the first half of the story what we know is reality—the accident, the operation. And that the rest corresponds to the death he would have liked. In that case, the story would be autobiographical, since my grandfather got himself killed after Mitre's surrender at La Verde in 1874. I too would have liked a death like that—the death of a man of action. But I have not been a man of action and do not wish to be one either . . . So we have this feeling for the South.

Now, there's another South, the quarter called Barrio Sur in Buenos Aires (the other quarters have changed so much). In the South, things have been preserved or tried to be preserved. For me, this South is not a quarter that is different from the others but an essential one, fundamental to Buenos Aires. Many things link it to me. I was once the director of the National Library (I resigned when he whom we know came to power). And, curiously enough—I don't know if I have said this before—I can be in Japan or in Edinburgh or in Texas or in Venice, but when I dream at night I am always in Buenos Aires, in Barrio Sur, in Monserrat parish to be exact. The parish of the milonga song:

> In Monserrat parish
> Where knives flash
> What I say with the sharp point
> I sustain with my skin

A part of me has stayed in Buenos Aires. And even when I believe that I am travelling, there's something in my—to say it in contemporary mythology—subconscious that stays in Buenos Aires, that stays especially in México Street between Perú and Bolívar. And at night, when I dream, I am always in that place.

FERRARI. In that way a version of the South would be, let's say, Monserrat by Rivadavia Avenue in the direction of Constitución Station.

BORGES. Yes, of course. And there would be another where I spent much of my childhood—Adrogué. The prettiest village in the South. A village of country houses or *quintas*, taking up whole blocks (they hadn't been divided up then), full of those green Australian trees, the eucalyptus (*laughs*).

FERRARI. Then we have the literary South, across the Salado river, especially in Argentina's nineteenth-century literature.

BORGES. That's right. I would be tied to it in some ways. I say this without great pride for I am a distant relation of Rosas, whose memory is linked to the Salado because he had his estancia there.

FERRARI. But beyond geographic details concerning the South, it seems that the South . . .

BORGES. There's another very important reason and it's that *Sur*, Spanish for South, is a monosyllable. In English, West is one syllable and sounds good. 'To the West', for example. But the Spanish for West, *Oeste*, is difficult to pronounce. Same goes for *Este*. The Spanish for North, *Norte*, is better. The best is the Spanish for South, *Sur*, acute and brief. On the other hand, if you use a similar word in Spanish, *Sud*, with the *d*, then the word loses its power. Many people say *Sud* instead of *Sur*. 'Ferrocarril Sud' is written into the facade of Constitución Station, which is a shame, and in our national anthem—'al gran pueblo argentino salud' (Hail to the great people of Argentina) because that ending *salud* has to rhyme with *Sud*.

FERRARI. There must be a spirit that corresponds to that region. And it seems to me that, somehow, this spirit has been transmitted to all of us. You will recall Ezequiel Martínez Estrada who said that the spirit of the land—what he called the spirit of the pampas—was what made up our deeper self, the depths of our personalities.

BORGES. Well, I guess that he was born in the pampas of Santa Fe. It was in San José de la Esquina, wasn't it? I knew him but he died in the South, he died near Bahía Blanca. I was in his house. It was packed with birds. He would call them, bread crumbs in the palm of his hand, and they would flock to him (*both laugh*). I think William Henry Hudson did the same. He identified so much with the birds that they didn't see him as a man but as one of them, as another bird.

FERRARI. Hudson, whom Estrada so admired.

BORGES. Yes, he did. I think that he was wrong about Hudson, though, because he defined him as a gaucho. That was false. By the way, Hudson's Spanish was very flawed. He knew the Spanish that was used to order a farmworker about, the Spanish used by farm owners to order their workers, but no more. Cunningham Graham knew Spanish very well but Hudson didn't. You see that in the Christian names he used—he got them wrong, gave them impossible names. Of course, he worked from memory and memory is usually too inventive. What is called literary invention is really memory work, not like dreams which are made up of fables woven by our memories. That is, dreams are the work of memory and the imagination is an act of memory, a creative act of memory.

FERRARI. That's true. But that version of the South as an empty desert, which Estrada describes, can be found in a story by Carmen Gándara that states—humanizing the meaning—that 'we are desert,' the Argentines are desert. What do you think of that?

BORGES. It's good.

FERRARI. You said that we were exiles. This is similar to your idea.

BORGES. No, no, no, no. My idea is that we are Europeans in exile. But to say 'we are desert' is a different idea. We would have to ask her exactly what she meant.

FERRARI. *Desierto*, desert, sounds close to *destierro*, exile . . .

BORGES. Perhaps a literary phrase cannot be explained without it losing something. If I say 'We are desert,' that is enough. There is no need to dig around it.

FERRARI. If you recall what José Ortega y Gasset said about us when he wrote about the Argentinian as 'a defensive man'—I immediately associate it with the desert.

BORGES. Yes, I recall. At the time many people were offended: 'In the battle of Chacabuco,' they said, 'we were not on the defensive but on the offensive' (*both laugh*). Well, that's natural but that's not what he meant. He was not referring to battles but to the fact that people here are not at all spontaneous, that they are somewhat reserved despite their boasting and their extravagance. In a sense, people here are rather hypocritical.

FERRARI. You seem to have a penchant for the South that is not only literary but also emotional.

BORGES. That could be explained by the fact that a large part of my childhood was spent in Adrogué. Also by the fact that if one thinks, let's say, of places close to here, like Tigre or San Isidro, they do not seem to be part of Buenos Aires province. One thinks more about the river's proximity. If then one thinks about regions in the West or in the South—the plains, really—then one understands what literary people call the 'pampas' and that it is actually part of Buenos Aires.

FERRARI. In Buenos Aires, we are surrounded by the South in the shape of Buenos Aires province.

BORGES. I think so.

FERRARI. That is pampas but also Buenos Aires.

BORGES. Of course, the pampas are in the South and the West.

FERRARI. The plains?

BORGES. The shore is not the plains, it's something else.

FERRARI. Well, this does not coincide with what Estrada said when he spoke of Buenos Aires as 'Goliath's head'. He said that the plains or the pampas invaded Buenos Aires in many ways. I don't know if you know that book.

BORGES. No, I do not but this also happens in the world. Buenos Aires invades the plains because Buenos Aires, all of it, is the plains invaded. The place where we stand (*both laugh*) is, in fact, on the pampas. The pampas with many houses, some with attics, but still the pampas.

FERRARI. You said in a story that as you cross Rivadavia Avenue you enter an older, more solid world.

BORGES. I said that? I must have said so many things! It's best not to allude to my work. I try to forget it and that's easy for me to do. In my house you won't find any book written by me. Not one. I try to forget my past, I try to live projecting myself into the future. If not, I would be living a sickly life. Memories might be useful for elegies, an admissible and forgivable genre. I try to think about the future and that's why I am always plotting stories and polishing lines that will never be completely polished. I try to fill the loneliness of a blind octogenarian. I try to fill it with fables, with dreams and projects. Now I am to realize my dream of travelling the world again.

FERRARI. So, recently, you have distanced yourself a bit from Plato.

BORGES. Yes, so it seems (*laughs*). Well, who knows, maybe travel will lead me to the archetypes.

FERRARI. We always come across archetypes. You told me that during your first trip to Japan you came across realities that you never thought you'd see or perceive.

BORGES. Well, I don't know if I really perceived them or if I had the illusion of perceiving them. But if they were real to my emotions, then they were real. Given that there's no other way to measure things than through our emotions about them.

FERRARI. Of course. You are about to begin your second trip to Japan and we have been talking about the South. In some way, we are confirming what we have said in other radio talks—that universal vocation that shows that people from Buenos Aires and all Argentines are knowledgeable about the world.

BORGES. Luckily we live in a country that's still very, very curious. It's one of our best qualities, isn't it? It is the universe and not our plot of land that interests us.

FERRARI. Very well said, Borges, we will talk again next week.

BORGES. Very well.

7

Conrad, Melville and the Sea

●

OSVALDO FERRARI. Every now and then, we have recalled two writers who have dealt essentially with the sea. The first is . . .

JORGE LUIS BORGES. Joseph Conrad?

FERRARI. Joseph Conrad, and the second is the author of *Moby-Dick*.

BORGES. Yes, and they have nothing in common, nothing at all. Conrad cultivated an oral style or, rather, a fictitiously oral style. Of course, they are the stories of that gentleman Marlowe, the narrator of nearly all of them. On the other hand, Herman Melville, in *Moby-Dick* . . . though it's a very original book it reveals two influences—two men are projected onto that book in a favourable way . . . or, better put, two voices resound in him: one voice belongs to Shakespeare and the other to Thomas Carlyle. I believe you can detect these two influences in his style. And he has benefitted from them.

In *Moby-Dick*, the theme is surely the dread of whiteness. He could have been led, he could have first thought that the whale that mutilated the captain had to be singled out from the other whales. Then he must have thought that he could render it different by making it white. But that is a very mean hypothesis. It's better to suppose that he felt a dread of whiteness. The idea that white could be a terrible colour. Usually we associate the idea of terror with the dark, with what is black, then with red and blood. But Melville saw that the colour white may be terrible too. Perhaps he found a hint of it in a book he was reading . . . reading is no less vivid than any other human experience.

I think that he found the idea in Poe's *Narrative of Arthur Gordon Pym*. Because the theme of that novel's last pages, which begins with the water of the islands, that magical water, that veined water, is by the end about the dread of white. And that's explained by the Antarctic land which was once invaded by white giants which is hinted at in the last pages. Pym declares that anything that is white terrifies those people. And Melville took advantage of that for *Moby-Dick* ('took advantage' is a pejorative phrase I lament using). Anyway, that's what happened. And there's that especially interesting chapter called 'The Whiteness of the Whale' where he eloquently expands—an eloquence I cannot repeat here—on whiteness as terrible.

FERRARI. And as immense, perhaps.

BORGES. And immense. Well, I have said white and, as I like etymologies so much, I will remind you of a fact not sufficiently divulged about the English word 'black', the Spanish *blanco* and, of course, the French *blanc*, the Portuguese *branco* and the Italian *bianco*—these words have the same roots. In English I believe that an Anglo-Saxon word was the origin of both 'bleak' and 'black'. And 'black' in English and *blanco* in Spanish have the same root. Initially, 'black' in English and *blanco* in Spanish did not mean black but something without colour. In English, this not having colour suggested darkness or 'black' while in the Romance languages it suggested light and clarity. Thus *bianco* in Italian, *blanc* in French and *branco* in Portuguese, meaning white. It's odd that this word branched out into two opposite meanings— we tend to see white as opposed to black. But the word it proceeds from means 'without colour'. So, as I've said, in English it suggested the dark, meaning black and in Spanish clarity, meaning white.

FERRARI. There's chiaroscuro in the etymology.

BORGES. That's right, chiaroscuro, an excellent observation. A while ago, more or less when I discovered *La Divina Commedia* I also discovered that great book *Moby-Dick*. I believe that the latter, upon publication, remained invisible for some time. I have an old and excellent edition of the *Encyclopaedia Britannica*, the eleventh edition published in 1912. In it there's a not-too-long paragraph about Melville, describing him as a writer of travel novels. And though it mentions *Moby-Dick*, it is not distinguished from the rest of his books. It's in the list but there is no mention that *Moby-Dick* is far more than a traveller's tale or a book about the sea. It's a book referring to something essential. It amounts, according to some, to a struggle against evil but taken on in a mistaken way which is Captain Ahab's manner. But what is curious is that he imposes his madness onto his crew, onto everyone in the whaling boat. And Melville was a whaler who knew that life thoroughly and intimately. Although he came from a great New England family, he was a whaler. And in many of his stories he speaks, for example, about Chile, islands close to Chile, that is, he knew the seas.

I would like to make another observation about *Moby-Dick*, something I don't think has been pointed out, although almost everything else has been said about it—*Moby-Dick's* last page repeats in a more wordy fashion that famous canto from *Inferno* in which, alluding to Ulysses, Dante says that the sea closed over them. And the last line of *Moby-Dick* says exactly the same thing though with different words. Now I don't know if Melville had this line from the Ulysses episode in mind, that is, the ship that sinks, the sea that closes over the ship, but you do find it in the last page of *Moby-Dick* as you do in the last line of that canto (I can't recall which one), the one in which the Ulysses episode, the most memorable in *La Divina Commedia*, is narrated. Although, what isn't memorable in *La Divina Commedia*? Everything is, but if I had to choose a canto, and there's no reason to have to, I would pick the Ulysses episode. That moves me more than the Paolo and Francesca episode, because there's something so mysterious in the fate of Dante's Ulysses. Of course, he's in the circle that corresponds to swindlers and fraudsters, to the deceit of the Trojan horse. But you feel that that is not the real reason.

I have written an essay in my book *Nueve ensayos dantescos* in which I state that Dante must have felt that what he had committed was perhaps forbidden to men because, for literary ends, he had to foresee decisions that Divine Providence would take on the day of the Last Judgement. Somewhere in *La Divina Commedia* Dante says that no one can predict God's decisions. But he does just that in his book when he condemns some to Hell, some to Purgatory and some others to Paradise. He could have thought that what he was doing was not blasphemous but it was not completely licit either that a man take those decisions. And so, in writing that book, he took on something forbidden.

In the same way, Ulysses, wanting to explore the southern hemisphere and navigating by the stars, was doing something forbidden for which he was then punished. If not for this reason, then I do not know why. So I suggest that, consciously or unconsciously, there's a link, an affinity between Ulysses and Dante. And I reached that through Melville who doubtless knew Dante. During the long American Civil War, the greatest war in the nineteenth century, Henry Wadsworth Longfellow translated Dante's *La Divina Commedia* into English. I first read Longfellow's version; much later I dared to read the Italian. I had the very mistaken notion that Italian wasn't very different from Spanish. Well, when spoken it is, but not when read. In any case, you have to read it as slowly as required by the book. The editions of the *Commedia* are excellent and if you do not understand a line, you can refer to the commentary. In the best editions, there's a note for each line, so it's hard not to understand the two (*both laugh*). Goodness, we have moved away from Melville . . .

Melville is evidently a great writer, in *Moby-Dick* and in his stories. A few years ago, in Buenos Aires, a book was published on the best short story. The title was obviously commercial. Four Argentine writers—Manuel Mujica Lainez, Ernesto Sabato, and perhaps Julio Cortázar and I—chose a story each. Sabato picked Melville's 'Bartleby', I picked Hawthorne's 'Wakefield'. I think someone picked a Poe story.

That is, there were three American writers. I think Mujica Lainez picked a Japanese or Chinese story. They were published in a volume with our photographs and the reasons for our choice. It was rather successful and revealed four admirable stories.

FERRARI. Yes, a great idea.

BORGES. A great publisher's idea.

FERRARI. As for Conrad—you once told me that his stories reminded you not only of the sea but, to be specific, of the Paraná Delta.

BORGES. In Conrad's first books, when he resorted to Malayan landscapes, I used my memories of Tigre as illustrations. Thus when I read Conrad, I slipped in or inserted remembered landscapes from Tigre, as it was the most similar. By the way, Buenos Aires is an odd case—a great city that has an almost tropical or Malayan archipelago near it. That's very rare, isn't it? and with reeds. I was recently in Brazil and rediscovered something that Eça de Queiroz's novels had revealed to me. Something called Bengala, doubtless due to the Bengala reeds. Someone once said to me 'Your bengala,' which is Irish-made, and handed me my walking stick, and I remembered that word (*laughs*). It seemed so lovely that a walking stick is called *bengala*, because 'walking stick' doesn't recall anything in particular. In Spanish, a *bastón* suggests clubs, a long ace of clubs. While *bengala* brings back a whole region; and in Bengali, the word 'bungalow' is also derived from *bengala*.

FERRARI. Borges, I see that the sea, through Conrad and Melville, is very close to you, that you often bear it in mind.

BORGES. Yes, always. It's so lively and mysterious—the theme of *Moby-Dick*'s first chapter, the theme of the sea as something alarming, something alarming in a terrible as well as in a beautiful way . . .

FERRARI. Beauty creates this sense of danger.

BORGES. Yes, danger is created by beauty and beauty is, in any case, one of the forms of danger and anxiety.

FERRARI. Especially if we recall Plato's phrase from *The Symposium*: 'Facing the immense sea of beauty'.

BORGES. Ah, what a lovely phrase. Yes, important words.

FERRARI. The sea.

BORGES. The sea, yes, that's so present in Portuguese literature and so absent in Spanish literature. For example, *Quixote* . . .

FERRARI. Set on a tableland.

BORGES. The Portuguese, on the other hand, the Scandinavians and—yes—the French since Hugo, feel the sea. Baudelaire felt it; Rimbaud in his 'Le Bateau ivre' felt a sea that he had never seen. Coleridge wrote 'The Rime of the Ancient Mariner' without having seen the sea; when he did see it, he felt betrayed. And Rafael Cansinos Assens wrote an admirable poem about the sea. I congratulated him and he answered, 'I hope one day to see it.' That is, the sea in Assens' imagination and the sea in Coleridge's imagination were superior to the mere sea of geography (*laughs*).

FERRARI. As everyone's noticed, for once we have strayed from the plains.

BORGES. That's true.

8

On Politics

●

OSVALDO FERRARI. In a way very different from Lugones, who in good faith changed his political position over time, you, Borges, seem to have maintained a constant attitude of independence or equidistance from politics and have only attended to it, I believe, as an ethical imperative.

JORGE LUIS BORGES. Yes, at least over the last half-century—unfortunately, I can only speak of half a century. Yes, at the moment, I would define myself as an inoffensive anarchist, a man who seeks a minimum of government and a maximum of individuality. But that is not a political position, of course.

FERRARI. Your independent attitude is perhaps related to your way of seeing the importance of the individual confronted by the State.

BORGES. Yes, of course, and now the State surrounds us everywhere, on both sides—the extreme right and the extreme left, both support the State and the State's interference in every moment of our lives.

FERRARI. And the classifying of the cultured man in one or other of those two great political divides.

BORGES. I have repeated so many times that a person's opinions are of least importance. Art and its practice are so mysterious that opinions are unimportant; I don't think intentions are important either. What counts is the work and the work is by its nature mysterious. The poet works with words but the dictionary meanings of words are of least importance. What is really important is the atmosphere of words, the connotation and the cadence of words, the intonation . . . one is dealing with intangible and extremely mysterious elements.

FERRARI. Of course.

BORGES. Even the poet does not know whether he dominates them or is carried along by them.

FERRARI. Insofar as he's the instrument.

BORGES. Insofar as he is the instrument, yes, for reality is fathomless. Language is a series of rigid symbols, and to suppose that these symbols can be completely explained by dictionaries is absurd. I here recall what Alfred North Whitehead called 'the fallacy of the perfect dictionary', that is, the fallacy of supposing that for each feeling or for each idea or for each moment of our changing and growing lives there is a symbol. As in Gustave Flaubert's 'le mot juste'. To suppose that there's a symbol for everything is to suppose that the perfect dictionary exists. And naturally, dictionaries are mere approximations, aren't they? The same applies to the idea of a synonym. There are, in fact, no synonyms, because the atmosphere of every synonym is different. I do not even know if one language can be properly translated into another, especially one poetic language into another. Perhaps with a conceptual language it's possible, but not with an aesthetic language. If we translate a poem literally, we give its verbal meaning—but what about its verbal cadences? And the atmosphere of its words? Perhaps that is lost and perhaps that is what is essential.

FERRARI. All this is very mysterious.

BORGES. Yes, the art of literature is mysterious. No less mysterious than music. Perhaps literature is a more complex music, because you have not only the cadence of words and sound but also the connotations, the atmosphere, the meaning. Senseless poetry is, after all, not acceptable. We must think that this has meant something for someone, for someone's emotions. And that is untranslatable.

FERRARI. As untranslatable as music?

BORGES. As untranslatable as music, yes, it's another kind of music. I recall a phrase now, perhaps by Kipling or quoted by Kipling from some Indian poet—it's the same, I suppose. In one of his stories set in India . . . I have forgotten it and only remember that a character says, 'If I hadn't been told this was love, I would have believed that it was a naked sword.'

FERRARI. Amazing!

BORGES. What's amazing is the form. If I say 'Love is inexorable like a sword,' I have said nothing. The same applies if I compare love to a weapon. That impossible confusion is possible only for the imagination. Clearly, no one will confuse love with a naked sword, but there it is, given by the syntax of the sentence. Because it does not open with 'At the beginning I thought it was a sword and then I saw it was love.' That would be ridiculous! But 'If I hadn't been told this was love, I would have believed that it was a naked sword'—that is perfect.

FERRARI. It's a lovely sentence.

BORGES. Yes, the sentence is competent even if I say it in Spanish or English or even Hindi, a language that Kipling would have heard. It would have another power which is lost in translation.

FERRARI. Despite your independent stance, in the second half of the 1930s, due to what was happening in Europe, I notice your stand against Nazism and Fascism.

BORGES. Indeed, when many people here were not declaring theirs.

FERRARI. In 1937, you wrote a page entitled 'A Pedagogy of Hate'.

BORGES. Yes, I was referring to a book that María Rosa Oliver had lent me. She was obviously a communist and did not oppose other pedagogies of hate—only the one against Jews seemed evil to her.

FERRARI. Against German Jews?

BORGES. Yes. It was a very strange book. I still recall it and remember the prints made for children. There was a Jew who seemed more like some kind of Arab or fantastic Turk, I'm not sure which . . . I think he had a ring in his nose. Then a German who was really an Irish peasant and as tall as a Scandinavian. How odd! For Germans, Jews were essentially dark. What was important was to make them different in order to hate them more easily. That's all it was.

FERRARI. In 'A Pedagogy of Hate' you pointed out that teaching hate was corrupting German civilization.

BORGES. Yes, an extraordinary thought, that German civilization was being corrupted. But I think that the whole thing had its roots in the dreadful Versailles peace. If they had followed Woodrow Wilson's idea of a democratic peace . . . but that didn't work out. France annexed Alsace and Lorraine; Italy was annexed; England kept its German blockade for a year or two after the German surrender which was terrible . . . I think I read in one of the Kafka biographies that he was a victim of that blockade, that is, hunger continued after peace had been agreed upon. A terrible thing.

FERRARI. You adopted the same attitude in another page written in 1939 called 'Essay on Impartiality'.

BORGES. I don't remember that.

FERRARI. Well, there you say that you detest Hitler because he did not share your faith in the German people.

BORGES. Really? Did I say that? Then I do not regret having written it because at the time it was supposed . . . one was called a Germanophile not because one was fond of Germany but because one followed the German government . . .

FERRARI. Oh, I see.

BORGES. Yes, a Germanophile meant a follower of Hitler—not a friend of Germany. The German spirit is a category that includes, Germany, England, Sweden, Norway, Denmark, Holland, Iceland, et cetera. We could go on indefinitely, Scotland also, yes, why not?

FERRARI. But what is very clear is the concept you expressed in 1945 with reference to Nazism, when you said that it was a prejudice of superiority about one's country, one's language, one's religion . . .

BORGES. Well, this has spread around the whole world. It seems that people everywhere are proud of their minimal differences, aren't they? Local colour is what is accentuated everywhere. Here, luckily, we do not have any local colour but it will be invented. In any case, the reverence for the gaucho is also a form of nationalism. Those who founded this country did not share this, of course—the word 'gaucho' was pejorative when I was a boy.

FERRARI. Are they exacerbated forms of nationalism, then?

BORGES. Yes, that's one of the great evils, the greatest evil of our times. There are others, like the unfair distributions of spiritual and material goods . . . What I have said about our planet divided into countries and these countries possessing frontiers, loyalties, prejudices . . . are dangers, I agree, but we will survive all this. I will not see this survival, but I'm sure . . .

FERRARI. That these dangers will be relegated.

BORGES. Yes, I think so, all that will be relegated. But it won't be immediate. My father believed, his generation believed, that this change would happen very soon. I remember when we went to Montevideo, that would be around 1905, my father told me to look hard at the uniforms, at the flags, at the barracks, at the customs houses, at the churches (*laughs*), because all that would vanish and that I should be able to tell my children about it. On the contrary, not only has it not vanished but it has been exacerbated. My father, though, had faith that the change would happen.

Macedonio Fernández was studying law when he asked his fellow students to abandon their studies because the whole world would soon be one country and there would be other laws. Why study statutes which would soon be archaic? Sadly, that didn't happen; the statutes remain valid and more have been passed. Nothing has been simplified. It has become more complex.

FERRARI. Getting back to the theme of the presumed racial superiority—you said it was one of literature's traditional themes.

BORGES. Yes, you find it everywhere. For example, in the United States, the blacks are convinced that the black race is superior. I attended a conference on Negritude in Berlin. I was asked to deliver the opening address. I began with the notion that, in the end, the differences between one race and another were minimal, that there were certain passions and capacities in man that lay beyond race. But an African nationalist present at the congress—I remember that he had a lance and a leopard skin—told me I was wrong, that their culture, as everyone agreed, was peculiarly African. Though the others applauded his speech, Mallea and I were astounded. Mallea was with me then . . .

FERRARI. What year was that?

BORGES. I don't recall exactly . . . there were two congresses. One was on Negritude and I had suggested the word *noirceur* . . . it's more attractive, don't you think? Because blackness is better than Negritude which is a horrible neologism. Then there was another in Berlin for Latin American and German writers. The congress was opened by three characters brought by Roa Bastos, wearing bright red ponchos, wide-brimmed hats and playing guitars. Again, the Germans all applauded whereas Mallea and I had to admit that this spectacle was quite unusual for us (*both laugh*). We'd never seen gauchos with bright red ponchos and guitars! The Germans were enchanted, so Mallea and I said that we were just as amazed as they were, that we had never seen anything like it though we were the ones who had come from South America. Everything was immediately accepted as a symbol of South America!

FERRARI. Now, coming back to our country, there's an auspicious sentence of yours about individualism being an old Argentine virtue.

BORGES. Yes, and that we should take advantage of it. But that didn't happen. In fact, quite the opposite.

FERRARI. Do you think it's applicable now?

BORGES. At this moment it would be insane, but why not imagine a future in which it could be applied, since the future is flexible? We can manipulate the future, the future depends on us. This manipulating could be useful, even beneficial. The fact is that when we think of the future . . . we all think of what we want, 'wishful thinking'. But that kind of auspicious thinking could be effective as well.

FERRARI. Anyway, I think we should underline autonomy and inde-pendence and not the pigeonholing that we are capable of in a period that needs the contrary.

BORGES. Yes, I try to do that, many of my friends try to do it as well. But it is rather hard.

FERRARI. Let's hope that it's continued.

BORGES. Yes. Anyway, we will remain two individualists, Ferrari, you and I, won't we?

FERRARI. At least that.

BORGES. Let others be typecast and lose their diversity. Regrettably, that is to be expected.

9

Macedonio Fernández and Borges

●

OSVALDO FERRARI. This time, Borges, I would like to talk about a man whom the Argentinians are always on the verge of understanding and about whom you have said that there is as yet no biography—Macedonio Fernández.

JORGE LUIS BORGES. I inherited Macedonio's friendship from my father. They studied law together and I remember, as a boy, returning from Europe in 1920 and seeing Macedonio waiting for us at the dockside. There stood my country in person. When I set off for Europe, my last great friendship was my tutelary friendship with Assens. I thought: Now I am saying goodbye to all of Europe's libraries. Because Assens told me, 'I can greet the stars in seventeen classic and modern languages.' What a lovely way to say that I can speak, that I know, seventeen languages, isn't it? 'I can greet the stars' which gives some sense of eternity and immensity, doesn't it? When I said farewell to Assens in Madrid, near Morería Street, where he lived above a viaduct (I wrote a poem about this), I thought: Now I'm returning home. But when I got to know Macedonio I thought: Really, I haven't lost anything. Here is a man who in some ways can replace Assens. Not a man who can greet the stars in many languages nor a man who has read much but a man who has dedicated his life to thinking, to thinking about those essential problems that are ambitiously called philosophy and metaphysics.

Macedonio lived and thought in the same way as Xul Solar—to recreate and reform the world. Macedonio told me that he wrote to help himself think. He never thought of publishing. It's true that in his lifetime one of his books was published, *Papeles de Recienvenido* (Papers of the Recently Arrived), but that was more because of the generous conspiracy plotted by Reyes who has helped so many Argentine writers. He has helped me too. I 'stole' some of those papers from Macedonio. He gave little importance to his manuscripts; they moved with him from one cheap hotel to another (for easily guessable reasons) in Tribunales or in the Once where he'd been born. We would reproach him for that—he would escape from a hotel and leave behind a pile of manuscripts and they'd get lost. We would say, 'But Macedonio, why do you do that?' He would answer, genuinely surprised, 'But do you believe that I could think of something new? You should know that I always have the same thoughts. I do not lose anything. I will think of the same things again in such-and-such a hotel in the Once. What I will think of on Jujuy Street will be the same as what I thought on Misiones Street.'

FERRARI. But you have said that conversations with Macedonio impressed you . . .

BORGES. That was the main point. I have never met a person whose dialogue impressed me more or who was more laconic than he. Almost mute, silent. We would meet to listen to him every Saturday in a cafe, La Perla, that is or was on the corner of Rivadavia and Jujuy. We would meet around midnight and stay till dawn, listening. And he spoke four or five times each night, and everything he said he would attribute courteously to his questioner. He would always begin by saying—he was a traditional Argentine in the way he talked—'You will doubtless have observed . . .' and then make an observation that others had never thought of (*both laugh*). Macedonio preferred to attribute his thoughts to others, he never said, 'I have thought such-and-such.' That seemed to him presumptuous or vain.

FERRARI. He would attribute his intelligence to the intelligence of all Argentinians.

BORGES. Yes, that also.

FERRARI. I recall that you compared two men to Adam.

BORGES. That's right.

FERRARI. Whitman and Macedonio.

BORGES. That's right.

FERRARI. In Macedonio's case, it was because of his ability to think and solve fundamental problems.

BORGES. In Whitman's case, it was because his discovery of the world. With Whitman, you have the sense that he saw everything for the first time, which is what Adam must have felt. And what we all feel when we are children. We slowly discover the world.

FERRARI. And that admiration you felt for Macedonio was somehow equivalent to what you felt for Xul Solar, according to what you have said several times.

BORGES. Yes. Things amazed Macedonio and he wanted to explain them. On the other hand, Xul Solar felt a kind of indignation and wanted to reform everything. That is, he was a universal reformer. Xul Solar and Macedonio had nothing in common. They knew each other, and we expected much from their meeting but then felt cheated, because Xul Solar thought that Macedonio was just another Argentinian. While Macedonio said, in a somewhat cruel way, that 'Xul Solar is a man worthy of respect and much pity.' Thus, they did not really 'meet'. I think that though they later became friends, that first meeting was a non-meeting, as if they hadn't seen each other. They were two geniuses but at first glance each was invisible to the other.

FERRARI. That's odd. Now, you have said that Macedonio identified dreams with the essence of a being. You have also compared the act of writing with dreaming.

BORGES. It's that I do not know if there's an essential difference. I believe the phrase 'life is a dream' is strictly true. What should be asked is: Is there is a dreamer or is it just a self-dreaming? That is, if there's a dream that is dreamt, perhaps it is something impersonal, like rain or snow or the changing seasons. Something that happens but it doesn't happen to just anyone. That means there is no God but there is a long dream that, if we want to, we could call 'God'. I suppose that's the difference. Macedonio negated the ego. David Hume negated it and so does Buddhism. Which is strange, because Buddhists do not believe in the transmigration of the soul. They believe, rather, that each individual, during life, constructs a mental organism or 'karma'. Then this mental organism is inherited by another. In general, though, it's supposed that's not the case. The Hindus, on the other hand, imagine that there is a soul that passes through several transformations, that lodges in different bodies that are reborn and that then die. That's why the god Shiva—you can see an image close by—is a dancing god, with six arms, the god of death and regeneration. Because the Hindus suppose that both are identical, that when you die another person is engendered; so if you engender, you engender for death. The god of regeneration is thus also the god of death.

FERRARI. Right. The meaning you give to Macedonio's solitude also seemed significant to me. You associate the nobility of that solitude with the Argentinian character prior to the arrival of radio, television and telephone.

BORGES. That's right. Earlier, people were perhaps more accustomed to solitude. Estancia owners lived alone for a good part of the year or for their lives, because the farm hands were usually uncultured people with whom dialogue was impossible. Each estancia owner was a kind of Robinson Crusoe on the plains or hills or wherever. Perhaps we have now lost the ability to be alone, haven't we?

FERRARI. I think so.

BORGES. Above all, today people always need to be accompanied, accompanied by the radio, by us (*laughs*). What can be done about it?

FERRARI. Illusorily accompanied.

BORGES. Yes, illusorily accompanied but I hope, in this case, pleasantly so.

FERRARI. There's something real about being accompanied by the radio.

BORGES. If that wasn't the case, if they were not pleasing for others, what sense could our talks have?

FERRARI. Naturally. It struck me also that you attribute to Macedonio the belief that Buenos Aires and its inhabitants could not make political mistakes.

BORGES. Well, they could never be wrong. But perhaps that was made worse by Macedonio's nationalism, a silly notion, really. For example, he wanted—though luckily never succeeded—us to sign our names and add 'artist from Buenos Aires'. But no one did this, it's obvious anyway (*both laugh*). Another example: if a book was popular, he said its author was good because Buenos Aires couldn't make a mistake. In that way, he could pass, literally overnight, from supporting Hipólito Yrigoyen to supporting José Félix Uriburu. From the moment the revolution was accepted, he could not censure it. And he thought the same about popular actors—from the moment they were deemed popular, they had to be good. That is an error. As is evident, we are all capable of making mistakes.

FERRARI. You said that your mother pointed out that Macedonio had been a supporter of all the presidents of Argentina.

BORGES. Yes, he supported each one, not to obtain anything from them but because he refused to suppose that a president could be elected in anything but a fair election. And this allowed him to accept everything (*laughs*). Well, I'd better not give too many examples.

FERRARI. Now, if this is a country with a sense of metaphysics, and if Buenos Aires is a city which from its origins is related to metaphysics, I link Macedonio with a metaphysical perception grounded in Buenos Aires.

BORGES. I am not sure. Is that perception right? Maybe, but I haven't observed this.

FERRARI. Well, I see it in the way I read Macedonio.

BORGES. Ah, well, that could be so. But I do not know if Macedonio isn't an exception.

FERRARI. I believe that he is.

BORGES. Like any genius, of course.

FERRARI. You have always felt what could be called a need to state your views on Macedonio.

BORGES. Yes, but I haven't done it completely. Precisely because it's so personal I am unsure if it can be communicated. It's like a taste or a colour. If someone hasn't seen that colour or tasted that taste, definitions are useless. In Macedonio's case, I believe that those who have not heard his voice when they read him do not really read him. And I can; I remember exactly what Macedonio's voice was like and I can lift the printed word back to the oral word. Others cannot; they find it confusing or incomprehensible.

FERRARI. Yes, have you noticed? its very strange . . . I could say that if you understand or notice Macedonio, it's easier to understand the peculiarities of members of our society, of our family, of our kind of person? I see it in some way . . .

BORGES. He would really have appreciated that idea. He would have approved. I do not know if it's true or not, for Macedonio is so unique. I could say this: we saw him every Saturday. I had to wait a whole week before I could see him again. I could have gone to visit him because he lived near our home and I had been invited. But I would tell myself: I won't, I won't use that privilege, I'll wait the whole week and know that the week will be crowned by a meeting with Macedonio. So I desisted from seeing him. I would go for walks, go to bed early and read—I read an enormous amount, especially in German. I didn't want to forget the German I'd been taught in Geneva in order to read Schopenhauer. So I read an enormous amount. I went to bed to read or went for walks alone—in those days, you could do that without any danger; there were no assaults, nothing like that, it was a far more tranquil time. I'd think: What does it matter if something happens to me tonight? If I get to Saturday, I'll be able to talk to Macedonio. My friends and I would say to one another how lucky we were to have been born in the same city, in the same period, in the same environment as Macedonio. We could have lost that, which is what a lover thinks too, isn't it? What luck to be alive at the same time as so-and-so, unique in space and time! Well, that's what our little group felt about Macedonio. After his death, 'intimate' friends of his began to appear, friends we'd never seen during his lifetime. But that always happens when an illustrious or famous person dies. Unknown people turn up and claim to be friends. I recall the case of a person—there's no reason to mention his name—who'd heard us talk of Macedonio. That person delighted in nostalgia and so claimed, and indeed believed, that he had been Macedonio's friend. That he fondly remembered, and missed, the Saturday meetings in La Perla when in fact he had never been there, never known Macedonio, not even by sight. But it doesn't matter—he had a need for nostalgia and that is how he fed it. When he talked about Macedonio with me, even though I knew that they had never met I let him talk on.

FERRARI. A creative nostalgia.

BORGES. Yes, a creative nostalgia.

FERRARI. Borges, I would continue chatting with you about Macedonio for ever but . . .

BORGES. Why not for ever? And about everything?

FERRARI. We must stop for today. Shall we say goodbye until next Friday?

BORGES. Why not, but I will anxiously await Friday.

10

Borges with Plato and Aristotle

●

OSVALDO FERRARI. Well, Borges, now that you are back, I am going to recall the topics we touched upon before your trip—we talked about the possible identity of the Argentinians; about order and time; about the differing meanings that the south of Buenos Aires and the south of the province have through history; about your voyage to Italy, Greece and Japan; about Macedonio Fernández; about how a Borges text is born and created. Now, naturally, we will talk about the experience of your journey to Italy, Greece and Japan. The first impression one has on seeing you is that this trip has suited you very much and that you have the air of having made new discoveries.

JORGE LUIS BORGES. I'm not sure whether they were discoveries or confirmations. I have returned with excellent impressions and with wonder—that people respect me so much, that they take me seriously. I'm not sure that my work deserves that attention, I think not. I think that I am a kind of international superstition now. But I am very thankful and have not ceased being amazed. Receiving those prizes, those honours! You are now talking to an honorary doctor of the

University of Crete! All of it seems so fantastic, as fantastic to me as to the others, does it not? I am astonished by it all. I think they have read me in translation, translations that may have even improved my texts. Or perhaps there is something between the lines that I haven't managed to grasp. But there it is. If not, then I don't know why I deserve all this.

I have returned with the best impressions of those countries. I didn't know the south of Italy, though I knew it was part of Greater Greece. I was in Crete too, and had the chance to use that expression, Greater Greece, a term that's applied to Asia Minor, the south of Italy and certain islands; it could be applied to the whole world; in any case, certainly to the West. We are all part of Greater Greece. I said that there—that we are all Greeks in exile, in an exile that isn't necessarily elegiac or miserable for it allows us to be more Greek than the Greeks or more European than the Europeans. I didn't know the south of Italy; I was surprised to hear its popular music. I heard a man playing a guitar, a peasant I was told, playing Sicilian themes, and I heard those Creole tunes that come from Buenos Aires province or from Uruguay. Tunes played to Elías Regules' words in 'La Tapera' or 'El gaucho'. That was the music I heard in Sicily. The people in Vicencza were splendid to me too, in Venice as well. In Japan, I reconfirmed the splendid experiences of my previous journey. It is a country that practises both Eastern as well as Western culture. In the Western sense, its technology seems to be leaving us far behind.

FERRARI. That's true. I saw somewhere that in Italy they have designated you Master of Life.

BORGES. Well, if only that could be applied to my actual life, which has been a sequence of mistakes, hasn't it? But perhaps you can teach what you do not know or have not put into practice (*laughs*).

FERRARI. Yes. It's odd, though, that after your recent travels to countries where the latest technology has arrived in its most modern forms, like America and Western Europe (the northern part), you convoke the south, the ancient West, Crete, Greece and Sicily.

BORGES. Well, what is not Crete or Greece or Sicily is a reflection of those places, an extension of those places. When I spoke in Crete, when they made me a doctor of that Greek university, I remembered a rather curious fact. One thinks of the north as opposed to the south. Yet, when Snorri Sturluson in the eighth century once referred to the god Thor—the god who gave his name to Thursday, for Thor's day, that is, Jove's day (*jueves* in Spanish)—he offered that etymology which is, of course, false. Sturluson said that Thor was Priam's son and, by the resemblance of the sounds, Hector's brother. Obviously that's false, but it doesn't matter. What does matter is that it reveals the desire of his people to incorporate the south in the north. He wrote in Iceland and in some way wanted to bind himself to the south, to get close to the *Aeneid* which is what they knew about the south because they couldn't have known the later Homeric poems. But, in the end, they wanted to be a part of Mediterranean culture. That can also be seen, for example, in the German word *Vaterland* or in the English 'motherland' which seems very Germanic and yet, what is *Vaterland* if not a translation of 'fatherland'? It is not an idea that the Germans had, for what was crucial for the Germans was to belong to such-and-such a tribe, to be loyal to such-and-such a leader.

FERRARI. Land of the fathers?

BORGES. Yes, land of the fathers. *Vaterland* or motherland in English, so as not to confuse it with *Vaterland* which is uniquely German— both with the same idea, *patria*, translated from the Latin. Curiously, Paul Groussac suggested the possibility of *matria* but that was rather late, an artificial word, that would be motherland in English. Perhaps the idea of a 'land of the mother'? In the end, perhaps it seems safer to say 'fatherland' (*laughs*). Paternity is an act of faith, as Goethe said, while maternity is an act that animals recognize, that everyone recognizes.

FERRARI. You have evoked Scandinavian and Greek myths and I have been reading Simone Weil, a French writer who, recalling Greek and Eastern myths, claims that Plato was the West's first mystic, inheriting the Eastern mystic tradition.

BORGES. I'm not sure of the first—that would be Pythagoras and he was somewhat earlier. I think that there's a bust of Pythagoras that has him wearing a Thessalonian hat, that is, an Asian hat. The Stoic and Pythagorean ideas of transmigration and cyclical time must be something that came from the East. In the East, the idea of cycles makes sense, because people, well, souls, the transmigration of souls through several cycles, are always improving or getting worse, always changing. On the other hand, the idea of exactly equal cycles, held by the Pythagoreans and Stoics, seems senseless, because in reality it had no use at all. I don't see how we can talk of a first, second or third cycle because there's no one who can perceive the differences between any of the cycles. Perhaps the Greeks poorly grasped the theory of circular time from Asian doctrines where there probably were cycles but different ones.

FERRARI. The Greeks may have poorly understood that tradition but, also, the West could have misunderstood the Greeks. Because if we say that Plato, and perhaps Pythagoras, is the first mystic in the West . . .

BORGES. I think that the word 'first' doesn't have an important meaning as it cannot be proved, but . . .

FERRARI. Just that our philosophy began there, but instead of taking Plato we took Aristotle as our starting point, and we will have to try to find out, one day, what was right or wrong about that, because everything would have been different . . .

BORGES. In any case, they represent two very different facts for us— Aristotle thought by reasoning while Plato thought through myths.

FERRARI. Exactly.

BORGES. And you see that in Socrates' last dialogue where he uses reason and myth at the same time. Since Aristotle, we use one or the other system—we are no longer capable of using both. I, personally, am almost unable to think by reasoning. It seems that I reason, knowing it's a dangerous and fallible method . . . I tend to think through myth, through dreams or my own inventions.

FERRARI. Or through intuitions, as in the East.

BORGES. Yes, or through intuitions. But I know that the other system is more rigorous. So I try to reason, although I know I am not capable of it. On the other hand, I am told that I am able to dream and I hope to continue doing so. After all, I am not a thinker—I am a mere short-story writer, a mere poet. I am resigned to my fate but that fate clearly need not be inferior to any other.

FERRARI. But you pointed out that, instead of mysticism and poetry as a tradition, we have opted for reason and method.

BORGES. Yes, but we are ruled by mysticism and poetry.

FERRARI. Ah, I see.

BORGES. Of course we are ruled unconsciously but we are ruled.

FERRARI. It's odd, because Western philosophers like Wittgenstein end up talking about mystical or divine possibilities after a rational journey that has lasted centuries.

BORGES. Perhaps if you exercise reason exclusively, you end by becoming sceptical of it, for everyone becomes sceptical of what they know. Poets faced with language, for example, are easily sceptical of language precisely because they handle it and know its limits. I think Goethe said, 'I have been given the worst material' when he spoke of the German language (though I think he was mistaken about that). In the end, he had to struggle with German, he knew its limits. If it's not boastful to say so . . . my fate was the Spanish language and thus I am very sensitive to its obstacles and awkwardness precisely because I have to handle it. Other languages I simply receive. I receive them with gratitude, of course—I try to receive everything with gratitude and not notice the defects. But if my fate had been another language, I would have noticed its deficiencies or weaknesses.

FERRARI. It's curious that, of late, you have been talking more and more about acceptance and gratitude.

ory of the Greek Democritus who

BORGES. I believe, like Chesterton, that you should be grateful for everything. Chesterton said that the fact of being on Earth, of having your feet on Earth, of seeing the sky, of having been in love, are all gifts for which you shouldn't cease to be grateful. And I try to feel this, I have tried to feel that my blindness is not just a misfortune—it is, but it has also allowed me, has given me time for solitude, for thought, for inventing fables, for fabricating poems. All that is a benefit, isn't it? I remember the story of the Greek Democritus who ripped out his eyes in a garden so that they would not disrupt his contemplation of the outer world. In a poem I wrote, 'Time has been my Democritus.' It's true. I am now blind but perhaps being blind is not a sad fate. Although just the thought that books are at hand and yet so far away makes me want to see. Should I recover my sight, I think I would settle down and read all the books I have here, books I barely know, although I know them from memory but that modifies everything.

FERRARI. Not too long ago I told you that you were distancing yourself from Plato. Now I see that you are closer than ever to the mystical Plato I mentioned earlier.

BORGES. Perhaps to distance yourself from Plato is dangerous. And from Aristotle as well. Why not accept both? Both are benefactors.

FERRARI. Perhaps its best to have a synthesis of both.

11

Art Should Free Itself from Time

●

OSVALDO FERRARI. Today we will talk about beauty. But before we do so, we will transcribe your views about the place of art and literature in our times as discussed in an earlier conversation.

JORGE LUIS BORGES. Art and literature . . . should try and free themselves from time. Often, I have been told that art depends on politics or on history. I think that's untrue. It escapes, in some way, from the organized causality of history. Whether art happens or doesn't, neither depend on the artist.

FERRARI. Another matter not usually talked or thought about, apart from the spiritual life, is beauty. It's odd that, these days, artists or writers do not talk about what is supposedly always their inspiration or objective, that is, beauty.

BORGES. Perhaps the word has been worn out but not the concept— because what purpose does art have other than beauty? Perhaps the word 'beauty' is not beautiful though the fact is, of course.

FERRARI. Certainly, but in your writing, your poems, your stories . . .

BORGES. I try to avoid what's called 'ugly art'—sounds horrible, doesn't it? But there have been so many literary movements with horrible names. In Mexico, for example, there was a literary movement frighteningly called Stridentism. It finally shut up, which was the best thing it could do. To aspire to be strident—how awkward, isn't it? My friend Manuel Maples Arce led that movement against the great poet Ramón López Velarde. I remember his first book—without any hint of beauty, it was called 'Inner Scaffolding'. That's very awkward, isn't it? (*Laughs*) To possess inner scaffolding? I remember one line of a poem, if it was a poem at all: 'A man with tuberculosis has committed suicide in all the newspapers'. It's the only line I recall. Perhaps my forgetfulness is kind—if that was the best line in the book, one shouldn't expect much from the rest of it. I saw him many years later in Japan. I think he was the Mexican ambassador there, and that had made him forget not only literature but his literature. But he has remained in the histories of literature, which collects everything, as the founder of the Stridentist movement (*both laugh*). Wanting to be strident—one of the most awkward of literary desires.

FERRARI. As we are talking about beauty, I would like to consult you about something that has caught my attention. Plato said that of all the archetypal and supernatural entities, the only visible one on earth, the only manifest one, is beauty.

BORGES. Yes, made manifest through other things.

FERRARI. Caught by our senses.

BORGES. I'm not sure about that.

FERRARI. That's what Plato said.

BORGES. Well, of course, I suppose that the beauty of a poem has to appeal to our ears and the beauty of a sculpture has to pass through touch and sight. But these are mediums and nothing more. I don't know if we see beauty or if beauty reaches us through forms which could be verbal or sensual or, as in the case of music, auditory. Walter Pater said that all the arts aspire to the condition of music. I think that is because form and content fuse in music. That is, one can tell the plot of a story, perhaps even give it away, or that of a novel, but one cannot tell the story of a melody, however straightforward it may be. Stevenson said, though I think he was mistaken, that a literary character is nothing but a string of words. Well, it is true, but at the same time it's necessary that we perceive it as more than a string of words. We must believe in it.

FERRARI. It must, in some way, be real.

BORGES. Yes. Because if we sense that a character is only a string of words, then that character has not been well created. For example, reading a novel, we must believe that its characters live beyond what the author tells us about them. If we think about any character in a novel or a play, we have to think that this character, in the moment that we see him, sleeps, dreams and carries out diverse functions. Because if we don't, then he would be completely unreal.

FERRARI. Yes. There's a sentence by Dostoyevsky that caught my eye as much as one by Plato. About beauty, he said, 'In beauty, God and the devil fight and the battlefield is man's heart.'

BORGES. That's very similar to one by Ibsen, 'That life is a battle with the devil in the grottoes and caverns of the brain and that poetry is the fact of celebrating the final judgement about oneself.' It's quite similar, isn't it?

FERRARI. It is. Plato attributes beauty to a destiny, a mission. And among us, Murena has said that he considers beauty capable of transmitting an other-worldly truth.

BORGES. If it's not transmitted, if we do not receive it as a revelation beyond what's given by our senses, then it's useless. I believe that feeling is common. I have noticed that people are constantly capable of uttering poetic phrases they do not appreciate. For example, my mother commented on the death of a very young cousin to our cook from Córdoba. And the cook said, quite unaware that it was literary, 'But Señora, in order to die, you only need to be alive.' You only need to be alive! She was unaware that she had uttered a memorable sentence. I used it later in a story: 'You only need to be alive'—you do not require any other conditions to die, that's the sole one. I think people are always uttering memorable phrases without realizing it. Perhaps the artist's role is to gather such phrases and retain them. George Bernard Shaw says that all his clever expressions are the ones he had casually overheard. But that could be another clever feature of Shaw's modesty.

FERRARI. A writer would be, in that case, a great coordinator of other people's wit.

BORGES. Yes, let's say, everyone's secretary—a secretary for so many masters that perhaps what matters is to be a secretary and not the inventor of the sayings.

FERRARI. An individual memory of a collective.

BORGES. Yes, exactly that.

12

Tigers, Labyrinths, Mirrors and Weapons

●

OSVALDO FERRARI. Borges, for a while now I have wanted to refer to an idea you have articulated several times.

JORGE LUIS BORGES. I have very few ideas and always express them poorly (*laughs*).

FERRARI. That's how they become strong (*both laugh*). You have said that every writer, especially every poet, is fated to have a personal universe. That he is somehow conditioned by a personal universe that has been allotted to him and to which he must remain loyal.

BORGES. I don't know if he must but in fact he does stay loyal to it. It might be impoverishing but one has to live. We write in a rather limited world, don't we? That's a fact, even if it might be better if we didn't.

FERRARI. In your case, you conjure up tigers, steel blades, mirrors and labyrinths, among others.

BORGES. It's true. I'm easily monotonous. Do I have to give a reason for this? I did not choose those themes—they choose me.

FERRARI. Of course.

BORGES. But I believe that this can be applied to all themes. I think it's a mistake to look for themes, and it's a mistake journalists rather than writers make. A writer should let the themes seek him out, he should start by rejecting them and then, grown resigned to them, he can write them down and pass them on to others. Isn't that it?

FERRARI. That's why some themese are fated to be yours.

BORGES. Yes, because they return. I know that if I write the word 'tiger', it's a word I have written hundreds of times. But I also know that if I write 'leopard', I am cheating and the reader will realize that it's a slightly disguised tiger, a tiger with spots and not stripes. One grows resigned to things like that.

FERRARI. Yes, but in your poem 'The Panther' you have managed to establish something completely different from a tiger.

BORGES. Well, for 14 lines perhaps, but not more (*both laugh*). I think that you, or the reader, can clearly see that it's a variant of a tiger.

FERRARI. If you agree, I would like to read 'The Panther' so that our listeners can see if it is really different from a tiger.

BORGES. I think it's exactly the same.

FERRARI. Behind strong bars the panther
Will repeat his monotonous journey
Which is (but he ignores it) his destiny
Of a black jewel, ill-fated, a prisoner

BORGES. Goodness, not bad. Go on.

FERRARI. There are thousands that pass by
And thousands that return, but the panther
Is one and eternal, fated in its cave,
He traces the straight line that eternal Achilles
Traced in the dream dreamt by the Greek.

BORGES. Of course, Achilles and the tortoise—the two in Zeno of Elea's paradox.

FERRARI. He does not know there are fields and mountains
Of deer whose quivering entrails
Will delight his blind appetite.

Borges, Silvina Ocampo is surely right in saying that at times you have a cruel streak.

BORGES. She's very right. This poem, and I've just realized this, can be seen as the opposite of 'Captive Lion', a vastly superior sonnet by none other than Lugones. The captive lion thinks about the deer that go down to the river . . . the alarmed trotting of gazelles. I don't believe it happens that way—I imagine an animal living a moment. But Lugones imagines a lion conscious of his imprisonment, remembering a past through memories not personal but inherited . . . then he writes something about the decline of empires or the decadence of empires. So it's the opposite. In my poem it's nothing like that. My animal is conceived of as living a moment, without memory—without a sense of past or future. My panther is travelling up and down his cage and that is his destiny. The panther doesn't know this but the reader does.

FERRARI. It's the idea that a cat that lives in the eternity of the moment inspired in you.

BORGES. Yes, it's the same idea. The idea that animals do not know time, that time is peculiar to man. Yeats exaggerated that idea in that splendid poem which ends:

He knows death to the bone—
Man has created death.

Man is conscious of death which also, of course, means that he is conscious of the past and the future.

FERRARI. 'The Panther' ends with these two lines:

In vain is the orb various. The day's journey
That each of us completes was already fixed.

BORGES. Ah, that's an extension of that idea about man. Because he reaches, in the end, the idea of fatality, an Islamic and Calvinistic idea about everything being prefigured. That is, not only is the lineal life of the panther in its cage fixed but also our lives and this dialogue with you, Ferrari. Everything is fixed.

FERRARI. Let's hope so.

BORGES. This does not imply that someone has fixed it. Because the two ideas are often confused. I think that you can believe in predestination yet not suppose that someone has knowledge about predestination . . . it's something given in a fatal game of cause and effect . . .

FERRARI. In that case, this dialogue, as you say, would be cosmic and ordered.

BORGES. Certainly. Moreover, it's being fixed by a machine, I think (*both laugh*).

FERRARI. As for labyrinths, I was thinking that not long ago you stood in perhaps the most famous of them all . . .

BORGES. In Crete, yes. Strangely, it is not known if Knossos was originally a labyrinth. I don't think so. It seems it was a palace and then Herodotus' idea of a labyrinth was brought over. He speaks of labyrinths in Egypt—I'm not sure he speaks of labyrinths in Crete. I don't think so. That would come later . . . I'm not sure of this, it's so easy to be mistaken.

FERRARI. Back from your travels, you also showed me some beautiful steel blades, knives brought from Greece, one of them with an amazing goat-horn handle.

BORGES. It's that people, thanks to my 'literature'—let's call it that, using that word in quotation marks—associate me with steel blades so they give me daggers as presents which I like a lot. Although I never learnt how to knife fight for I am very awkward. *Vistear* is the Spanish word, it is very exact and better than the verb *barajar* used in Uruguay. You concentrate on your adversary's eyes and not the hand that holds the weapon, and by looking into the his eyes you can guess his intentions. And then your hands do their work. I have been given knives from many parts of the world as presents.

FERRARI. They should give you swords as presents too. It seems to me that there are more swords mentioned in your work than daggers.

BORGES. That's right, but swords are more cumbersome, aren't they? (*Laughs.*) It's easier to travel with a dagger.

FERRARI. As for mirrors . . .

BORGES. They corresponds to the idea of the double, the idea of another self. And refers to another different idea—the idea of time. And the idea of time is this—the idea that the self lasts and that everything else changes. Yet there's something mysterious about memory which is both actor and spectator. So, the idea of the mirror, yes, there's something terrifying about mirrors. I recall Poe's *Narrative of Arthur Gordon Pym* in which the characters reach a region in the Antarctic where people faint when they see themselves in a mirror. Doubtless, Poe felt that way too; there's an essay on the topic of how a room should be decorated in which he claims that mirrors should be hung in such a way that a person sitting down cannot see his reflection. Poe must have been afraid of mirrors. If he wasn't, how do you explain that precaution about a mirror not reflecting a seated person? Without a doubt, he'd felt this horror—it's there in two of his texts, two unmistakeable allusions to a mirror as terrifying. It's odd that he didn't write more about it.

FERRARI. As we mentioned when we were talking about dreams, in a mirror we have a worrying split of personality.

BORGES. In front of a mirror, of course. And, doubtless, that phrase 'alter ego', another self, attributed to Pythagoras, is exactly that idea and was conceived from a reflection in a mirror. Later it was applied to friendship, though that is false—a friend is not another self. If a friend was another self, it would be very monotonous. A friend has to be another person with his own set of characteristics.

FERRARI. Naturally. What philosophy now calls a 'relation with alterity' would be an approximation with the other, differentiated from one's self.

BORGES. Yes, it wouldn't be another self. The stress would be on 'self', not on 'other'.

FERRARI. Tigers, steel blades, mirrors and labyrinths . . . what other elements in your personal universe stands out as a constant in your later work?

BORGES. In dreams?

FERRARI. Or when awake?

BORGES. Well, now there's the theme of death. Because now I feel a kind of impatience. I think I should die and die soon. I have lived too long. And I am very curious too. I think, but am unsure, that death must have a special taste, something unique, something one has never experienced. The proof is . . . I have seen many people in their death throes, people who knew they were going to die. Recently, Alberto Girri told me that he had been with Mujica Lainez a month before his death and Lainez told him that he was about to die, that he had no fears—only a great certainty. That certainty could not be grounded in reason but in death's peculiar taste. That we will feel it and know it's something we have never experienced . . . that it cannot be communicated, goes without saying. You can only communicate that which can be shared. Words presuppose shared experiences. In the case of death, not yet.

FERRARI. Yet, what you brought back from your journey, the mood on your return, contradicts that approximation to death that you have pointed out.

BORGES. Well, that approximation arrives anyway. Also, I'm not talking about an immediate approximation but a specific impatience. But, perhaps, when death's moment comes, I will find out that I am a big coward. Although I have seen many dying people . . . by the time you are 84 you do see many die, and whoever is dying always feels this impatience. They want to die once and for all.

FERRARI. Despite everything, from each trip, you have come back with something completely new. That could indicate that your wish to travel is greater than your anxiety to die (*laughs*).

BORGES (*laughs*). Well, death may be a journey, obviously better than Sinbad's seven journeys. It would be far longer, wouldn't it?

13

Kafka Could Be Part of Human Memory

●

OSVALDO FERRARI. Before you go abroad again, Borges, I would like to discuss your travel plans. You'll start in France, continue to England and then to the United States, right? France will be first, then?

JORGE LUIS BORGES. France first. There will be a congress on a person who would have been astounded by the thought of a congress about him, and that is Kafka. His works are a wonderful subject for discussion and an infinite one too. Works based, according to what Carlos Mastronardi told me, on Zeno of Elea's paradoxes. The idea, for example, of the infinite race of the tortoise whose aim is to never reach the finishing line. Kafka, as Mastronardi rightly told me, poignantly adopted that theme—that was Kafka's great invention. I will have to talk in front of an organization that sounds at first to be very tedious but isn't—the Academy of Sciences and Arts. I have been told that I can choose the topic. Let's see if we can agree on what I would prefer—a conversation with the public that would hopefully be like this one with you, that is, an easy-going dialogue.

Then I have to receive my honorary doctorate from Cambridge University. Then I am to receive some honour from the Marquis of Ricci in New York. I don't know what it will be but I will feel duly amazed and pleased. Especially with the chance to tour, or just be in, those three countries. I would like to spend some days rummaging about in bookshops, especially in London. And then New York.

Really, a less varied trip than the last one which covered Sicily, Venice and Vicenza, then Greece and Crete which are very different regions. Of course, the Cretans believe they are far more ancient than the Greeks and view them as garrulous. Nationalism prospers everywhere—someone is born two metres to the right or two metres to the left and has made a mistake by not being born in the required centre . . . That's the case, sadly, in Sicily. They insist on being Normans. I have no idea why they chose the Normans, rather than . . . well, why not, I have some Norman blood too. On my last trip I was in Japan too, and flew over the North Pole twice. It's a peculiar experience which is actually nothing more than an awareness that you are flying above the North Pole—you don't really see anything, do you? (*Laughs.*) Apparently you can see some icebergs—that's what María Kodama told me—but that's all. And then, knowing that you are flying over the North Pole although it doesn't know it's the North Pole, naturally (*laughs*).

FERRARI. Borges, as your journey begins in France, and begins with Kafka as well, I would like to talk about him. I don't know if you have decided on a way to expound the theme there. You have, I know, often written on Kafka . . .

BORGES. Yes, I have and I'll do my best not to plagiarize myself (*laughs*)—it's better to plagiarize others. But sometimes, at the age of 84, because I do not reread what I have written, I plagiarize myself, that too badly. Matters I have more or less articulated well I now repeat poorly. Well, that can happen . . .

When you read the great writers, you constantly have to make allowances—you have to keep in mind that this was written in such-and-such a period and so on. Take Shakespeare, the greatest example. In his case, you have to bear in mind that he was writing for a public he didn't choose, that his work had to last for as long as what we now call five acts (they were continuous then). That is, an extension in time. For his starting point, he represented or borrowed traditional arguments that were not his own. Then he had to fit his characters into these arguments and the discord is evident. For example, I believe in Hamlet but I am not sure, despite my best efforts, that I believe in Hamlet's ghost. And I am not sure I believe in the Danish court and its intrigues either. Not at all. In Macbeth's case, I believe in Macbeth and in Lady Macbeth. I am ready to believe in the Parcae, who are also the witches, but I don't know if I believe in the fable. As for the other writers, you have to remember that they wrote in such-and-such a period, under such-and-such conditions . . . you have to situate them in literary history. Only then can you forgive or endure certain things.

In Kafka's case, I think that he can be read beyond his historical circumstances. And there are two very important ones. Kafka writes a good part of his work during the 1914–18 war. One of the worst wars ever. He must have suffered it greatly. Also, he was a Jew at a time when anti-Semitism was growing. He lived in Austria, well, Bohemia which was then part of Austria. He died in Berlin, I think. All these circumstances—living in a besieged city, in a country that was winning but was then defeated—reverberates in his work. Yet if a reader did not know about this, he wouldn't notice it. Kafka transmuted all this.

The other circumstance is that Kafka was a friend of the Expressionists. The Expressionists led the most important aesthetic movement of the twentieth century, far more interesting than Surrealism or Cubism or Futurism or mere Imagism. It was a total revision of literature. The same goes for painting. We can think of Ernst Barlach, of Oskar Kokoschka and others. Kafka was their friend. They wrote, they continuously renovated language, wove metaphors. You could say that the greatest Expressionist work was Joyce's, although he didn't belong to the movement and he wrote in English and not German (or rather in his English, a different English with made-up words). Expressionism was a great literary movement and Kafka published in one of its two magazines—I'm not sure if it was in *Die Aktion* or in *Sturm*. I had a subscription to both in the years 1916 and 1917. That's when I first read a text by Kafka. I was so insensitive that I thought him tame, slightly anodyne compared with the verbal splendours of Expressionism (*laughs*). But Kafka went on to become the great classic writer of our tormented century. He will possibly be read in the future too, and it will be forgotten that he wrote at the beginning of the twentieth century, that he was a contemporary of the Expressionists and the First World War. All that will be forgotten. His work can become anonymous, and perhaps in time deserves to be so. It's the most that a work can aim for, isn't it? Few books attain that status.

When you read *The Arabian Nights* you accept Islam. You accept the fables woven by generations as if they were by one single author or, better still, as if they had no author. And in fact they have one and none. Something so worked on, so polished by generations is no longer associated with an individual. In Kafka's case, it's possible that his fables are now part of human memory. What happened to *Quixote* could happen to them. Let's say that all the copies of *Quixote*, in Spanish and in translation, were lost. The figure of Don Quixote would remain in human memory. I think that the idea of a frightening trial that goes on for ever, which is at the core of *The Castle* and *The Trial* (both books that Kafka, of course, never wanted to publish because he knew they were unfinished), is now grown infinite, is now part of human memory and can now be rewritten under different titles and feature different circumstances. Kafka's work now forms a part of human memory. I think that's what I will say in France, I will point out that the works are classics and the fact that we can read them and forget their circumstances—that happens with very few authors . . .

FERRARI. The paradox is that with this status of a classic, we are constantly told that the bridge that Franz Kafka tends between previous epochs and ours is unavoidable, as it is with James Joyce, Marcel Proust and Henry James.

BORGES. Perhaps James is closer to him. Proust would not have been interested and Joyce not at all—Joyce corresponds to Expressionism, to the idea of art as something passionate as well as verbal. For Joyce, what mattered was every line he wrote. But Kafka lived surrounded by people who were or tried to be Joyce, without realizing it, of course. Yet Kafka himself wrote in a rather straightforward German. So straightforward that I, while learning German, could understand it. Other writers have given me considerable trouble. For example, the Expressionists. Johannes Becher, whom I much admire, became the epitome of Expressionism. I did not understand Becher, I could not understand what I was reading through his verbal games.

FERRARI. But we are told that we cannot make a faithful interpretation of our times without Kafka's help.

BORGES. Yes, but Kafka is more important than our times. It's lamentable that Kafka has to survive this period and its simplifications. Of course, we endure this century without much pride. With a little nostalgia for the nineteenth century, which also feels like nostalgia for the eighteenth century. Perhaps Oswald Spengler was right about the decline that we are nostalgic about—obviously, we can talk of *mon vieux temps* and perhaps we are right. There's a reference to this in Jorge Manrique's *Coplas* but it's ironic: 'As it seems to us, any time in the past / was better.' 'As it seems to us' followed by 'any time in the past was better'—yes, that's what Schopenhauer said. We see the past as better but we also see it as something that has stopped. We are no longer actors but spectators. In what is called the present we are actors, there's an idea of responsibility and, associated with it, an idea of danger. The past, even if it was terrible . . . we can even think of Rosas' times nostalgically because, although it was terrible, it has passed. It has been fixed in time and so have its terrible images. On the other hand, the present can threaten us, just as life threatens us every second we're alive.

FERRARI. That's right and this was another point I wanted to mention with regard to Kafka. A writer you know wrote a very significant essay on Kafka, which I recently glanced at. I am referring to Carmen Gándara.

BORGES. I knew her and have fond memories of her. I read a story of hers, 'The Inhabited'. I'm not sure but isn't it similar to Julio Cortázar's 'House Taken Over'? Or is the theme different?

FERRARI. The scope is different. She refers to Kafka and says something that struck me—that throughout his life, Kafka sought a God 'absent' in our times.

BORGES. Yes, I have been asked that many times. I do not understand that question.

FERRARI. She means that, despite everything, Kafka might have had a religious spirit.

BORGES. Yes, but a religious spirit need not believe in a personal god. For example, the Buddhist mystics do not believe in a personal god but that doesn't matter. The idea of believing in a personal god is not a necessary factor in a religious spirit. The pantheists are an example or Spinoza—he was essentially mystical and he said 'Deus sive natura,' God or Nature. The two ideas were identical for him. That's not the case for a Christian because Christianity needs to believe in a personal god, in a god who judges your acts. In Emerson's *Representative Men*, the mystic is Swedenborg. He didn't believe in a

personal god but he chooses between Heaven or Hell. After dying—
he actually says this—Man finds himself in a strange region and is
addressed by unfamiliar people; some attract him and some do not.
He goes along with those who do. If he is an evil man, then those
who attract him are devils. Because he will be more at ease with devils
than with angels. And if he is a just man, he will be at ease with
angels. He chooses his company accordingly. Once he's in Heaven
or Hell, he doesn't want to be anywhere else because he will suffer
too much. Swedenborg believed in a personal god, that's certain. But
the pantheists, in general, didn't. What matters is that there's an ethical proposition in the universe. If there is an ethical proposition, and
if you feel it, then you have a religious mind. And I believe that we
should try to believe in an ethical proposition, although it doesn't
exist. But in the end, it depends on us, doesn't it?

14

Modernismo and Rubén Darío

●

OSVALDO FERRARI. We have talked many times about the most important literary movement in our language . . .

JORGE LUIS BORGES. Modernismo?

FERRARI. Yes, and about its influence on the other side of the ocean. We have talked about Modernismo and about some of its personalities but we have not referred in particular to its great central figure. He has remained implicit or implied . . .

BORGES. Rubén Darío?

FERRARI. Exactly.

BORGES. I recall talking to Lugones four or five times in my life. And each time he deflected the conversation to talk about 'My friend and master Rubén Darío'. He liked accentuating that filial relationship. He was so proud, so authoritarian as a man, yet he felt the need to recognize that relationship. I have heard that Darío was scandalized by what he called the excessive liberties in Lugones' *Lunario sentimental*. Yet *Lunario*—whose date of publication I don't recall, it must have been between 1900 and 1910—was dedicated to Darío and other 'accomplices' (*laughs*). What an odd word 'accomplices', isn't it?

FERRARI. Of the movement . . .

BORGES. Yes, but it seemed to Darío that he had gone too far. It seemed that Lugones thought the same about Freyre. But he then surpassed Freyre's liberties in his *Lunario sentimental*. In Darío's case, I find his work so uneven . . . his best is based purely on the cadence of his lines, isn't it?

FERRARI. In the music . . .

BORGES. In the music, yes. I think there's no doubt about that because in the end, when he began to express them, his political opinions were rather trivial. For example, that ode 'To Roosevelt' begins well: 'It's with a biblical voice or Whitman's verse that I will reach you, Hunter.' But in the end, he says, 'The Spanish Lion has let a thousand puppies loose,' which doesn't convince me and nor does the following: 'And, as you count on everything, the one thing you lack is God!' Well, rhetorically, it's fine, but . . . I would say that the weakest bit of Darío's work—and I state this publicly—is that elegy he wrote after the death of Mitre. One can tell that it's not stimulated by the slightest emotion, that he wrote it to keep in with the newspaper *La Nación*. His 'Ode to Argentina' is very weak too. The line 'Exodus saved you, there's only one Argentina on earth!' has no poetic value. The poem to Mitre contains some stanzas that can make one feel personally ashamed:

> The work where you did so much,
> Civil triumph over souls

> Progress full of palm trees
> Freedom above the ombú!

Yes, it's better to forget them.

FERRARI. A bit forced.

BORGES. Completely forced. Against this, Lugones wrote his 'Ode to Cattle and Grains'—it's on the same topic but written with so much more emotion. Clearly, there was no reason for Darío to feel any emotion and that's exactly how his poem is written.

FERRARI. He felt obliged . . .

BORGES. I would say that if I had to choose a piece by Darío, and there's no reason to have to for there are so many that are excellent, I would chose his 'Response' to Verlaine's death: 'Father and master magician, celestial lyrical dreamer.' And his 'I Was a Slave Who Slept in Queen Cleopatra's Bed' written in the 1880s, that is, before his famous poems. His most famous is perhaps his worst, 'Sonatina': 'The Princess is sad. What ails the Princess?' And more of the dross follows: 'Sighs escaped her strawberry mouth'—hardly admirable! 'She has lost her laughter, has lost her colour' is worthless, but then we have a magical line: 'The Princess is pale in her golden chair,' which is so attractive that it forces your voice to slow down, and then:

> The keyboard of the sonorous clavichord is mute
> and in a vase, a forgotten flower faints.

This is not particularly good and then that dreadful line: 'A sleepless greyhound and a colossal dragon'—that colossal dragon makes everything seem like a lie, doesn't it? You know there's no colossal dragon. Moreover, 'colossal' seems to shrink it, somehow.

FERRARI. The dragon?

BORGES. Yes, or makes it look like cardboard. Yet it was one of the lines that staggered his readers the most.

FERRARI. Many writers suffer due to the obligatory teaching of their work in schools.

BORGES. I have a strange example of this. I was talking to an Italian gentleman who told me that at school he had learnt two or three cantos from *La Divina Commedia* by heart. At that time he had hated Dante and the *Commedia*, but years later he reread it and discovered that it was rather good (*both laugh*), despite that loathing that the obligatory reading had inculcated. Reading should not be obligatory.

FERRARI. When he could read the cantos freely, he liked them.

BORGES. Yes, what happens with obligatory reading is the same as what happens with street names—they are named after people and thus imply a kind of ill-fated transmigration, that is, a person turned into a street.

FERRARI. Yes.

BORGES. In 50 years, Lavalle will be Lavalle Street or Lavalle Plaza, unless substituted by some other notable leader. This happens with time. We talk every day about Esmeralda Street but I'm ashamed to admit that I haven't a clue about Esmeralda. I suppose it has something to do with Chile but I don't know why. The same goes for Florida Street. I don't think it refers to the American state—there must be some other reason.

FERRARI. The obligatory reading is damaging, especially in Darío's case because recent generations do not approach him—because of his statuesque name, they feel it would be tedious to stop before him.

BORGES. Perhaps the worst that can befall a writer is for him to become a classic, for then he is truly dead (*both laugh*), which is what happened to Marinetti in Italy. Now he and his work are museum pieces. I'm not sure if that would have made him happy or indignant—after all, he had wanted to destroy museums.

FERRARI. We do not know. But as important as your perception of the validity of music in Darío's poetry is your appreciation of the way he renovated metre and metaphor . . .

BORGES. And themes, language . . .

FERRARI. And sensibility.

BORGES. Sensibility, yes, of course. One can feel things in a different way, a way more delicate way than Darío. All this, of course, thanks to Hugo and Verlaine. How odd, because Hugo and Verlaine are perceived in France as antagonistic. Here, on the other hand, Spanish literature was so impoverished that it welcomed them like two helpful guests and didn't think that between them . . . I don't think that Verlaine liked Hugo much though Hugo appreciated Verlaine. That was because Hugo was so sure of himself. And he had such a generous soul—he praised everyone, even Baudelaire, he said that Baudelaire had brought a *frisson nouveau* to poetry's firmament.

FERRARI. Yes, 'a new thrill'.

BORGES. Yes, it was very generous of Hugo to say that, and very just. What a pity that Hugo and Whitman never got to know each other.

It's possible that Hugo died without having heard Whitman's name. I think he died in the 1880s, I'm not sure, and Whitman's work dates from 1885. By then Hugo was already famous. But they didn't know each other. I'm sure they would have liked each other.

FERRARI. Surely.

BORGES. Because they complement each other in some ways.

FERRARI. At the same time, it's heart-warming to see Darío's devotion to Verlaine, as seen in his 'Response'.

BORGES. Ah, yes. The fact is that if you do not feel Verlaine in your guts, you do not feel him at all.

FERRARI. Yes.

BORGES. Just one of Verlaine's lines is sufficient: Le vent de l'autre nuit a jeté bas l'amour (Last night's wind has knocked love down), which refers to love and to an image, a statue, of love, and it can be read both ways because they are not mutually exclusive. Dante comes to mind. In his letter to Cangrande de la Scala, Dante said his work could be read in four different ways. That was also supposed to be applicable to the Holy Scriptures. Now people ignorantly criticize Dante, ignorantly assume that he believed that the other world was exactly like this one. Curiously, one such was Paul Claudel: 'We certainly expect different marvels in the other world from Dante's.' But Dante already knew that. He didn't assume that each one of us would meet all those people speaking Italian and in tercets—that's absurd!

FERRARI. I agree. The other aspect that interests me is that you seem to regard Modernismo as a movement that aims at freedom.

BORGES. Yes, I think so. I think that all that has been done since wouldn't have happened without Modernismo. Though, in some ways, it would be extremely unfair to blame Modernismo for the Ultraist Movement, which was nonsense, or for Creationism. Yet these movements wouldn't have happened without Darío.

FERRARI. But what has freedom to do with this? Is it because it breaks with previous forms?

BORGES. No, because I believe that since the Golden Age, perhaps even in the Golden Age, Spanish poetry has been in decline. To me, Conceptismo and Culteranismo are already forms of decadence. There's something . . . In the end, everything becomes rigid. On the other hand, in the ballads, in Fray Luis de León, in St John of the Cross, in Manrique, the forms are not rigid—everything flows. Later, especially in Quevedo or Góngora or Gracián, it's already rigid. Then we have the impoverished eighteenth and nineteenth centuries. Then along comes Darío and everything is renewed. The renovation happens in America and then reaches Spain and inspires great poets, like the Machado brothers and Juan Ramón Jiménez, to mention a a few. I'm sure there are more.

FERRARI. So we could think of Darío, Lugones and Freyre as liberators within poetry?

BORGES. Yes, I think so. According to Lugones, the first was Darío.

FERRARI. Of course.

BORGES. No one doubts this today. In fact, that's why it seems trite, precisely because he was the first of the renovators. Under Poe's influence, of course. How odd—Poe is American, he was born in Boston and died in Baltimore, but he reached our poetry because Baudelaire translated him.

FERRARI. That's true.

BORGES. Because without him, it wouldn't have happened. So those three influences are really French influences.

15

Doubts about a Personal Divinity

●

OSVALDO FERRARI. Many people still ask whether Borges believes in God, because at times they feel he does and at times that he doesn't.

JORGE LUIS BORGES. If God means something in us that strives for good, yes. If he's thought of as an individual being, then no, I don't believe. I believe in an ethical proposition, perhaps not in the universe but in each one of us. And if I could I would add, like Blake, an aesthetic and an intellectual proposition but with reference to individuals again. I'm not sure it would apply to the universe. I remember Tennyson's line: 'Nature red in tooth and claw'. He wrote that because so many people talked about a gentle Nature.

FERRARI. What you have just said confirms my impression that your possible conflict about belief or disbelief in God has to do with the possibility that God may be just or unjust.

BORGES. Well, I think that it's enough to glance at the universe to note that justice certainly does not rule. I recall a line from Almafuerte: 'With delicate art, I spread a caress on every reptile, I did not think justice was necessary when pain rules everywhere.' In another line, he says, 'All I ask is justice / but better to ask for nothing.' Already to ask for justice is to ask for much, too much.

FERRARI. Yet, you also recognize in the world the existence of happiness—in a library, perhaps, but other kinds of happiness too.

BORGES. That, yes, of course. I would say that happiness can be momentary but that it also happens frequently, it can happen, for instance, even in our dialogue.

FERRARI. There's another significant impact—the impact that prompts most poets to hold on to the notion of another world, a world apart from this one. Because there's always something in the poet's words that seems to send us beyond what is mentioned in the writing.

BORGES. Yes, but that beyond is perhaps projected by the writing or by the emotions that lead to the writing. That is, that other world is, perhaps, a beautiful human invention.

FERRARI. But we could say that in all poetry there's an approximation to something else, beyond the words and the subject matter.

BORGES. Well, language does not match up to the complexity of things. I think that the philosopher Whitehead talks of the paradox of the perfect dictionary, that is, the idea of supposing that all the words that a dictionary registers exhaust reality. Chesterton also wrote about this, saying that it is absurd to suppose that all the nuances of human consciousness, which are more vast than a jungle, can be contained in a mechanical system of grunts which would be, in this case, the words spoken by a stockbroker. That's absurd and yet people talk of a perfect language, of a rich language, but in comparison to our consciousness language is very poor. I think that somewhere Stevenson says that what happens in ten minutes exceeds all Shakespeare's vocabulary (*laughs*). I believe it's the same idea.

FERRARI. Throughout your writing, you have referred to what's divine, including the supernatural. You have also accepted, in one of our dialogues, Murena's words about beauty being able to transmit an otherworldly truth. That is, you seem to admit that transcendence exists but you don't call it God.

BORGES. I do think that it's safer not to call it God. If we call it God, then we are thinking of an individual and that individual is mysteriously three, according to the doctrine of the Trinity which to me is quite inconceivable. On the other hand, if we employ other words, perhaps less precise or vivid ones, then we could approach the truth, if an approach to truth is possible. Or it could be something that we ignore.

FERRARI. That's exactly why one could think that you do not name God. Even though you believe in the perception of another reality, besides the everyday one.

BORGES. I am unsure if this reality is an everyday one. We don't know if the universe belongs to a realist genre or a fantastic one, because if, as idealists believe, everything is a dream, then what we call reality is essentially oneiric. Schopenhauer spoke of the 'essence' (oneiric sounds pedantic, doesn't it?). Let's say, 'The dream-like essence of life'. Yes, because 'oneiric' suggests something sad—like psychoanalysis (*laughs*).

FERRARI. Besides faith or its absence, another question is whether you consider love in universal terms, as a power or a necessary force for the fulfilment of life.

BORGES. I don't know if it's necessary but, yes, it is inevitable.

FERRARI. I don't mean love between two human beings but what men receive or do not receive, as they receive air or light. A love that is eventually supernatural.

BORGES. At times I feel, how can I put it? mysteriously grateful. When I have an idea that will later, sadly, become a story or a poem, I have a sensation of receiving something. But I do not know if that 'something' is given to me by something or someone or if it bursts out on its own. Yeats held a doctrine of a great memory and thought that it wasn't important for a poet to have many experiences because he inherited memory from his parents, his grandparents, his great-grandparents. This multiplies itself in geometric progression until he inherits humankind's memory and this 'something' is revealed to him. Now, De Quincey thought that memory is perfect, that is, I have in myself everything that I have felt, everything that I have thought since childhood. But there must be an adequate stimulus to find this memory. He thought—he was a Christian—that would be the book used in the Final Judgement, the book of everyone's memories. And that could lead us eventually to Heaven or Hell. But, deep down, that mythology is alien to me.

FERRARI. How odd, Borges, it seems that we are talking constantly through memory. Sometimes, our conversations remind me of a dialogue between two memories.

BORGES. In fact, that's what it is. If we are something, we are our past, aren't we? Our past is not what can be recorded in a biography or in the newspapers. Our past is our memory. That memory can be hidden or inaccurate—it doesn't matter. It's there, isn't it? It can be a lie but that lie becomes part of our memory, part of us.

FERRARI. As we have talked about faith or its absence, I want to mention something about our times that seems strange to me. Over the centuries, men in the Protestant and Catholic West have worried about the dilemma of the soul's salvation. But it seems to me that recent generations do not think that it is even a dilemma.

BORGES. That seems pretty serious to me, that a person or people do not possess an ethical instinct or sense, doesn't it? Moreover, there's a tendency, or a habit, of judging an act by its consequences. Now that seems immoral to me, because when you act you know if your acts are evil or good. As for the consequences of an act—they ramify and multiply and perhaps balance out in the end. I do not know, for example, if the consequences of the discovery of America have been good or evil, because there are so many. Even as we are talking, they are growing and multiplying. Thus, to judge an act by its consequences is absurd. But people tend to do this. For example, a contest or a war is judged according to failure or success and not according to whether it's ethically justified. As for the consequences, as I said, they multiply in such a way that, perhaps in time, they balance out and then become unbalanced again. It is a continuous process.

FERRARI. With the loss of the ideas of salvation and damnation, there's the loss of the ideas of good and evil, sin and virtue. That is, there's a different version of things that excludes the earlier world view.

BORGES. People now only think about whether something is advantageous. They think as if the future doesn't exist, or as if there is no future other than an immediate one. They act according to what counts in that moment.

FERRARI. And that way of being, of being preoccupied with immediacy, has turned us into 'immediate' beings, perhaps even into futile ones.

BORGES. I completely agree.

16

Concerning Love

●

OSVALDO FERRARI. Borges, in several of your poems and stories, especially in 'The Aleph', love is the theme or, rather, the dynamic factor. Love for a woman takes up plenty of space in your work.

JORGE LUIS BORGES. Yes, but in relation to that story that's not the case. In that story something unbelievable happens—the Aleph. There's the possibility that it's a hallucination, and it's important that the spectator of the Aleph is moved. And what better motive than the death of the woman he loved but who hadn't reciprocated that love? When I wrote that story, the woman I called Beatriz Viterbo had just died.

FERRARI. Really?

BORGES. Yes, it served my story well, for I experienced the same emotion. She too never paid any attention to me. I was in love with her and that was useful for the story. It seems that if you want to tell an unbelievable story, you must have a prior emotion. That is, the observer of the Aleph couldn't just be there as a casual spectator—

he had to be someone deeply affected. Only then do we accept that feeling and accept the Aleph as a marvel. That's why I did that.

H. G. Wells said that if there is a fantastic fact, it's best that it's the sole fantastic fact in the story, because the reader's imagination, especially today, does not accept many fantastic facts at the same time. Take his *War of the Worlds*, dealing with a Martian invasion, written at the end of the nineteenth century. Then *The Invisible Man*, also written around that time. In both, except for the essential fact of an invasion by beings from another planet—something that no one had thought of before but that we now see as possible—and an invisible man, we have trite and trivial circumstances. Their purpose is to help the reader's imagination, for the reader, especially the reader of today, tends to be sceptical. In spite of having invented it, Wells would have sensed how hard it would be to make it all believable. Ordinarily, he would have discarded the idea of an invasion of our planet by invisible Martians. That would be demanding too much. And that is precisely where science fiction today errs—it accumulates prodigies and we don't believe in any of them.

Anyway, I thought that in my story everything else had to be trivial. So I picked Garay Street, one of the dullest streets in Buenos Aires, and put in the ridiculous character of Carlos Argentino Daneri. I began with the circumstance of a girl's death and then introduced the crucial fact, the Aleph—that is what lasts in memory. You believe in that fact because until then you have been told a series of possible facts. The proof of this lies in one of my visits to Madrid when I was asked if I had seen the Aleph. I was aghast! The man, clearly not a subtle person, said, 'But why not, if you gave us the street and street number?' 'But what is easier,' I replied, 'than naming a street and putting a number?' (*Laughs*) 'So you haven't seen it?' he asked again, wanting to make sure. When he realized that I was a hoaxer, a mere writer, that he needn't take into account what I had said (*both laugh*), he went away.

FERRARI. He couldn't accept it was something you'd invented?

BORGES. Yes. Something similar happened a few days ago—someone asked me if I had the seventh volume of the Tlön, Uqbar, Orbis Tertius encyclopaedia. I should have said yes, or that I had lent it to someone, but I made the mistake of saying no. So he said, 'It's all a lie then?' 'You could have used a more polite word,' I said in reply, 'you could have said fiction.'

FERRARI. If we continue like this, imagination and fantasy will be banned at any moment.

BORGES. That's right. But I interrupted what you were saying.

FERRARI. I said that the emotion behind what you write, in this case the emotion we find in the Platonic tradition, is creative in itself, although today it is no longer seen that way. That is, as opposed to that Platonic tradition that elevated you through love. Love has been degraded to two sexes who meet and who are almost nothing more than that—two sexes.

BORGES. Yes, it has been degraded to that.

FERRARI. The poetry has been stolen.

BORGES. Yes, well, poetry has been stolen everywhere. Last week I was asked in several places—two people asked me the same question—

what's the use of poetry? And I answered them with: What's the use of death? What's the use of the taste of coffee? What the use of me? What's the use of us? What an odd question, isn't it?

FERRARI. Everything is seen through utilitarian eyes.

BORGES. Someone reads a poem. If they are worthy of it, they receive it, they are grateful and they feel an emotion. And that's not too little a use. To feel moved by a poem is not an insignificant event—it's something we should be grateful for. But it seems that these people are not—it seems that they read in vain. If they read at all. It's something I'm quite unsure of.

FERRARI. Instead of a poetic consciousness about life, there is now only a sociological and psychological one.

BORGES. And political.

FERRARI. And political.

BORGES. And poetry makes sense only if it serves a cause.

FERRARI. Utilitarian.

BORGES. Yes, utilitarian. If not, no. It's incomprehensible that a sonnet may exist, or a rose.

FERRARI. Incomprehensible. But they will both survive this, let's say, this desacralizing and anti-poetry trend.

BORGES. Despite it, I believe that poetry doesn't run any risks.

FERRARI. Of course.

BORGES. It would be absurd to suppose that it did. Another very common idea in our times is that a poet signals something special.

Because, one may ask: What is the poet's function in this society and this period? The function is, always, to write poems. This cannot change, and it has nothing to do with political or economic circumstances, absolutely nothing. But this is not understood.

FERRARI. We return to the question of utilitarianism.

BORGES. Yes, it is seen in terms of utility.

FERRARI. It's what you were telling me not long ago, that everything is seen in terms of success or lack of success, of acquiring or not acquiring that which you desire.

BORGES. Yes, it seems that everyone has forgotten that Kipling poem which talks of success and failure as two impostors. Which says that you should recognize them and face them. Clearly, no one fails as much as they think and no one succeeds as much as they think. Failure and success are truly impostors.

FERRARI. That's true. Now, coming back to love. Among poets, love continues to be a way in, a path.

BORGES. And so it should be, the more it spreads to people and things, of course. It's not necessary, though. It is enough to believe in a person. That faith vindicates us, exalts us, leads us to poetry.

FERRARI. I recall Octavio Paz saying that counter to different fashions and differing risks that these created in society, the poet always defended love. And I believe that is real. But the other tradition that we have diverged from, besides the Platonic one, is the Judaeo-Christian proposition—that love structures or shapes the family and, indeed, society itself.

BORGES. It seems as though our epoch has discarded all versions of love, hasn't it? As though love is something that must be justified, which is very strange because it doesn't occur to anyone to have to justify the sea or a sunset or a mountain. These need no justifying. But love is far more intimate than those things which merely depend on our senses. Love curiously seems to need justification now.

FERRARI. Yes, but when I referred to love I was thinking of its role in your work as inspiration and as a thread through several poems and stories.

BORGES. Well, I think that I have always been in love, throughout my life, even in first memories. Always. But, of course, the pretext or theme (*both laugh*) has not been the same woman. There have been several women and each one unique. That's how it should be, isn't it?

FERRARI. Of course.

BORGES. The fact that they change appearance or name is not important. What counts is that I sensed them as unique. Sometimes I have thought that when, someone is in love, one sees the other person as God sees us, that is, in the best possible way. You are in love when you realize the other person is unique. Perhaps in God's eyes everyone is unique. We can stretch this theory to a kind of 'reductio ad absurdum'. Why not suppose, then, that each of us is irrefutably unique or believes that he is irrefutably unique . . . why not suppose that in God's eyes every ant is an individual? We may not perceive these differences but God does.

FERRARI. Each individuality?

BORGES. Yes, even an ant's. And why not a plant's or a flower's? A rock's, a boulder's? Why not suppose that everything is unique? I deliberately chose the most humble thing. That each ant is unique and that each ant shares this prodigious and inextricable adventure that is the cosmic process, that is the universe—why not suppose that each one serves an end? I have written a poem about this . . . but what else remains for an 85-year-old to do but repeat himself? Or try variations, which comes to the same thing.

FERRARI. Of course, precious variations. But, Borges, seen this way, as you evoke it, love could be a form of revelation.

BORGES. Yes, it's the moment when a person reveals himself to another. Macedonio said, how can I put it politely? that the sexual act is a greeting that two souls exchange.

FERRARI. That's magnificent.

BORGES. A splendid saying.

FERRARI. It's obvious that he had attained that deep understanding of love.

BORGES. Yes, he said to me that it was a greeting, the greeting of one soul by another.

FERRARI. Naturally, in this case, love, as it should, precedes sex.

BORGES. Of course, well said. Yes, sex is one of the means. Another could be perhaps a word or a look or something shared—a moment of silence, a view of the sunset. These could also be forms of love. Or friendship which is, of course, another expression of love.

FERRARI. That's magnificent.

BORGES. And it could be true. It runs the beautiful risk of being true.

FERRARI. Socrates recommended expertise in love as a form of wisdom. Naturally, he meant the vision that arises from love, the Platonic vision.

BORGES. Yes, I understand.

17

On Friendship with Alfonso Reyes

•

OSVALDO FERRARI. Borges, for a long time I have wanted to talk to you about two Mexican writers—Alfonso Reyes, very close to Argentina as well as to you, and Octavio Paz.

JORGE LUIS BORGES. I can speak about Paz with little authority. I have read nothing by him though I have excellent memories of him as a person. Let's talk about Reyes.

FERRARI. Good.

BORGES. I met him at Victoria Ocampo's San Isidro house. I met Reyes and immediately recalled another Mexican poet, Othón. I remember this line of his: 'I see your back and already have forgotten your forehead.' It seems as if it's by Almafuerte, doesn't it? Then Reyes told me that he had met Othón and that Othón frequented his father's house. His father, General Reyes, had allowed himself to be killed in the Mexican Revolution. A death rather similar to that of my grandfather Francisco Borges who let himself be killed after Mitre's surrender at La Verde in 1874. Reyes said he had seen Othón many times. I was stunned, because when you think of authors you think of books—somehow, you do not think that the authors of those books were human and that there were people who had met them. How did you really meet Othón, I asked him. Without a moment's hestitation, Reyes found the apt quotation, lines from Browning: 'Ah, did you want to see Shelley play?' Which is the same situation: some-one was amazed that someone else had met Shelley in person. I was stunned that he had met Othón and that he had discovered the quo-tation . . . How odd that in Japanese novels, one of the customs of people in court is that when they want to say something they do not say it directly but quote a line from a Chinese or Japanese poem which anticipates what they want to say. And so everything is said indirectly. A further merit is to recognize immediately which poem the other refers to.

Well, Reyes, then, in those first words he exchanged with me, moved from 'But, how, did you really meet Othón?' to 'Ah, did you want to see Shelley play?' from Browning's 'Memorabilia'. And from that moment we became friends and he started taking me seriously. I wasn't used to being taken seriously. Perhaps it's a mistake to do so. Although this mistake seems to have spread . . . At that time, it was new to me. We became friends, united by Browning's great reputation and that apt quotation. He invited me out to eat. He invited me every Sunday to the Mexican Embassy on Posadas Street. There he was, with his wife and son and me. We talked until late in the night, ''til the small hours'. About literature, specially English literature, about Góngora . . . I did not share, and still don't completely, the cult he professed for Góngora. We talked about literature . . .

I took him to Ricardo Molinari. When we were leaving, Molinari said, 'This has been the happiest night of my life.' Well, it's a set phrase but at that moment it was true, 'I have met Alfonso Reyes.' Indeed, he had. I also went to see him with Francisco Luis Bernárdez. It was through me that they met him. Then Reyes founded a literary review called *Cuadernos del Plata*. He asked me to collaborate but I declined. Later he said he regretted what I'd said about Leopoldo Marechal and Francisco Luis Bernárdez collaborating on his magazine . . . I was Bernárdez's friend, I knew Marechal somewhat. And I knew that both were nationalists. And I didn't want to publish in a magazine which also published the nationalists. People easily confuse matters—they would have said that I had become a nationalist too. Reyes said that he regretted my absence but indicated, without stating clearly, that my not publishing in his magazine would in no way ruin our relationship. Later, he published one of my books, one he should have rejected and one I try to forget now—*Cuaderno San Martín*, illustrated by Silvina Ocampo, I think.

FERRARI. Was it dedicated to Wally Zenner?

BORGES. No, there was a poem dedicated to her but no more. The book isn't dedicated to any one. I did dedicate a rather weak poem to Zenner which I later took out because it really did not honour her and could, in fact, dishonour me. It was very, very weak.

FERRARI (*laughs*). But you were telling me that Reyes, besides looking after you and supporting you, also took care of other writers.

BORGES. Of course.

FERRARI. Including Macedonio Fernández.

BORGES. Well in Macedonio's case I took the texts to Reyes. He knew nothing about Macedonio but he accepted the texts for *Cuadernos del Plata*. And he published Macedonio's book, *Papeles de Recienvenido*, the one I had 'stolen'. I corrected the proofs with Reyes. Macedonio, of course, wasn't interested in publishing—he said he wrote to help himself think and he never thought his work could have any literary value. Many were letters he had written almost in jest. Later, years after Macedonio's death, I read a biography of Emily Dickinson where she is quoted as saying that publishing is not a necessary part of literary destiny—that a writer need not publish. Mybe she was right. I remember a similar case concerning one of England's greatest poets, which means something: John Donne. I believe he published hardly anything. He wrote poems and addressed sermons and these circulated as manuscripts. I do not think that he published anything, although I could be wrong. In Dickinson's case, she published about four or five poems in her lifetime; the rest were found in drawers in her bedroom. And one of Melville's best stories, 'Billy Budd', was, as you had mentioned, found in one of the boxes in his study. Melville had not intended to publish it, although, of course, he published many books.

Today, on the other hand, I note that people think of publishing, or think of writing, as a means of getting noticed or promoted. It happens, and seems unbelievable. In another age, this would not be understood but today this is what happens. Spoken words or words in manuscripts are unreal, but what is printed is real. Well, the truth is that what's printed does give a certain validity, doesn't it? And Reyes told me, 'We publish so as not to spend our lives correcting drafts.'

That is, you publish a book to rid yourself of it—what happens in my case. And the truth is that once my book has been published, I do not know if the criticism is negative or positive nor do I know if any copies have been sold. That's the booksellers' or publishers' concern—not the writers'.

FERRARI. You got rid of the idea of success, of the idea of publicizing your name through the printed word.

BORGES. Yes, it was natural for it to be this way because a writer matters very little. I recall Arturo Cancela telling my father, 'My enemies say I sell many books to discredit myself because then I become a popular writer, meaning a bad one.' The truth was that he did sell a lot but he didn't like saying so. It was understood that a writer wrote for a minority. Those lines by Stefan George—I know them through Enrique Díez Canedo's Spanish version, another great friend of Reyes—'the select few are rarely given a prize'. George takes an image from James, from his short story 'The Figure in the Carpet'. It's about a writer who compares his work to a Persian rug. At first sight the rug looks chaotic. Then, as one looks closely, one sees a pattern, one understands that in all the writer's work there is a pattern. A pattern which James, naturally, does not reveal. In the last scene, the narrator, who is a critic, is in a room on the floor of which is a Persian rug. Surrounded by his master's books, he thinks that he is about to discover the pattern that has been deliberately hidden by the writer . . .

I talked about this story with Reyes. I talked about so many things with Reyes! One person he wanted to meet was Ricardo Güiraldes but they never did meet. He wrote a poem about that failure to meet, which was, in an ideal way, a kind of meeting. And he used such a lovely phrase for a gate in the middle of the country—the country is so vast (he was referring to the plains that writers translate as the pampas) that on each side of the gate you're outside. Very nice and magical, isn't it? On either side of a gate on the plains you are outside. And Reyes employed that image in his poem dedicated to Güiraldes.

FERRARI. There's a very important aspect that you share with Reyes. We can recall 'Sun Dial' or 'Anáhuac Vision' or that poem of his called 'Homer in Cuernavaca'.

BORGES. I am not familiar with that one but I know 'Sun Dial'. I recall its epigraph: 'Sun dial that modestly strikes each hour'. It's very nice. No bells, no noise of any kind. 'Modestly strikes each hour'. There's an anthology that mentions inscriptions on sun dials—I'm not sure if Dorothy Sayers compiled it. A classic one is 'I only enumerate clear hours,' which is fine because it refers to hours of happiness. Another one in an English garden says, 'It is later than you think.' There's a slight threat there, isn't there? 'It's later' as if death threatens whoever reads it. 'It's later than you think,' implying, I suppose, that death is closer.

FERRARI. There's another poem relevant to all this—Octavio Paz's 'Sun Stone'.

BORGES. I do not know it but I think that 'Sun Stone' refers to a sundial.

FERRARI. Yes, to the Aztec sun stone.

BORGES. Yes, that's it. 'Sun Stone' is a fine title.

FERRARI. What you have in common with Reyes is that . . .

BORGES. We share a love for literature, for all literatures.

FERRARI. Of course.

BORGES. He had read much more. He taught me many, many things. And he worshipped Homer. For me, it's a great effort to admire *The Iliad*, except for the last cantos. On the other hand, I read and reread *The Odyssey*. It's an advantage that I do not know Greek for it allows me to read the many translations that exist. In the same way, my ignorance of Arabic has allowed me to read six or seven versions of *The Arabian Nights*. Maybe we can agree to ignore languages for then we can read several versions of the same work. The languages I ignore are Greek and Arabic . . . really, all the world's languages. Because one man can know very little.

FERRARI. Borges, because of time we must come to a stop.

BORGES. Yes, I just want to remind you of one of Reyes' complimentary remark to Victoria Ocampo when he told her 'In later times, they will talk of a Victorian age.'

FERRARI. Terrific.

BORGES. Yes, it was very good. It was a joke, but a polite one, a tribute.

18

The East, I Ching *and Buddhism*

●

OSVALDO FERRARI. Borges, you may remember a certain man and a certain book. A man who placed one of your poems on the first few pages of that thick book that he translated from Chinese into Spanish through German. I'm referring, of course, to the *I Ching* and to David Vogelmann and to your poem 'For a Version of the I Ching'.

JORGE LUIS BORGES. Yes, David Vogelmann translated Richard Wilhelm's German version. I read in the English sinologist Arthur Waley's work that Wilhelm had been criticized for not translating it faithfully, for translating according to the interpretations by contemporaries of Confucius. Waley said that Wilhelm did that deliberately. Well, he didn't translate the hexagrams, which are whole or broken lines, but the commentary. And the commentary makes the book, not the drawings, although, the commentary is also used for purposes of divination. In a Chuang Tzu translation, the commentaries are called 'wings' and are not at the bottom of the page or at the end of the volume but inserted in the text in a different typeface. There's a commentary by Wilhelm in *The Book of Changes* that, according to the

Chinese, every process or act is possible in 64 different ways. I would say that is a rather moderate calculation; there must be more. Following that logic, let's say, a person about to begin a journey, about to embark upon a loving or friendly relationship, an emperor about to undertake a campaign, opens the *I Ching* by chance and discovers which of those 64 forms concerns him. Clearly, the 64th form corresponds to the total number of forms available with the hexagrams; you cannot go beyond 64. Some hexagrams consist of six straight lines, others of six broken lines and yet others inserted in diverse ways, with broken lines and complete ones. Each one has a rather arbitrary moral interpretation. For example, one begins, 'This line suggests a man walking behind a tiger.' Well, that's impossible, isn't it? (*Laughs.*) Also, there are no other interpretations that talk of men walking behind or before tigers.

FERRARI. As in Greece where the choice appears to have been between Plato and Aristotle, in China it appears to have been between Confucius and Lao Tse who symbolize completely contrary world views.

BORGES. Yes, although some have tried to unite them. For example, in some Taoist book it's said that Confucius conversed with Lao Tse and said, when he left, 'At last, I've seen the dragon.' That's all he could say to explain the meeting. It seems to me, however, to be evidently false. Ah yes, it's in Chuang Tzu's book.

FERRARI. That's very interesting.

BORGES. Yes, but it must be false. Also, it would be very odd for Confucius to say that because he was a thinker totally opposed to Lao Tse. We don't even know if they were contemporaries.

FERRARI. Chuang Tzu wanted to unite them.

BORGES. I think that's right. He also wanted that meeting to be in Lao Tse's favour and not Confucius'. The word 'Confucius' was invented, I believe, by the Jesuits. It should be Master Kong or Kung, but they gave it a Latin form, Confucius, and it has remained thus.

FERRARI. In recent years, perhaps because of your trips to Japan, you seem to have got closer to Eastern cultures and beliefs.

BORGES. Well, it has always been like that. Also, I think that what we call 'Western culture' is not completely Western—there are Eastern influences on Pythagoras and the Stoics. And our culture is, in some ways, the dialogue between the Greeks (let's call them that) and the Holy Scripture, something no less varied than the Greeks because we are dealing with books written by different people in different periods, every one of them very diverse. It seems impossible that the Ecclesiastics could have been written by the author of the Book of Job, even less by the author of Genesis.

FERRARI. It's curious that Vogelmann and Murena also had a conversation on this very radio station, towards the end of both their lives, which could be called esoteric by those who later read it when it appeared in book form.

BORGES. I had no idea that Murena was interested in these topics. I thought he was rather a realist novelist.

FERRARI. He was extremely keen on it and had become an expert like Vogelmann.

BORGES. I didn't know that about Vogelmann either.

FERRARI. They talked about the Torah, the Tao, the *I Ching*, Hinduism, Hasidism, et cetera.

BORGES. I didn't know that. All I know about this, as in their case, is second- or third-hand. But you must know about such matters. Better to know them third-hand than be ignorant, isn't it?

FERRARI. If it is all right with you Borges, I would like to read that brief poem of yours: 'For a Version of the I Ching'.

BORGES. Yes, that poem was read and corrected by Vogelmann. I recall that he made me realize one line was weak—I had given up on that line. But he insisted that I correct it. He got involved with the correction and it helped. I must thank him for it.

FERRARI. And he placed it on the first pages of his *I Ching*. As you know, Vogelmann's is the best version we have in this part of the world.

BORGES. Well, he took it from Wilhelm, didn't he?

FERRARI. Yes, he did.

BORGES. Of course he did.

FERRARI. If it suits you, I'll read your poem.

BORGES. Why not, though I'm not sure I'll understand it (*both laugh*). Yes, I was asked to do a prologue, so I gave in. But I do not know exactly what I said, let's see . . .

> The future is as irrevocable
> as rigid yesterday . . .

Well, that's the idea of fate, I think.

> As rigid yesterday. Not one thing
> that isn't a silent letter

of the eternal indecipherable scripture
Whose book is time . . .

That's Carlyle's idea, that universal history is a book we are cease-lessly obliged to read and write. Later he adds, and this is terrible, 'in which we also do not write'. That means, not only do we write and read but that we are letters in that text, given that each one of us, however modest, forms a part of that vast cryptography that's called universal history.

It is the game of forgetting and remembering

Yes, why don't you start at the beginning again?

FERRARI. Why not.

The future is as irrevocable
as rigid yesterday. Not one thing
that isn't a silent letter
of the eternal indecipherable scripture
Whose book is time . . .

BORGES. Clearly, it's Carlyle.

Whose book is time. Whoever leaves home
has already returned.

That's well put, isn't it?

FERRARI. Not only that, but a Buddhist would approve of it.

BORGES. Also, it is written in a slightly amazed tone, because it doesn't say 'he knows that he will return'—no, it says that on leaving he returned which is like a magical act. That hint of magic does not bother me, it has an aesthetic virtue that the other lines do not.

FERRARI. It's followed by an idea that reverts to the same meaning:

Our life

is a future path already travelled.

BORGES. 'A future path already travelled'. I'd like to recall one of my favourite writers, Oscar Wilde. Wilde said and possibly believed, or at least believed at that moment, that every man is, at every moment of his life, all that he has been and all that he will be. In Wilde's case, that's terrible. It means that he, in times of prosperity, of happiness, was already the man in jail. At the same time, it means when he was in prison he continued to be the fortunate man from before.

FERRARI. The author of *The Picture of Dorian Gray* was already the author of *The Ballad of Reading Gaol* and *De Profundis*.

BORGES. Yes, and the, let's say, villainous man was already the loved and applauded one. Also, each one of us is the child he has been and has forgotten, isn't he? as well as the old man. Perhaps, also, his fame—if he has any—is posthumous.

FERRARI. I will continue with your poem:

Nothing bids us goodbye. Nothing leaves us

Do not surrender. The ergastulum is obscure,

the firm plot is ceaseless iron . . .

BORGES. That's the line that Vogelmann made me change or improve. 'Ceaseless' is fine, isn't it? If I had put 'firm' or 'solid' it would not have any force, but 'ceaseless' has force because it seems that iron is something that lasts, that lives. It's as if iron was, perhaps, time, a river of iron.

FERRARI. But in some corner of your prison
   there can be a fault, a crack
   the path is as fatal as an arrow
   but God lurks in the cracks.

BORGES. Now I remember—the word 'ergastulum' that Vogelmann contributed. I did not know that word but it was just what I wanted. According to Flaubert—it's one of his personal theories—the melodious word is always the right one. But I allow myself to doubt this. Perhaps it seems appropriate because it is melodious. Otherwise it would be odd, wouldn't it?

FERRARI. Borges, I don't know if you noticed that you do not speak of God so specifically in any other poem as in this one. And you say he lurks.

BORGES. Yes, but . . . there was also the necessity to construct a sonnet (*laughs*), to finish it in a convincing way. The word 'God' is obviously convincing. There's that too.

FERRARI. Perhaps you remember that Arnold Toynbee said that one of the most important events in our century was the arrival of Buddhism in the West, the knowledge of Buddhism by Western man.

BORGES. Well, that is happening now. There are Buddhist monasteries in the United States, in Brazil. There are places for retreats, for Buddhist meditation, in many Western countries. I recall a book—I only remember its title—*The Discovery of the West by the Chinese* or *The Discovery of Europe by the Chinese*, which points to the opposite. You think that Europe is continuously discovering the East, you think of Marco Polo, the Crusades, *The Arabian Nights*, the discovery of Indian and

Chinese philosophy in the nineteenth century, which is still going on. Recently, Japanese literature has been discovered. All this is part of a game that should make us forget whether we are from the East or from the West and unite us all. Perhaps the sources of our culture are various.

FERRARI. Perhaps by the year 2000 we will reach a contemporary synthesis of a Western and Eastern world view.

BORGES. Yes, that would begin with Christianity and, of course, the Middle Ages are a kind of reconciliation of Aristotle and the authors of the Holy Scriptures, don't you agree?

FERRARI. Yes. Borges, we have remembered, the *I Ching*, Vogelmann, the East and the West and your approach to the Eastern world over the last years.

BORGES. I would like to know more about it, of course. Among my books, there's one on the Ramayana in two volumes. I must find someone who knows German to read it to me. I have always been keen on the East since *The Arabian Nights* and my reading of a poem by Matthew Arnold on Buddha's legend.

19

About Dreams

●

OSVALDO FERRARI. Borges, I would like to come back to the theme of dreams that you've developed in books, poems and conversations. I recall your *Book of Dreams* as well as your poem 'The Dream' which I would like to read aloud. I recall also that you recently linked the act of writing with that of dreaming.

JORGE LUIS BORGES. Yes, the act of living as well as the act of dreaming. Also, of course, idealistic philosophy. Now, as for the act of writing, I recall a passage from Joseph Addison, collected in the *Spectator*, more or less in the middle of the eighteenth century, in which he says that when we dream we are, all at once, the theatre, the actors, the play and the author, we are all those simultaneously. That image can be found in Góngora too: 'The dream, author of representations in your theatre, built by wind, dresses in shadows of beautiful shapes.' José Bianco picked that bit, 'dresses in shadows', as the title of one of his books. Now, if the fact of dreaming is a kind of dramatic creation, it would make the dream the most ancient literary genre, even earlier than humanity, because—as a Latin poet reminds us—animals also dream. It would be a fact of a dramatic nature, of a play in which we are the author, the actor and the building itself, the theatre. That is, at night, we are all some kind of playwright.

FERRARI. We are both author and actor, because the dreamer splits into the actor on the dream stage.

BORGES. Yes, we would be all that every night. That is, all men have this aesthetic capacity, specifically dramatic, of dreaming. Now, this is what happens to me. Of course, unfortunately, as I have passed 84 years, I now know my dreams. From long ago I know I am dreaming when I dream. This is at times scary because I fear the terrible things that may happen. But I also have learnt to recognize and, in certain ways, domesticate my nightmares. For example, in my case the most recurring nightmare is the one about a labyrinth. The labyrinth can have different settings. It could be this room we are talking in. It could be, and often is, the Biblioteca Nacional building on México Street, a place I particularly liked. I was director of the National Library for many years. And no matter what part of the world I happened to be in, I was usually in Monserrat district at night, dreaming about the Library on México Street, between Perú and Bolívar. My dreams usually take place there. Sometimes I dream that I am in any old place but from where I want to get out. I manage to escape but find myself back in an identical place or even the same place. This is repeated a few times and then I know it's a labyrinth dream. I know that it will go on repeating itself indefinitely, that the room will always be the same and the room next door the same and the one next to that. So

I say to myself: This is a labyrinth nightmare. What I must do is touch a wall. I try to touch it but I can't. What happens is that I really can't move my arm but dream that I can. And after a while, in making that effort, I wake up. Or if not, this too is frequent, I dream that I have woken up but have woken up in another place, in a dream place (*laughs*).

FERRARI. I guess that you would recognize dreams of tigers, knives and mirrors.

BORGES. Mirrors, yes, but not about knives or tigers. I used to dream them ages ago but not any longer. They have lost their power, they have lost their terror.

FERRARI. But they repeat themselves in your 'personal universe'.

BORGES. Yes, in my literature but not in my nightmares. My nightmares are the labyrinth. Now, speaking of labyrinths, I was not long ago in the palace at Knossos which is supposed to be a labyrinth in Crete. It would be very odd to find two almost infinite buildings, the labyrinth and the palace, one next to the other . . . and it is the labyrinth that has been lost.

FERRARI. If you don't mind, I would like to read your poem 'The Dream' so that we can comment on it.

BORGES. I do not remember it completely.

FERRARI. I'll remind you of it.

BORGES. All right. I will doubtless regret having written it.

FERRARI. When the clocks of midnight squander
   a generous time,

I will go further than Ulysses' oarsmen
to the realm of dreams, inaccessible to human nature.
From that underwater region, I rescue fragments
that I do not begin to understand.

BORGES. Of course, inaccessible to human memory because it's possible that when you recall a dream you modify it. That means perhaps the dream world is very different. An English writer thought that dreams were not continuous. But because it's a habit, and because we live in time, which is continuous, we give dreams a narrative, a continuous form when we do remember them. But perhaps when we dream, we do not. Perhaps when we dream everything is somehow inside us or all at once. Let's go on.

FERRARI. Simple botanical herbs
Somewhat diverse animals
Dialogues between the dead . . .

BORGES. 'Simple botanical herbs' because I imagine that the plants I dream of are rather vague, aren't they? (*Laughs.*)

FERRARI. Faces that really are masks,
Words from very ancient languages . . .

BORGES. Yes, 'Faces that really are masks' because they are surfaces— there is no one behind those faces; they are simply faces. That's why in another poem I speak of a 'deer with only one side'—because that is the side I see. On the other side there's nothing.

FERRARI. And at times an incomparable horror
which day can give us . . .

BORGES. I think a nightmare has a special taste, diffeent from the horror we experience when we are awake. It could be proof that hell exists, that you glimpse something beyond human experience.

FERRARI. It's a plausible theory.

BORGES. Yes.

FERRARI. In the last part of the poem:

> I will be everybody or nobody. I will be the other
> that I am without being aware of it, he who has looked
> At that other dream, the state of being awake.
> I judge it,
> Resigned and smiling.

I was struck by the marvellous splitting between he who dreams and he who acts in the dream. That is, the person dreaming himself.

BORGES. That's right. Did I write that poem? I must have, even though I have completely forgotten it.

FERRARI. There's no doubt it's yours.

BORGES. Well, I'll resign myself to being its author. It's not that bad.

FERRARI. Of course not, it's very good. You could also think that beauty, which we have talked about before, is more accessible to man's sensibility when he is dreaming than when he is awake, especially if we think of the perfection of the archetypes that Plato conceived as being more real in dreams.

BORGES. Well, I would say that beauty and horror too, for dreams imply nightmares.

FERRARI. That's true.

BORGES. But they would be two perfections or two intensities. Although there are also languid dreams.

FERRARI. I've just remembered a line from a Silvina Ocampo poem: 'With beauty and horror as guides.'

BORGES. That's good. Both beauty and horror.

FERRARI. United.

BORGES. Both can stimulate. Well, anything could be a stimulant for a poet. All experience should stimulate. There's a passage in *The Odyssey* where the gods gave misfortune to man so that subsequent generations had something to sing about. That would be a poetic way of saying what Stéphane Mallarmé said more prosaically: 'Everything for a book.' I prefer the Homeric image of 'human generations' and 'something to sing about'. 'Everything for a book' is a merely literary idea and rather unpoetic. Although the idea is the same, the idea that everything happens for aesthetic reasons. Now, we could stretch that idea to the gods or God. We could suppose that everything happens not for our pleasure or pain but because it has some aesthetic value. With that, we would have a new theology based on aesthetics. Many things could emerge from our speculations.

FERRARI. Now another thought occurs to me while we reflect. If we Argentines are, as we have speculated before, 'Euroamericans' because we come from Europe . . .

BORGES. I do not have any doubts about that. As for me, I feel far from being a Pampa or a Guaraní Indian, although I've been told I have a drop of Guaraní blood, but that hasn't caused me any worries.

FERRARI. If an Argentine has, for example, 30 generations in Europe and only two or three or four in Argentina, in his memory . . .

BORGES. I go back many generations in this country but, of course, these generations were not especially American; they were Europeans in exile. As we all are.

FERRARI. You would have fewer generations in America than in Europe as you came from Europe.

BORGES. Yes, far fewer.

FERRARI. Then, what I am trying to formulate is that in an Argentine's memory and dreams, he can dream of Europe in a special way through his ancestral memory that has recorded an eternal Europe.

BORGES. And we are continuously thinking about Europe. We read European books. Our imagination is more European than Araucanian, which, let's admit, has nothing to do with Europe (*laughs*).

FERRARI. Despite novelties from the United States and Japan . . .

BORGES. North America shares our situation as well. North America is also a Europe in exile. Few Americans are 'redskins' and even those redskins barely have their own culture. They have a European one but not their own.

FERRARI. What I mean is that if Europe persists in us, it has also to persist in ancestral memory and, thus, in dreams.

BORGES. In dreams, in ancestral memories and in our daily experiences, as our daily experiences are more similar to European ones than those that Pincén or Catriel might have had, don't you agree?

FERRARI. Yes, because even if we embody the American world—if we can define it—in some ways it's an Euroamerican integration because an undeniably European part is mixed with American soil.

BORGES. I would go further. I would say that the idea of America is not an Indian one but a European one. The proof is the following: when *The Winning of the West* took place in the United States (here we had the Conquest of the Desert) there were tribes that were friendly. That implies that they had no awareness of a war between races. Coliqueo and Catriel's Indians were friendly and fought other Indians. They did not conceive of all that, as we did later, as a war between races. No, those Indians were loyal to a specific cacique or leader and he was friendly with the Christians.

FERRARI. Except in countries like Mexico or Peru, where a war between races was resolved by the mixing of two races, forming a third one that exists today. In Peru and Mexico.

BORGES. Yes, I suppose. But I do not know how long the Mexican or the Aztec or the Inca culture in Peru lasted. They lasted as curiosities, nothing more. But anyhow, longer than here.

FERRARI. Longer than here, yet . . .

BORGES. Not that much longer.

FERRARI. But there was a concrete, not imaginary, racial symbiosis between the Spaniards and the Indians.

BORGES. Yes, there was that.

FERRARI. Unlike in Argentina.

BORGES. Of course. But that is up to them.

20

Concerning Ricardo Güiraldes

●

OSVALDO FERRARI. The other day, Borges, I associated 25th May with the memory of Ricardo Güiraldes, a man very dear to both of us.

JORGE LUIS BORGES. Yes, it's an easy association.

FERRARI. Very dear and well remembered, even officially, as he is part of the compulsory reading texts in school.

BORGES. Well, I am not sure that suits a writer. I was talking to an Italian who told me that he had been forced to read Dante at school and that, naturally, because all compulsory reading is unrewarding, he didn't like it. Years later he read it again and discovered that it was rather good. That's why I am not sure if compulsory reading is worth the while, as compulsory and reading are two contradictory words. Reading must be a pleasure and pleasure cannot be compulsory. It really must be something spontaneous.

FERRARI. You have remembered Güiraldes more as a friend than as a writer who you refer to . . .

BORGES. It's just that my personal memories are more vivid than the ones of his work.

FERRARI. In Güiraldes' case.

BORGES. Yes. I once emphasized, in a forgettable and forgotten sonnet, that his politeness was the most visible aspect of his kindness. I want to add now that the word 'politeness' reminds me exactly of *Don Segundo Sombra*. Nearly all the writers who had dealt with the gaucho until then had picked out one of Sarmiento's gaucho types—the evil gaucho, the outlaw. Hilario Ascasubi was an exception, he praised the gaucho: 'Gauchos of the Argentine and Uruguayan Republics sing and battle to topple the tyrant Rosas and his henchmen.' He would have remembered the gaucho as a soldier in the Unitarian armies or in the Colorado party of the Uruguayan Republic, when he celebrated the victory of Cagancha. But later, in *The Twins of La Flor*, he too describes the gaucho as treacherous and curiously employs the word 'outlaw'. In *Martín Fierro*, of course, the gaucho is an outlaw as well as a deserter and a killer who crosses over to the Indians and so on. In Eduardo Gutiérrez's novels, the chosen characters Black Ant, the Barrientos brothers, Moreira are also outlaw types. Güiraldes, on the other hand, wanted to emphasize the gaucho as a peaceful, quiet and polite person. He chose Don Segundo Sombra as the foreman from Santa Fe of the La Porteña farm in Buenos Aires province. And that was new. And I noticed something else. When I got to know Güiraldes, he asked me—it was almost his first question—if I knew English. In those days to know English was rather rare. That's not the case now—everyone more or less knows it, or guesses its meaning (which is what happened with French at the time). So, he asked me if

I knew English and I answered that I did, more or less. 'How lucky you are,' he said, 'you can read Kipling in the original.' I think that when he spoke of Kipling—he had read French translations because he couldn't read English—he was thinking of *Kim*. Now, it's curious that the setting for *Kim* and *Don Segundo Sombra* is the same. I mean, a society and a country glimpsed through the eyes of two friends, one of whom is advanced in years, an old man—the lama in *Kim* and the cattle herdsman Don Segundo Sombra in Güiraldes' novel. The other one is a boy. It's the same scheme in Mark Twain's *Huckleberry Finn*. Through Don Segundo Sombra we see Buenos Aires province, not the province of the time of writing but the province of his childhood; we understand that everything took place long ago. That means we have in *Kim* the lama and the boy (Kimball) and in *Don Segundo Sombra*, the narrator, a boy from San Antonio de Areco, and the herdsman Don Segundo. That's why the overall plot is the same. Through *Don Segundo Sombra* we see the rather peaceful life of Buenos Aires province, its farms, some typical criollo scenes. Through *Kim* we see the vast and abundant India (*laughs*). In both cases, there's a society glimpsed through two friends with a great difference in ages.

FERRARI. Now that you mention vastness, I recall that no one has talked about the pampas in the mystical way in which Güiraldes did.

BORGES. I asked Güiraldes why he had used the words 'pampas' and 'gaucho', which no one in the country uses. He said to me, 'Well, I write for *Porteños*.' He knew that no one in the country said pampas and gaucho which is a rather pejorative term.

FERRARI. But would you agree that the dimension he gives to the plains is completely original compared with what previous writers had written? He sees a mystical perspective, a purificatory perspective for the people of this country, an area for regeneration.

BORGES. Yes, but I am unsure if that's what happened. Spanish and Italian smallholders have inhabited Buenos Aires province. I don't think that the plains have made them especially pure.

FERRARI. Güiraldes said the plains . . .

BORGES. The plains are the same the world over. For example, I have been in Oklahoma as well as in Buenos Aires province, and, doubtless, had I been to the steppes I would have found them to be the same too. On the other hand, every mountain is different. The Pyrenees are not similar to the Alps and the Alps are not the same as the Rocky Mountains. The Rocky Mountains are quite similar to the Andes but also different. The plains are the same everywhere.

FERRARI. However, Güiraldes said the following in particular: that in this appearance of flat terrain in which nothingness stands out, there had been thousands of accidents, invisible at first glance. But knowing this, you could begin to appreciate and value it.

BORGES. That is what the trailfinder knows. The countryside is something the country people do not feel. Of course, one of *Martín Fierro*'s merits is that the plains are never described and yet one feels them, doesn't one?

FERRARI. Of course.

BORGES. You arrive as if asleep
 when you return from the desert
 let's see if I can explain

amongst such odd people
if when I play my guitar
I wake up from my dreams.

When a clear dawn
had arisen
the last huts
and two large tears
rolled down Fierro's face.

The last settlement, the last huts and then the desert region where
nomadic Indians roamed, but not the gauchos who were sedentary.
But we must talk some more about Güiraldes who has been extraor-
dinarily kind to me. Also, I was so amazed that he took me seriously.
I don't think I am yet used to that. Perhaps not. I was recently awarded
a doctorate in Crete, which amazed me. I thought: How strange. I
arrive in a country where there are very generous people in a university who honour me, goodness, but they are quite mistaken. The same
happened with Güiraldes when I met him through Brandán Caraffa.
He lived in a hotel on San Martín. I don't remember the hotel's name,
it was between Córdoba and Viamonte. I met him through a trick
played by Brandán: Brandán came to see me and said that he had
been chatting with Pablo Rojas Paz and Güiraldes about the possibility
of launching a magazine to represent the young writers of the time.
I'm speaking of the year 1925, or perhaps 1926. The three of them
had apparently agreed that 'No, this magazine cannot do without
Borges.' I felt very flattered. So he took me to the hotel where
Güiraldes was staying. I met him and he said, 'I am very flattered. I

know that you have been talking to Brandán Caraffa and that you think a magazine of young writers cannot do without me.'

FERRARI. So that's how *Proa* began.

BORGES. That's how *Proa* began. A little later Pablo Rojas Paz arrived. He said, 'I am very flattered.' So I looked at Brandán and said to him, 'Yes, we were talking to Brandán and Güiraldes and thought that a young magazine could not do without you' (*laughs*). So with Brandán's pious lie, the four of us became friends and *Proa* was founded. But we had to make a small sacrifice. There were four of us. Each had to contribute 50 pesos. That's how the magazine was born. It cost us 200 pesos for 200 copies. Life was different then. I became friendly with Güiraldes, and he was welcome at my house. I remember that he came to lunch once. My mother reminded him that he had forgotten his guitar. He played it well and sang like a country singer. Then Güiraldes said, 'Well, I forgot it on purpose. I am off to Europe soon, as I told you, and I wanted something of mine to remain in this house.' So, very elegantly, he left his guitar. We kept his guitar at home and people who came to see us played it, because on those days many would play the guitar, something that's no longer the case.

FERRARI. I understand that politeness that you are talking about.

BORGES. Yes, it was a very delicate trait.

FERRARI. Indeed.

BORGES. I remember seeing Güiraldes' library. I remember two rooms. One was for French and Belgian Symbolists and all Lugones' works, because Güiraldes worshipped Lugones, as did my generation. We attacked him in order to defend ourselves against our own worship. So that no one would notice the attraction we felt for him. And the other room was for books on theosophy. For example, there was Madame Blavatsky. All in French. I spoke a bit about the Germans with Güiraldes, but he held a prejudice from the 1914 war and thought: Of course, the Germans, thickheads, what can they understand? It was useless for Xul Solar or me to repeat that all the research that had been done on Buddhism had been done by German writers. He refused to accept the Germans. A concept like that belonged to that first European civil war known now as the World War of 1914–18. So I remember Güiraldes' politeness and his irony. And his cult of friendships. For example, he was a close friend of Valery Larbaud's, a French writer more or less forgotten today. So, every time we talked about Paul Valéry, he pretended we meant Valery Larbaud (*laughs*). So we would explain who Paul Valéry was and he'd say, 'Oh, that vulgar man!' He wasn't hostile to Paul Valéry, only loyal to Valery Larbaud. That's why one of the farmhands in *Don Segundo Sombra* is called Valerio—that was Güiraldes winking to Valery Larbaud.

FERRARI. That's interesting what you say about Güiraldes' initiation into theosophy and mysticism.

BORGES. He was very keen on theosophy.

FERRARI. Because, in a way, he ended up applying it to our landscape.

BORGES. That's true.

FERRARI. You can see in his book *The Path* how clearly he applies this. That's why I talked about the dimension that he gave to the pampas, he was probably applying his theosophical and mystical knowledge to our landscape.

BORGES. Yes, it's a likely interpretation. I do know he was very interested in that subject, he wrote a chapter in *Don Segundo Sombra* in which Don Segundo exorcizes a possessed person. According to him, 'Given Don Segundo's modest possibilities, I couldn't go further than that. But I do believe that evil spirits can possess you.' He believed in all that. Of course, he was not a Catholic, but mysticism, especially Indian mysticism, fascinated him. Proof of which is that his widow Adelina del Carril went to live in Bengal for ten years and then adopted a boy from India.

FERRARI. His other book *Raucho*, a book of his youth . . .

BORGES. *Raucho* was somewhat autobiographical, wasn't it?

FERRARI. Yes, and there's a kind of confrontation—I guess you can see it that way—between Americanism and Europeanism. Raucho discovers Europe and later rediscovers, after his European discoveries, his own land.

BORGES. Yes, 'crucified by peace' is how I think the book ends?

FERRARI. 'In his same old land.'

BORGES. 'In his same old land', yes, I remember that. Now Güiraldes insisted, sometimes aggressively, in using Gallicisms. Some were quite ugly, like *eclosionar*, from the French *éclore*, to open—hardly an attractive word. He used them defiantly, because neither he nor his wife wanted to be, as they said, 'Ah, so-and-so is Spanishifying.' This was applied to writers like Calixto Oyuela or perhaps Ricardo Rojas who used Spanish phrases. And he refused that. Although professionally he didn't use South American words either. I believe if an Argentine writes spontaneously, he doesn't write like a Spaniard, because he is so far off from them; there's no point trying to be Argentine as you already are one. If you try to be one, as I did at first, you'll immediately notice how artificial it is.

FERRARI. What's important is to be natural.

BORGES. I think that's right. I think that we are naturally not similar to Spaniards. The Spaniards tend towards emphasis and interjection. The Argentine or Uruguayans tend towards understatement, that is, not too much, but less.

FERRARI. A kind of sobriety . . .

BORGES. Also I believe that Spaniards tend towards interjections, towards exclamations, while Argentines tend towards narrating or explaining—not interjecting.

FERRARI. Although they may suddenly fall into neutrality, a sober neutrality.

BORGES. Yes, a sober neutrality. I think that an interjection can be seen in Spanish music as well, especially in Andalusian music, which is a music of complaints, of interjections, of screams. On the other had, I have been friendly with folksingers like Luis García and their way of singing is more monotonous, like the English sing-song which doesn't raise the voice.

FERRARI. Now, there was an unfair delay in recognizing Güiraldes, because if you recall his *Cuentos de muerte y de sangre* (Stories of Death and Blood) . . .

BORGES. But I do not believe that his *Cuentos de muerte y de sangre* is worth recalling . . .

FERRARI. But they are valuable, splendid stories. Perhaps you do not like the title but do you recall any of the stories?

BORGES. No, I don't remember any. I also tried to read *Xaimaca* and failed. Güiraldes thought that *Xaimaca* was his best book. I remember that he handed either the manuscript or the proofs of *Don Segundo Sombra* over to my mother. The next morning, my mother called him. He asked her, 'What did you think of the book?' She answered, 'I loathe criollo folklore, yet I stayed up reading it until two in the morning.' 'In that case,' said Güiraldes, 'it must be good.' 'Yes, I think so,' she said. Then the book was published and, backed by Lugones' article, became a classic.

FERRARI. But that was when Güiraldes was about to die . . .

BORGES. Yes, he died soon after. It was very strange, almost dramatic, wasn't it? Sudden glory when the book was published—until then he'd been the prototype of the failed writer. Lugones consecrated it. Güiraldes goes to Paris, has an operation for throat cancer and dies. I can't recall the year, perhaps it was 1927.

FERRARI. It was between 1927 and 28, I think.

BORGES. I think it was 1927 because *Don Segundo Sombra* appeared in 1926, printed at Colombo in San Antonio de Areco. Then he moved to Calle Hortiguera.

FERRARI. But Güiraldes shared a visible characteristic with Lucio Mansilla: the plains, Paris salons, great tango dancer. You said that he could have been . . .

BORGES. I think so. Another important person is Saborido, Enrique Saborido, author of *La Morocha*. I was his friend and he wasn't a petty crook—he was a gentleman. He was from Montevideo but worked in customs here in Buenos Aires. He has left us two famous tangos: *La Morocha*, mentioned by Evaristo Carriego, and *Felicia*.

On Humour

●

OSVALDO FERRARI. Borges, there are several conjectures about the sources of your sense of humour, about your literary humour and your more general humour. George Bernard Shaw, for example, Samuel Johnson and some others.

JORGE LUIS BORGES. Well, I never knew that I was humorous but it seems that I am. I think that we live in a very superstitious country and it's sufficient for someone to say something against these superstitions—and there are many—for him to be taken as a joker. I also think that some people, in order not to take what I say seriously, accuse me of a sense of humour. I don't think I have one. I am a simple man and say what I think but because this tends to contradict many prejudices, people suppose that they're jokes. So my reputation is safe from danger as are the things that I attack. For example, I recently published an article titled 'Our Hypocrisies' and what I said there was completely serious. But it was taken as a kind of witty joke and the people I had attacked praised me.

FERRARI. Your sense of humour made it seem inoffensive.

BORGES. Yes, I think so. At the same time, I do admire humour, especially in others. In my case, I cannot recall a single joke.

FERRARI. But in Johnson's tradition . . .

BORGES. Indeed, humour and wit above all. But it does seem so hard to define things precisely because what's most obvious is impossible to define. To define is to employ different words and these words can be less expressive than what is being defined. Also, what's basic cannot be defined. How can you define, for example, the taste of coffee or the appealing sadness of twilight or that hope, doubtless an illusion, that one feels in the morning? These things cannot be defined.

FERRARI. They can't be defined.

BORGES. In the case of abstractions, things can be defined. You can define exactly a polygon or a congress. But I don't know if you can define a toothache.

FERRARI. But you can define a lack of humour. In our country, for instance.

BORGES. Yes, that's true. A lack of humour and solemnity, one of our worst traits, isn't it? It's evident in so many things. For example, there are few histories as brief as Argentine history—it has barely lasted 200 years—and yet few countries are as overwhelmed as we are with anniversaries, patriotic dates, equestrian statues, attempts at making amends for the illustrious dead.

FERRARI. And grievances.

BORGES. Grievances too. It's terrible and it's been encouraged.

FERRARI. You have characterized Argentine history as extremely cruel. Within its essential characteristics, you have pointed out cruelty.

BORGES. I think so. Today I was reading a statistic published by the police about murders committed over the last few years. Starting from a recent date, each year there's more crime. This corresponds, of course, with poverty. The poorer the people, the more likely it is that they will turn to crime.

FERRARI. It's typical of this period too.

BORGES. Violence? Yes, I agree.

FERRARI. Sadly . . .

BORGES. Yes, but I believe this ethical crime has an economic root.

FERRARI. As for humour, I was saying that I believe that you have admired, over many years, if not humour, then the irony of men like Shaw and Johnson.

BORGES. Yes, without a shadow of a doubt.

FERRARI. How would you define this trait in both of them? Because they are very particular and unique to English wit.

BORGES. Well, in both cases, that irony has its root in reason. I mean, it's not arbitrary. Personally, what Baltasar Gracián labelled wit is disagreeable, because it's about wordplay and playing with words only involves words, that is, conventions. A sense of humour, on the other hand, can be performed with facts—it is not simply about similarities between one syllable and another.

FERRARI. That's true. English humour is really reasonable.

BORGES. Very reasonable, yet, there's something fantastic about it . . . I believe that between wit and humour, even if humour criticizes real things, is something fantastic. There's always a fantastic element in the imagination which cannot exist in irony or in wit.

FERRARI. That's clear.

BORGES. Thus there's an onset of a fable, of a dream, something irrational in humour. And something slightly magical. That would be the difference. Unfortunately, no example comes to mind at this moment. But as I have thought about this theme, I hope that the conclusion I've stated remains valid.

FERRARI. You are in some ways the example. Unlike Lugones or Mallea and many Argentine writers with an obvious lack of humour, you have developed one.

BORGES. Well, Lugones sometimes tried it out but, I would say, with unhappy results: 'The schoolteacher, a skinny Scottish lady identical to an isosceles triangle, next to her obese mother-in-law.' Clearly, there's a humorous intention but the result is rather melancholic.

FERRARI. One cannot easily guess it.

BORGES. Well, the word 'isosceles' is funny, isn't it? This fits more with caricature than with a real image, which, by the way, is what Lugones sought. I can't remember any more of Lugones' attempts at wit. But I do recall Groussac's, whose irony is evident. For example, we see it in that controversy he had when he said, ' If you put that short tract by doctor so-and-so on sale, it would prove a serious obstacle for its circulation' (*laughs*). It's obvious there. Who would buy that book?

FERRARI. Borges, as I have already mentioned Johnson, I recall that you said that in England, if a national author could be chosen, it would naturally be him.

BORGES. Well, I could say Johnson or Wordsworth, but I could refer to another, and far more famous, book. If the convention is that every country be represented by a book, in this case that book would be the Bible. The Bible, as everyone knows, incorporates texts in Greek and Hebrew translated into English. Now those texts are part of the English language. A quotation from the Bible in Spanish or in French can seem pedantic or not immediately understandable. But colloquial English is packed with biblical sayings. And my grandmother, who came from a family of Methodist preachers, knew the Bible by heart. You could quote a biblical sentence from anywhere and she would say, 'Book of Job, such-and-such chapter and verse' or 'The Book of Kings' or 'The Song of Songs'.

FERRARI. She remembered the sources.

BORGES. She'd read the Bible daily. Also, I don't know if you realize that in England every family has its Bible. That in the blank pages at the end they write their family history. Marriages, births, baptisms, deaths. Those Bibles have a judicial value, they can be used in court cases, they are accepted as authentic documents by the law. You can always say, 'In the family Bible, it says such a thing.' And in Germany, another country with a Protestant majority, they have an adjective *bibelfest*—'firm in the Bible', that is, the Bible is known by heart. The same occurs in Islam, people know the Koran by heart. I think that the name Hafiz, of the famous Persian poet, means 'the one who remembers', that is, the one who knows the Koran by heart.

FERRARI. The person with a good memory.

BORGES. Rather like poor Funes (*both laugh*).

FERRARI. Or you.

BORGES. In what way?

FERRARI. You were called 'the one with the good memory' in a Buenos Aires newspaper.

BORGES. Talking of Funes, I have been asked several times if I knew him, if Funes existed. But that's nothing compared with a Spanish journalist asking me if I kept the seventh volume of the Tlön, Uqbar, Orbis Tertius encyclopaedia.

FERRARI. Which belongs to one of your stories.

BORGES. Yes, one of my stories. And when I said that all of it was invented, the man looked at me so scornfully. He had thought it was history, and it turned out it wasn't, it was a mere personal fantasy, it had no reason to be taken into account. The same happened in Madrid with 'The Aleph'. The Aleph, if you recall, is a point containing all spatial points, as all the moments of time are in eternity. I took eternity as a model for 'The Aleph'. A journalist asked me if there really was an Aleph in Buenos Aires. I said, 'Well, if there had been such a thing, it would have been the most famous object in the world and would not be limited to a book of fantastic stories written by a South American writer.' And then he said, with a naivety that almost moved me, 'Yes, but you mention the street and the street number—it says Garay, such-and-such a number . . .'

FERRARI. He thought the street and its number were not invented.

BORGES. No, the street and number were certainly not invented but the fact that something like that happened there . . . he said to me that many people, from all over but above all from South America, went there to see Corrientes such-and-such a number, because a tango said Corrientes 1214 or something like that.

FERRARI. Three hundred and forty-eight.

BORGES. Ah, good, you've remembered it. Well, there are people who go seek it, so it's similar to a fable or to literature when taken seriously. It seems many people go to London to see Sherlock Holmes' house. They go to Baker Street and look up the number. So, to satisfy these people, or as a joke, there's now a Sherlock Holmes museum and tourists find there what they are seeking, for there's the coat hanger, the laboratory, the violin, the magnifying glass, the pipes and so on.

FERRARI. According to each visitor's degree of fantasy.

BORGES. Yes, all that attire linked to Holmes can now be found there. As Oscar Wilde famously said, 'Life imitates art.'

FERRARI. That's right.

BORGES. An example that Wilde gives is of a lady who refused to go out on a balcony to see the sunset because the sunset was there in a Turner painting. He added, 'One of Turner's worst sunsets' (*laughs*), because nature had not imitated Turner that well.

FERRARI. Borges, I see that without intending it, humour has sought us out again at the end of the interview.

BORGES. That's true.

Concerning Henry James

●

OSVALDO FERRARI. Borges, Guillermo de Torre reminds us of a North American writer, naturalized English, who in the course of time has produced what he called 'a return'. That is, after a period of apparent oblivion, he has been adopted by new generations. Published and read again with interest. I am talking about Henry James.

JORGE LUIS BORGES. Of course.

FERRARI. Guillermo de Torres adds something to what we touched upon with regard to Kafka. He says James is somehow a bridge between the end of the last century and our century.

BORGES. That is, James was already decadent, he belonged to a time of decline. Of course, what I say is acceptable and very reasonable and it's that our century is inferior to the one before. He would become the first slope down. But I don't think that way. He was an excellent writer and there's no reason to mix him up with this century.

FERRARI. It's better to associate him with the transition between two centuries.

BORGES. In general, I disbelieve in any historical criteria. As Keats said, 'A thing of beauty is a joy for ever.' In James' case, we can dispense with literary history.

FERRARI. Perhaps we can dispense with history but we must pay attention to some geography. James was born in the United States and during the First World War, around 1915 . . .

BORGES. He became an English citizen. He did that because he thought that the United States had the moral duty, the ethical duty, to enter the war. Then, to underline this, he became a British citizen. I believe he did it for that reason. Also he identified himself with England. His father had educated him and his brother William James in a deliberately cosmopolitan manner, he'd feared they might become provincial or, let's say, too narrowly American. They were given a European education and so were never 'national' in the narrow sense of the word. They were very generous. Now, on the whole, James believed that the Americans were ethically superior but intellectually inferior to the Europeans. You notice that in all his books. The Americans seem naive, surrounded by complex, even evil people. I think that he had that impression. There's a lovely novel of his—one of the earliest—that he wrote and rewrote, *The American*. The plot is more or less the following: A young American falls in love with an aristocratic French girl. Her family try to prevent the marriage and then work in horrible ways on the girl. He knows all this. He cannot take revenge but he wants to do something. I think the girl dies, I'm not sure, it's ages since I read the book. But I remember the last chapter. The protagonist knows what the countess of so-and-so, the girl's mother, has done. He meets a woman from the French aristocracy, a duchess, I think, and says to himself, 'Well, I know that this woman is a gossip. If I tell her what happened, she will spread it to all of Paris and the guilty ones will be found out.' So he writes to her and asks for an interview. She lives in a castle outside Paris and is rather surprised at his request for they have met only twice. But, as she is a gossip, she suspects there is more gossip behind his request. And so she invites him. There's another guest, a rather disagreeable Italian prince, who insists on staying but the lady more or less throws him out and invites the man, an American millionaire, to dinner. They eat but he says nothing. She thinks, 'Well, he won't say anything over dinner.' Then they go to a nearby room and have coffee. She waits for what he must tell her, for that would be the only reason for his unexpected visit. Time passes, still he says nothing. Then when the last train that could take him back to Paris is about to leave, he gets up, says goodbye, thanks her for her hospitality and returns to his hotel. The next day, or very soon after, he embarks for the United States, determined not to return to Europe, a place burdened with bad memories. Then, when he is on board, he asks himself, 'Why on earth didn't I say anything to the duchess?' He had acted as he did, and didn't know why. Then he has a revelation that is wonderful— he so hated the woman he was going to denounce, hated her so much that he couldn't take revenge on her because that would create a relationship between them. That is, revenge would tie him to her even more. That's why he remained silent. Only, at the time, he hadn't known why.

FERRARI. That's really original.

BORGES. It's a lovely idea. It seems that Henry James, who usually rewrote his books, did not make his character act deliberately in the first version because he preferred forgiveness to revenge. But the second version, the one I read, is far more attractive. Later, I found out that there had been an earlier one. It's the idea that he does not take revenge because revenge is a bond between the avenger and the person who he wanted to take revenge on.

FERRARI. Without a doubt, the second is more original.

BORGES. It is more original and it is the second one that I read. My mother read it too and liked it a lot. It's a long novel. One can see the perverse behaviour of the Europeans. That was James' idea of Europeans in general. The American is a naive man in that sense. Although, of course, he is a millionaire who made his fortune in an implacable way, as all fortunes are made. But he is a just man. He illustrates that general concept that James held about Americans. He thought not about people from Chicago or from San Francisco but from New England, that is, people who had inherited the best English tradition.

FERRARI. But all his life James struggled creatively with that spiritual conflict between America and Europe.

BORGES. Yes, but I believe that he saw that difference above all. He saw Americans as very simple and Europeans as very complex and, at the same time, perverse, that is, as intellectually superior and the Americans as ethically inferior.

FERRARI. All that became with time James' main trait, his ambiguity.

BORGES. Ambiguity, yes. When I wrote my story 'The South' I said to myself, 'I will try and write, within my extremely modest possibilities, a story in the manner of Henry James.' But, I said, I will look for a very different background. I sought this and found Buenos Aires province and wrote 'The South'. Now, this story can be read in various ways. It can be read realistically. It can be read as a dream. It can be read symbolically. Wilde said, 'Each man kills the thing he loves.' I think that the opposite happens too. You are killed by what you love, and that was the case where the South kills my character. But I wrote the story keeping in mind James' stories which are deliberately open to diverse interpretations. They are deliberately ambiguous. That's why many people questioned James about his most famous story 'The Turn of the Screw'. There's an admirable translation by Bianco called 'Otra vuelta de tuerca'; Bianco turned the screw one more time (*laughs*), and from 'The Turn of the Screw' it became 'Another Turn of the Screw'.

FERRARI. It became known by that title.

BORGES. Yes. Because he was working within James' ideas.

FERRARI. Now, about that ambiguity that we have mentioned concerning James . . . he assumed and accepted it. He used to say that the North Americans were not sure whether he was an Englishman writing about the United States, and the English were not sure if he was an American writing about England. This ambiguity seemed to him . . .

BORGES. But today that doesn't matter to us at all. We think of Henry James and not whether he was American or English. The essential point is that he's Henry James.

FERRARI. But to him that ambiguity seemed to be a trait of a civilized man. He said it in writing. That ambiguity he was accused of from both sides of the ocean was precisely the trait of the civilized man.

BORGES. Yes, it means that he felt richer, more diverse. That's good.

FERRARI. Exactly.

BORGES. He must have been a very unhappy man because I believe that an aesthetic work always obeys . . . emotions, and emotions deal with unhappiness. Because happiness is an end in itself, isn't it? In that sense, happiness does not have to be transmuted into beauty but misfortune does. And we return to what we were saying in an earlier conversation, to that sentence found somewhere in *The Odyssey*: 'The gods plot misfortunes so that later generations have something to sing about.' That means that the gods plot misfortunes with an aesthetic end in view. On the other hand, happiness is an end in itself and doesn't need to be transmuted into beauty. And James must have suffered a lot to write his admirable books. At the same time, none of them are confessions. A trait in James, doubtless often pointed out, is that he imagined situations—not characters. He's the extreme opposite of, say, Dickens. In Dickens, plot doesn't matter. The plot is a pretext to reveal character. It doesn't matter in *Quixote* either. All the adventures are one adventure. What matters is that we are constantly seeing Alonso Quijano who has dreamt of being Don Quixote; sometimes he achieves this and at other times he does not. In the end, what's important is Quixote himself. Jiménez said that one could imagine *Don Quixote* with other adventures and I think he was completely right. We could imagine a third part of *Quixote*, and possibly, as we've said about another book, if all the copies of the *Quixote* were lost, Alonso Quijano would remain in human memory and new adventures could be invented for him, maybe even better ones than Cervantes'. What's important is the character. That's what happens with Shakespeare's characters. One believes in them and not the fable. Now, in James' case, I believe he imagined situations and then the characters to fit the situations, quite the opposite of Cervantes or Shakespeare. Or perhaps Dostoyevsky, who imagined characters. But not James, no, he imagined situations and then created the adequate characters.

FERRARI. To fit those situations?

BORGES. To fit those situations. He also lacked any kind of visual imagination. An extreme opposite would be Chesterton—in his work when a new character appears it is like an actor arriving on stage. James' world is not like that. It seems to be a world without colours, without forms. He was first of all a writer, one drawn to situations and then to characters.

FERRARI. But you'll have noticed that T. S. Eliot qualified him as the most intelligent writer of his generation. That Julien Benda associates him, as in his own case, with that 'brilliant situation of an obscure writer'.

BORGES. That's good.

FERRARI. That's to say, mystery surrounds his life and work. And there's another aspect. James cultivated something that has been swept away to this side more often than not—a distinction or elegance, in his writing, in his life, in his characters. All his portraits are very distinguished. I do not think that was superficial.

BORGES. No, he was without a doubt a distinguished man. It's odd, though, that he tried theatre and failed. Because when Ibsen scandalized all Europe, James thought him a *primaire* writer, as the French put it. He found him primitive and rudimentary and, of course, he wasn't. James tried theatre and he was a complete failure.

FERRARI. Just as he did not understand Ibsen, he misunderstood Whitman.

BORGES. It's just that he couldn't understand him. They were so different.

FERRARI. However, towards the end of his life, he changed his view on Whitman.

BORGES. I didn't know that. I didn't know that he had even read him. Yet, he had to have because Whitman was popularized in England by the Pre-Raphaelites, by Dante Gabriel Rossetti and his brother who published a first, expurgated edition. It had to be that way— otherwise it would have been confiscated, wouldn't it? (*Laughs.*)

On Conjecture

•

OSVALDO FERRARI. Borges, there is a genre that you have invented. It's tied to both literature and philosophy and I think that you see it as that which allows us humans to think but not penetrate further. This genre is conjecture. We see it in your poems, in your thoughts, in your stories. You always use 'perhaps', 'maybe' or other expressions that invoke conjecture.

JORGE LUIS BORGES. Yes, that's true. I have no certainty, not even the certainty of uncertainty. In that way I believe all thought is conjectural. Especially so in the case of stories. As I have mentioned earlier, the beginning and the end of the short story, the starting point and the finishing line, are revealed to me. But all that happens between those two is conjectural. I have to ascertain the best historical period, the best style. I believe that the less one intervenes in one's writing, the better. I try to prevent my opinions from appearing, I try to prevent my theories—well, I do not have aesthetic theories—from appearing. I think that each theme demands its own rhetoric. I was rather dissatisfied with the style of 'The Circular Ruins', but friends tell me that the baroque style is what the theme demanded. So, every theme demands its own rhetoric and wants to be narrated in the first person. Well, it must occur in such a historical period, in such a country—all that is given by the theme. It is better to wait after the first revelation which give me the beginning and end of a fable. New insights will come along that will tell me if the story took place at the end of the nineteenth century or in the vague Orient of *The Arabian Nights*. Now, in general, I prefer the last years of the nineteenth century as well as places that are a little removed, not only in time and space, because then I can invent, I can freely imagine. What is contemporary ties you down. And literature's ancient tradition is like this: no one supposes that Homer fought in the siege of Troy; it's understood that everything happened later. Because the past can be so easily modified. Contrary to what is said about the past not being modifiable, I believe that each time we recall the past we modify it, given that our memory is fallible. And that modification can be beneficial.

FERRARI. Then the past is . . .

BORGES. I believe the past is malleable, as is the future. On the other hand, the present sadly isn't. If I feel a physical pain, it would be useless to think that I do not feel it—because there's the pain, isn't there? Or if I feel nostalgic for a certain person, I feel it in the present. But what can one know about the past, even one's own past? I can perhaps imagine that my adolescent years in Europe were painful. The proof is that once, like many young people, I contemplated suicide. I think all young people have at some time contemplated it. All have spoken

Hamlet's monologue 'To be or not to be'. Yet I recall those years as if they had been happy ones—even though I'm sure they weren't. But it doesn't matter, so much time has passed. The past is malleable and I can alter it. And what is history but our image of history? That image always improves the past, that is, it tends itself to mythology, to legend. Also, every country has its private mythology that perhaps does not correspond to anything in reality. It is very hard for the present to be always pleasing.

FERRARI. Then past and future are conjectural?

BORGES. Yes, I think so, although it is perhaps easier to alter the past than the future because we usually think about the future as 'well, such a thing will probably occur', 'no, such-and-such factors cancel each other out'. But the past, above all the distant past, is a very, very flexible matter. In the end, everything is apt for art. Especially unhappiness. Happiness, not so much, as it is an end in itself. That's why there are no poets of happiness. Although I think perhaps Jorge Guillén was one. Whitman less so, because with Whitman you feel that he imposed happiness on himself as if it is the duty of an American. And happiness is not like that, happiness has to be spontaneous, doesn't it? While, in Guillén's case, I think you feel happiness in those lines of his: 'All the air is a bird.' That could be a nightmare: 'All the air is a bird' but said by him it isn't, it feels like happiness. Otherwise, misfortune and elegies give one the impression of being easy, of being natural.

Conjecture in general . . . for example, it is not logically impossible for solipsism to be true. Logically, I could be the sole dreamer and I could dream all universal history, all the past, all my past, perhaps I begin to exist at this very moment. But at this moment I already recall that we met a quarter of an hour earlier, a quarter of an hour created by me now. Well, that is possible, nothing more. Not for the imagination—it would be terrible to imagine that. Also, you perceive that beyond the sensory data there's the presence of another. That's why John Locke's philosophy is false. He says we owe our knowledge to the senses. No. I believe that, along with the senses, one feels there is something else—one feels hostility, indifference, love, friendship, adversity. These things are felt beyond the senses.

FERRARI. Certainly. Conjecture is licit, according to your thinking. But there's another aspect. I am not sure whether it's developed recently or is far older, and that is your belief that poems, stories and thoughts are given to us . . .

BORGES. I believe that there is no doubt about that. Besides, it's the initial idea, it's the idea, for example, of the Muse. The Muse dictates its poems to the poet. The poet is the Muse's scribe. The Hebrews thought it was the spirit that dictated the diverse books of the Bible to diverse scribes over diverse periods and across diverse regions of the world. All of it is the spirit's work.

FERRARI. Curiously, your thinking about what is given to us when we create is a thought—I am aware that you'll find the word excessive— that's invariably mystical.

BORGES. It has to be mystical because it cannot be physical or logical. Poe's idea that aesthetic work was intellectual work was a *boutade* of his, a joke. He could not have believed that. No person who sits to write a poem does so by force of reason. There's always something that escapes him. Poe gives a series of reasons that, according to him, led him to write 'The Raven'. But always between each link of the chain there's a kind of interval of shadow or something that demands further links. That's why what he said doesn't explain anything. He could reduce 'The Raven' to a series of reasons but between each link in his reasons there will be something that's not clear, that's due to, let's call it, secret inspiration. That secret can be external or can come from our memory. Yeats too believed in the 'great memory'. He thought that all men inherit the memory of their elders. The elders, clearly, grow geometrically. Two parents, four grandparents, so many great grandfathers and so on until all humanity is included. He thought that in every man those virtually infinite ancestors converge which is why it's not necessary for a writer to have many personal experiences—everything is already there. Each one makes use of this secret receptacle of memories and that's sufficient for literary creation.

FERRARI. So when we are sometimes told, for example, that Elizabeth Browning was a poet of mystical inspiration, that is permissible.

BORGES. Ah, yes, without a doubt. Perhaps that could be applied to all poets, because I do not conceive of a poet as a mere intellectual.

FERRARI. Naturally.

BORGES. Now there are writers who perceive intellectual matters in an aesthetic way. For me, the best example of an intellectual poet is Emerson—he is not solely intellectual though he was always thinking. On the other hand, the case of other intellectual poets . . . I'm not sure if they really are. Robert Frost was. Emerson also.

FERRARI. Perhaps Valéry.

BORGES. In Valéry's case, one notices that he is most impressed by the external world but not by ideas. His ideas are vulgar. They are more images than ideas. That's why in the end every writer must resolve it in his own way. Valéry never struck me as an intellectual poet, but a poet, without a doubt. One of his poems defines exactly what taste a fruit is and how that fruit dissolves in pleasure.

FERRARI. Perhaps Valéry is associated with an intellectual vision for his link with mathematics.

BORGES. Yes, there is that.

FERRARI. So, on the one hand, we have conjecture and on the other, mysticism. There's a third aspect that interests me . . .

BORGES. Not only a third but I would guess thousands more. But what interests you at this moment, Ferrari?

FERRARI. What interests me is what you reflect on through your journeys, when you return and before you leave. Despite time, your love for life doesn't decline, which is what, in my view, is most essential in a poet.

BORGES. Yes, I do believe that if one is a poet, one should feel every moment as poetic. That's to say, one should live loving life, and in loving life love also its misfortunes, its failures, its lonely moments. All this is matter for a poet—without it he couldn't write and wouldn't feel justified. In my case, I do not like what I write but if I don't write or don't compose something, I feel disloyal to my destiny. My destiny is to conjecture, to dream and then to write and eventually to publish which is what's least important. But I have to live in continuous activity or have to believe that I live in continuous imaginative activity and, if possible, rational activity as well, but especially, imaginative. I must dream all the time, I must live facing the future. It seems sick to think of the past, although the past can grant us elegies which is not a negligible genre. But, on the whole, I try to forget what I have written, because if I reread all I've written I would lose heart. On the other hand, if I live facing the future—even if I forget what I have written, I can repeat myself—I feel alive and justified. Otherwise, I feel lost (*laughs*).

FERRARI. I believe that if you did reread all you have written that wouldn't happen . . .

BORGES. Yes, but it's a dangerous experiment and better not tried. The result might be a vow of silence, a call to silence.

FERRARI. Maybe you would discover that your love for life has also been constant, even if you haven't noticed it.

BORGES. Well, that's a conjecture, one of your generous ones.

FERRARI. The last conjecture in today's conversation.

BORGES. Ah, very well, we will continue to talk about other themes.

FERRARI. We will.

24

Westerns or Cinema Epics

●

OSVALDO FERRARI. Borges, we have talked about different cultures, literatures and religions. Today, I would like to approach something simpler but just as interesting, something you have cultivated as a spectator and at times an author—your interest in cinema over many years.

JORGE LUIS BORGES. Yes, I think that for obvious commercial reasons, Hollywood saved the epic at a time when the poets had forgotten that poetry began with the epic. Before that cinematography was like a photographed stage. With the arrival of the Westerns, movement was introduced. Horsemen rode from one side to another, shooting pistols. That movement that now seems intrinsic to cinema was created by the Western. I remember that Néstor Ibarra and I recommended that a friend of ours, Julio Medina y Vedia, a very intelligent man, watch a Josef von Sternberg's film, I can't recall which. I think it was *The Salvation Hunters* or perhaps *Underwood* or *The Dragnet*. He went to see it but said that he couldn't follow it because it was made in such an unartistic way. It was so uncomfortable—at times you saw a face from the front, then that face filled the screen; or you saw a character from the back; sometimes there was no character at all, only land-scape. Naturally, a film made in such a confused way could be followed by no one. Today, even a child could follow a film. In a sense, I worshipped cinematography, I could have written much on cinema. My cinematographic chronicles have been collected and published in a book, but only what appeared in the magazine *Sur* which wasn't much. There were other magazines too, to which I regularly contributed. Also, once you have seen a film, you have the urge to talk about it. In that way, I began . . . well, when I was a child, cinematography had certain conventions that everyone accepted, and once a convention is accepted it ceases being one. For example, if what you were seeing was in sepia you knew it was daytime, but if it was green it was night.

FERRARI. It was a code.

BORGES. Yes, and it was accepted and no one thought of it as artificial. You knew night was green and day was sepia (*laughs*). And then, as I was telling you, another way developed—a kind of room was photographed, always from the same angle and distance. Later, with Von Sternberg and others like King Vidor or Ernst Lubitsch, one began to photograph the room from different angles. And no one was upset. We accepted it as natural. One of the first films showed an actor attacking, I think, a girl. He had a kind of monkey face. They showed it in a close-up and people went to see that one scene where the huge face of that monstrous man filled the screen. Then the same happened with the talkies. I remember a film with Emil

Jannings playing a Russian tsar. He spoke once, asking his assassin to help him. I also recall the great poster for *Ana Christie* with Greta Garbo, based on a Eugene O'Neill play. 'Garbo Talks' it said. In that film, a series of inns were shown to stimulate our expectations, then there was mist, then a horse in the mist, then finally a woman arrived from Sweden and walked across the stage.

FERRARI. Was it Greta Garbo?

BORGES. Yes, she arrived at the bar and slowly strolled past a very long table. We all expected her to talk—we were waiting to hear Greta Garbo's voice, her never-heard-before voice. What we did hear was a hoarse voice that said, 'Give me a whisky.' It made us shiver with emotion. That was her first talkie.

FERRARI. You once wrote about Greta Garbo.

BORGES. Yes. All of my generation was in love with Greta Garbo. I think that the whole world was in love with her. My sister Norah said a lovely thing—'Greta Garbo will never be vulgar.' And it's true. A tall woman with broad shoulders. The other actresses of that time are forgettable. But not Greta Garbo. There was something solid as well as mysterious about her. She was called the Swedish Sphinx.

FERRARI. You know that Reyes divided people of that time according to before and after cinema?

BORGES. That could be true.

FERRARI. It characterized the times.

BORGES. Of course, the cinema. To start with, we saw many, extremely sentimental Italian films. I cannot recall the actress' name but she was famous and always died among flowers, among roses. Then there were the Italian comedies, a few French films and many North American ones. But the best were the Westerns, with shootings and riders. There was a special one—you must have seen it?—where the representation lasts the time of the action, called . . . .

FERRARI. *High Noon.*

BORGES. Yes, *High Noon.* Aristotle spoke about the three unities. But his unity was rather arbitrary because he stated that a representation should last a day. But in that film it was done in a far more rigorous way—the representation, the action, lasted exactly as long as the film. That's why every now and then a clock was shown, the station clock. And you could tell that time had passed. I believe that the only time the temporal unities have been so rigorously applied is in that Gary Cooper film. A wonderful Western. There were earlier ones too, like *Stagecoach.*

FERRARI. I believe you were a fan of Von Sternberg's before Marlene Dietrich.

BORGES. Yes. I think it was a pity that he met Marlene Dietrich. She was a very beautiful woman, she had a lovely voice but no dramatic talent. She didn't claim to possess any, either. But there's something so pleasing about seeing and hearing a beautiful woman. What role she plays hardly matters (*laughs*).

FERRARI. You wrote about Von Sternberg's *Docks of New York.*

BORGES. Yes, it would have been very odd not to have written about it. Those films where George Bancroft and Fred Coller appeared as two eternal antagonists. They could be adventurers or a sheriff or in other things but the two were always enemies. Also Evelyne Brench and William Powell, who started working during that time but lasted longer than the others.

FERRARI. We also have the scripts that you have written, for example, *Invasión* with Casares.

BORGES. Well, that's fine, but I had nothing to do with that. In *Invasión*, I provided two of the deaths. But I never understood the plot. When I saw the film, I understood it even less. It seemed to me a very confused film. Moreover, I think that the temporal or chronological order was inverted. That made it completely impenetrable. I thought that the film was very bad. It was titled *Invasion* and there's a group, including Macedonio and his disciples, and you cannot tell if it plots to invade the city or is secretly defending it. But why a city is not defended by proper soldiers and by 10 people is never explained.

FERRARI. Every time it's shown in cinemas it seems that it's twisted even more.

BORGES. That's right.

FERRARI. I have also read comments you have written on Argentine films.

BORGES. Yes, I do not think that any of them are good.

FERRARI. I'm not sure if you recall *Los prisioneros de la tierra* (*Prisoners of Earth*)?

BORGES. Yes, that was with Ulises Petit de Murat and based on several Quiroga stories, I believe.

FERRARI. Horacio Quiroga, yes.

BORGES. I met Quiroga and tried to befriend him. He was a man who seemed to be made of wood. He was very short and was sitting by the fire in Dr Aguirre's house, I think that was his name. I saw him that way, bearded and made of wood. He was sitting by the fire and I thought—he was so short—I thought: It's natural for me to see him so short, because he lives far away in Misiones. And that fire that I am seeing is not a fire in the fireplace in the house of a man living on Junín Street. No, it's a bonfire in Misiones. My impression was that only his appearance was with us; that he had really stayed behind in Misiones, out there, in the middle of the jungle. I tried several topics with him but he refused to answer. Then I realized that it was natural that he didn't answer because he was far away. There was no reason he could hear what I was saying in Buenos Aires . . .

25

Lugones, That Austere, Heartbroken Man

●

OSVALDO FERRARI. Borges, there's an Argentine writer who turns up in our dialogues without being summoned. You seemed to have had several meetings and disagreements with him but he inevitably turns up in our talks. Obviously, I am speaking of Lugones.

JORGE LUIS BORGES. Lugones, of course (*laughs*), I had no idea that he was turning up in our chats. I thought that he had stopped talking in 1938 (*both laugh*). I had dealings with Lugones five or six times in my life. Let's say five times, to be free from any errors. To converse with him was very difficult for I held him in such high respect that I dared not disagree with him. Dialogue was difficult because any topic one brought up was immediately killed by him. I don't know if we have already talked of a risky moment when Bernárdez dared to pronounce Baudelaire's name. Lugones said, 'He's worthless' and that was it. He never justified his dismissal, he gave no reasons for negating Baudelaire. As we held Lugones in such high regard, we let it pass. Another time, I dared speak of Groussac and he was more explicit and in seven words rather than two said, 'A French teacher,' then paused, then continued, 'he'll soon be forgotten.' Full stop and new paragraph.

Now, conversation becomes very hard with someone who condemns all topics to death. Though I would like to record that he always changed the conversation to talk tenderly and nostalgically about Darío. I can still hear his voice, with that Cordoban lilt. Chatting for him was a form of nostalgia for 'my friend and master Rubén Darío'. He enjoyed that filial relationship with Darío. Darío was a very loveable man. I have known people like Casares, for example, who spoke once in his life with Darío and never forgot it.

Dialogue with Lugones, on the other hand, was thankless. I grew tired of proposing topics and then watching them being killed off. So I stopped seeing him. I think the same thing happened to many others. We all respected Lugones—in those days we not only imitated him but we wanted to be him. I have since discovered that there are hundreds of ways of writing well that are not exactly his way. But in those days, we all felt his attraction and we attacked him precisely because, somehow, we wanted to free ourselves of him. That is, we were ungrateful to Lugones for he was everything in our eyes. And Lugones must have felt this. The first time I saw him I was with Eduardo González Lanuza and each of us feared that the other would consider chatting with Lugones as servile. This made us both impertinent with Lugones. But he realized that our impertinence was a mask for our shyness and ignored it and said nothing. I returned a few times and then finally stopped seeing him. When González Garaño telephoned me to say that Lugones had committed suicide I was extremely sad but not at all surprised. Suicide in such a haughty and lonely man seemed inevitable. He was a man who never stooped to friendship. Yet I know that he had some excellent friends, Alberto Gerchunoff, for example; a cousin of mine called Álvaro Melián Lafinur who with Eduardo Mallea tried to be his friend but failed. And there's a poet only remembered when Lugones is mentioned, who may still be alive, called Luis María Jordán; he wrote a play I haven't read called *La bambina*. According to Mallea, Jordán went to chat with Lugones every day. That's all I know about him, though I have read and inevitably forgotten some lines of his in some anthology. I mean by this that Lugones deliberately isolated himself. I must also emphasize that Lugones was, above all else, an ethical man. He was criticized for having been an anarchist, a socialist, a democrat and, finally, when he gave his lectures in the Círculo Militar, a fascist. But he never thrived with any of these changes. I know from a good source that Uriburu, in 1930 after the revolution, offered Lugones the directorship of the National Library. Lugones said that he had plotted with Uriburu but that he had done so for his fatherland and so could not benefit personally from the revolution's triumph.

FERRARI. He was an ethical man, even when he was wrong.

BORGES. Yes, and then a Venezuelan critic called Blanco Fombona criticized him for plagiarizing Julio Herrera y Reissig, a poet from Montevideo. Now, Fombona's argument seems irrefutable as Herrera y Reissig published his *Los éxtasis de la montaña* two years before Lugones' *Los crepúsculos del jardín*. The titles are similar, aren't they? But that argument is false because the poems that Lugones collected in his book, clearly sharing the same rhetorical devices, the same vocabulary, the same stylistic tricks as Herrera y Reissig, had been published earlier in magazines as widely known as *Caras y Caretas*. And Herrera owned a cylindrical phonograph on which Lugones had recorded those sonnets supposedly copied from Herrera. And that cylinder wore out because Herrera made everyone who went to his house listen to it. That is, the disciple was Herrera. But when Lugones was accused of plagiarizing Herrera, the latter's widow was still alive and Lugones thought that it would seem offensive to say that he had been the master and the dead man his disciple. So he allowed himself to be stained by that accusation of plagiarism, which still circulates in Europe and especially in Spain, and never said a word about it. That's how he was an ethical man.

I know this in many other ways. Now, regarding Lugones' work, it should be pointed out that reading a book impressed him as much as, if not more than, say, love for a woman or a landscape or any other fact. Reading a book was something memorable. As it was for Alonso Quijano, a man changed by his library, for Quijano chose to become Don Quixote after reading the chivalry novels in his library. Behind each of Lugones' books, except for his *Romances del Río Seco*, one can sense another author. For example, behind *Los crepúsculos del jardín* one finds Albert Samain; behind *Lunario sentimental* one finds Jules Laforgue; behind others one finds Hugo and, often, Almafuerte. Yet those texts are by Lugones, that is, one feels a tutelary presence which could be that of a French writer or a Belgian like Laforgue or Samain but one also feels that these poems are by Lugones. Thus he was an imitator but a conscious one, an imitator with his own voice. If one takes a poem from Samain's *Au Jardin de l'Infante* and one by

Lugones from *Los crepúsculos del jardín*, though both use the same rhetoric, one immediately notices that Lugones does uses that rhetoric differently. Now, Almafuerte, who was a kind of genius but also a rather straightforward man, what the French call *primaire*, felt that Lugones imitated him. He said, 'Lugones would like to roar, but he cannot. He is an Almafuerte for women.' That hurt Lugones. But Almafuerte failed to understand Lugones.

I recall that Lugones cited four poets in *Las montañas de oro*. These four poets, personally crucial, were Homer, Dante, Hugo and Whitman. However, in his prologue to *Lunario sentimental*, Whitman, is omitted. That was inevitable, for when Lugones published *Lunario sentimental* he believed that rhyme was an essential element in poetry whereas Whitman was one of the fathers of free verse. That is why he was omitted. In Homer, the verse form is the hexameter with short and long syllables—quite another matter. But in the case of the other two, yes, Dante and Hugo were Lugones' poets. I remember that in conversation, when he wanted to say that a poet was excellent he would say 'So-and-so is Victor Hugo,' that is, Victor Hugo was for him an obvious synonym for poet, something that many in France no longer recognize. Hugo tends to be very unjustly forgotten. It's been said that Lugones, Darío and Freyre did nothing but turn Hugo and Verlaine's music into Spanish. Maybe, but to transfer the music of one poet into another language is very hard. But they did so. The texts by Hugo and Verlaine were available to everyone, yet not everyone translated them. They did. For example, I know English pretty well, that is, my ears are attuned to the music of English, to German also, but I have been unable to transfer that music into Spanish. If I could have done that, well, I would have been as great a poet as Darío or Lugones whereas I'm sure I'm not. So, to transfer the music of one language into another is an achievement. Clearly, what did Garcilaso do but transfer Petrarch's music into Spanish? Nothing more, but, I would say, nothing more and nothing less! In Lugones' case, he brought so many voices, so many different kinds of music, to Spanish . . . that his work continues to enrich us. And as I am talking about Lugones, I would also like to talk about Ezequiel Martínez Estrada. Estrada's work is . . . unimaginable, inconceivable without Darío or Lugones' work. Yet, I would argue that Estrada's best works are better than Lugones' or Darío's best. Now that could be explained because Lugones invented a metrical scheme and style that was rather complex, especially in his prose and in *Lunario sentimental*, but his mind was naive and simple. On the other hand, that complex and impenetrable style precisely matched Martínez Estrada's complex and impenetrable mind.

FERRARI. Lugones, apart from being for us the leader of Modernismo, was a personal writer in his *Romances del Río Seco*. There Lugones is, perhaps, free from influences.

BORGES. I do not know if he is really himself. I would say that those ballads are written in an anonymous style, or almost anonymous. He has stated that in the prologue.

FERRARI. But they are your favourite poems.

BORGES. Yes, but it's a mistake to pick favourites in a work as rich as Lugones'. It's better to pick each stage in that work, isn't it? That would be to select *Las montañas de oro*, *Los crepúsculos del jardín*, *Lunario* *sentimental*, the *Romances del Río Seco* and perhaps some pieces from *Las horas doradas* as well.

FERRARI. Or the *Poemas solariegos*.

BORGES. Or also the *Poemas solariegos*—why not, of course. Yes, Lugones' work is so vast. It's curious that no book of his repeats any other. One book does not predict the next one. But in all of them, in very different ways, you hear Lugones' voice and intonation. Because, in the end, what do ideas matter? Metrical innovations can interest historians of literature but not a reader. In that sense, I would say that Lugones is one of Argentina's first writers, although he was not a man of genius like Almafuerte. Now about Almafuerte . . . What could be saved? Perhaps his *Confiteor Deo*, *El misionero*, some of the *Paralelas* and little else. I have often thought of writing a book about Almafuerte, especially about his ethics.

FERRARI. You make him stand out as a spirit among us Argentines.

BORGES. Yes, as a spirit, of course. It could be said that Almafuerte has written the best and worst lines in the Castilian language. The same goes for Lugones, because he abounds in lines that are hard to forgive, like:

> Poblóse de murciélagos el combo
> Cielo a manera de chinesco biombo

(Bats filled the bulging / sky in the shape of a Chinese screen.)

While, on the other hand, after that:

> Y a nuestros pies un río de jacinto
> Corría sin rumor hacia la muerte.

(And at our feet a hyacinth river / ran without sounds towards death.)

Those last two lines could be interpreted in several ways and, in addition to being accurate, are lovely.

FERRARI (*laughs*). I think that I struck the right note when at the start of this conversation I mentioned Borges and Lugones, because I have hardly said a word.

BORGES. Goodness, sorry!

FERRARI. No, on the contrary, I would like to thank you for your contribution, and Lugones', of course.

26

Classics at the Age of 85

●

OSVALDO FERRARI. Borges, beyond our century's fashions, you have fortunately declared in one of your pages that one should not follow an iconoclast's calling.

JORGE LUIS BORGES. Yes, that's true. I think that we should respect the past as the past is so easily changed from the present.

FERRARI. But you are distancing yourself from successive iconoclastic fashions . . .

BORGES. Yes, but the fact of thinking of literature in terms of schools or generations is a bad French habit. Flaubert said, 'When a line is good, it loses its school' and added, 'A good line by Boileau is the same as a good line by Hugo.' And it's true. When a poet gets it right, it's right for ever. It doesn't matter what aesthetic theory he follows or when it was written. That line is good and it's good for ever. And the same goes for all good lines. You can read them without taking into account that they may correspond with the thirteenth-century Italian language or the nineteenth-century English language or the political opinions of the poet. The line is good. I always quote Boileau's line where he astonishingly says, 'The moment when I talk is already far from me.' It's a melancholic line and also, while you quote the line, it stops being in the present and gets lost in the past and it's all the same as to whether it's a very recent past or a remote one—the line remains there. And Boileau said it. That line doesn't match our idea of Boileau but it would be as good if it were by Verlaine or by Hugo or by an unknown author. The line exists in its own right.

FERRARI. That's right. In this August of 1984, the month of your 85th birthday . . .

BORGES. Well, goodness, what can I do? I am still stubbornly alive. When I was young I wanted to be Hamlet, I wanted to be Raskolnikov, I wanted to be Byron. That is, I wanted to be a fascinating tragic character but not any more. I resign myself to not being interesting, to being insipid, but also on being serene or trying to be serene which is no less important. Serenity is something to aspire to always. Perhaps we do not attain it completely but it's easier to attain in old age rather than in youth. And serenity is the greatest good. That is not my original idea—the Epicureans and the Stoics thought that there are no original ideas. But, why not emulate those illustrious Greeks? What more could we want?

FERRARI. And exactly in relation to that persistent serenity and your refusal of iconoclastic fashions, I would like to chat with you about the classics.

BORGES. Well, I will have to repeat myself, there's no other way, for if I don't repeat others I repeat myself. Perhaps I am no more than a repetition. I do not believe that a book that is a classic is a book written in a particular way. For example, Eliot thought a classic became possible when language had reached a kind of perfection, when a period had reached a kind of perfection. But I do not believe that. I think a classic is a book that we read in a certain way. So it's not a book written in a certain way but read in a certain way. When we read a book as if nothing in it was due to chance, as if it had an intention and could justify itself, then that book is a classic. The most obvious proof is the *I Ching* or the Chinese *Book of Changes*, made up of 64 hexagrams composed of 64 complete or broken lines combined in 64 possible modes. This book has been given a moral interpretation and is one of China's classics. It's a book that's not based on words but on complete or broken lines, but it is read with respect. This is the same that happens with classics in every language. For example, it is supposed that every line in Shakespeare is justified. Obviously, many are the fruit of chance. It's supposed that every line in *Quixote* or every line in *Divina Commedia* or every line in the poems called 'Homeric' are justified. So a classic is a book read with respect.

I believe that a text changes in value according to where it is. If we read a text in a newspaper, we read it as something that is made to be forgotten immediately; even the expression 'daily' reveals its ephemerality. Each day there's a new newspaper that erases the previous one. If we read the same text in a book, we do so with a respect that changes the text. That's why I say that a classic is a book read in a particular way. Here, in our country, we have decided that *Martín Fierro* is our classic and that, without a doubt, has changed our history. I think that if we had picked *Facundo* our history would have been different. *Facundo* offers a different aesthetic pleasure but not inferior to the one offered by *Martín Fierro*. Both books have an aesthetic value and, of course, *Facundo*'s teachings, I mean the democratic idea, the idea of civilization against barbarism, is an idea that would have been more useful than taking a deserter, a criminal, a sentimental assassin, as an exemplary character, which is what happened and which is what Martín Fierro was. All of this doesn't spoil the book's literary virtues.

It pleases me to name Sarmiento as, you know, on 11 September I am being given a lofty and unwarranted honour—I am being made a doctor honoris causa of the University of San Juan, a recent branch of the University of Cuyo which is linked to Sarmiento's name, for me the greatest name in our literature and history. Why not risk saying that? Well, I am being given this in San Juan and I am feeling very, very honoured.

FERRARI. And that is linked to your first honoris causa doctorate?

BORGES. That's right. My first honoris causa still overwhelms me. I have others from ancient and famous universities such as Harvard, Oxford, Cambridge, Tulane, the University of the Andes, but the first was the University of Cuyo around 1955 or 1956. I owe this honour to my friend Félix Della Paolera who suggested the idea to the University of Cuyo's rector. I heard this from others—he said nothing about it to me. He's an old friend from Adrogué.

FERRARI. Returning to the classics, Borges, you pointed out two ways of interpreting them. The first, followed by Homer, Milton or Torcuato Tasso invoke an inspiring Muse or spirit . . .

BORGES. They are the ones who deliberately decided to write a masterpiece. Well, today we call it the unconscious but it's the same thing. The Hebrews spoke of the spirit, the Greeks of the Muse and our mythology speaks of the unconscious; during the nineteenth century, they spoke of the subconscious. It's the same, isn't it? It reminds me of Yeats who spoke of the Great Memory, in addition to personal experiences.

FERRARI. Then there's another process, also indicated by you, following the classics to reach the final form of a work. It's that untangling of a thread, or something starting from an apparent secondary or anonymous fact, as in Shakespeare's case, where you stated that the plot did not bother him as much as . . .

BORGES. The possibilities of that plot. Those possibilities are, in fact, infinite. This may seem strange in relation to literature but not with regard to painting and the plastic arts. For example, how many sculptors have felicitously attempted an equestrian statue? More or less variations on the horseman, they have led to results as diverse as the *Gattamelata* and the *Colleoni*. And the statues of Garibaldi which are perhaps best forgotten (*both laugh*). They are a somewhat melancholic example of the genre for they are also equestrian statues. And how many painters have painted 'The Virgin and the Child' or 'The Crucifixion'? Yet each painting is different.

FERRARI. Of course, these are precious variations.

BORGES. Yes, Greek tragedians dealt with themes already known to the public. That saved many explanations. When they said 'Prometheus bound,' they were referring to something everyone knew. Literature is in many cases a series of variations on some essential themes. One of these themes is the 'return', the classic example being *The Odyssey*.

FERRARI. That's true.

BORGES. Or the theme of lovers who meet, of lovers who die together. Essential themes that lead to different books.

FERRARI. You claim that the validity of a classic depends on the curiosity or apathy of generations of readers. That is, at first the work is not controlled by chance but by the spirit or the Muse, but then it is left to chance, to the readers.

BORGES. Who knows if it is chance? Yesterday I realized how important each person's reading is because I heard two analyses of my story 'El Evangelio según Marcos' (The Gospel According to Mark). Those two interpretations were two rather different stories, two very inventive interpretations made by a psychoanalyst and a theologian. Which means that there are, in fact, three stories. My draft of the story acted as a stimulus to theirs and I thanked them for that, for it's good that every text be protean and take on different forms through reading. Reading can be a creative act, no less creative than writing. As Emerson said, a book is one thing among things, a dead thing, until someone opens it. Then the aesthetic experience happens, something that was dead revives and revives in a form that is not necessarily the one it had when it appeared to the author. It takes a different form, a precious variation like the ones you spoke of earlier.

FERRARI. How strange that a psychoanalyst and a theologian understood each other over one of your stories.

BORGES. Well, his theology is close to Jung's myths, so they met in Jung's mythological world (*both laugh*).

FERRARI. Oh, that explains it!

BORGES. But it was a rather theological association in which the Father, the Son and the Holy Spirit appeared. I think they also introduced the Virgin Mary and the earth goddess. Importance was given to two elements, fire and water. But, since I was talking about the plains, the earth was present too and since my characters breathed, air as well.

FERRARI. The four elements.

BORGES. It would be hard to do without the elements, wouldn't it? Above all, they insisted on the presence of water, a flood, rain and the presence of fire that burns down part of the house. But they forgot that my characters did not suffocate, that is, there was air and there was earth, the obvious proof of which would be the region referred to by the literary people as the pampas.

FERRARI. You've always told us that getting involved with an author allows you, somehow, to become that author. Reading Shakespeare allows one, during the reading, to become Shakespeare.

BORGES. Yes, in the case of a sonnet, for example, one becomes who the author was when he wrote it or conceived it. That is, in the moment when we say 'We will be dust, but passionate dust,' we are Quevedo or the Latin writer Propertius who inspired Quevedo.

FERRARI. But you have been deeply affected by your chosen classics . . .

BORGES. Of course, because each person chooses his classic authors. I have failed with some. For example, I have completely failed with the classic novels, which is rather a recent genre, but also with some of the ancient classics. I remember acquiring François Rabelais' work in two different editions and thinking, 'I cannot read him in this edition, but maybe in another typeface and binding I can.' But I failed both times. Apart from some happy passages, including one that pleased Xul Solar, the one about an island with trees that produce instruments and tools—there's a tree that gives hammers, another that gives knives, another irons . . . a fantastic island. And Silvina Ocampo, Bioy Casares and I picked this chapter for our *Antología de la literatura fantástica*: 'The Island of Tools' or 'The Trees of Tools', I cannot exactly remember which, but it was by Rabelais and it was a very pleasurable read.

FERRARI. You somehow epitomize your favourite classics. It's said that you are already a living classic. What do you think?

BORGES. Well, that's a generous mistake. Anyway, I do have a love for other writers' classics. And some recent classics, a little forgotten already. For example, in different continents, I have conveyed my love for Stephenson, for Shaw, for Chesterton, for Twain, for Emerson, and perhaps that is what's most essential in what's called my work. Spreading that love. And teaching. My family is linked to teaching. My father was a psychology teacher, my great aunt was one of the founders of the Instituto de Lenguas Vivas. I think her name, Carolina Haslam de Suárez, has been engraved in stone or marble.

FERRARI. Then let us celebrate your birthday by remembering the classics.

BORGES. Yes, that's a good idea.

Dante, an Infinite Reading

●

OSVALDO FERRARI. Borges, there's a classic that always enters our conversations indirectly and which should now be dealt with directly. It's an Italian classic that sometimes reminds you of Ulysses' adventures in a distant place in the Aegean Sea. I'm talking about Dante, of course.

JORGE LUIS BORGES. A limitless topic.

FERRARI. Inexhaustible.

BORGES. In the letter to Cangrande de la Scala, Dante said that his book could be read in four ways, like the Holy Scripture. But there are doubtless more than four ways. He spoke of a four-sided reading though I can't now remember his divisions. He took the idea from the Holy Scriptures and from theologians of that period. According to the Kabbalists, the Holy Scriptures—the Old Testament—had been written with each of its readers in mind, each of the faithful. That was not so difficult as readers were/are are no less the work of God than the Holy Scriptures. God could have premeditated everything in the same moment, if we can speak of moments with reference to God.

FERRARI. That reminds me of something that Alberto Girri revealed to me about poetry not long ago—the idea that a poem seeks out its reader, creates it reader.

BORGES. Yes.

FERRARI. So it is possible for a specific poem to have a specific reader.

BORGES. Yes, I do believe that it's important that a book finds its reader. If it doesn't, it has been written in vain. The Kabbalists thought that every verse of the Bible had been written with each of its future readers in mind. Written especially for each individual. Because when you read the Bible you are in personal contact with the Divine. That's what it means, doesn't it?

FERRARI. From the Divine to each reader.

BORGES. Yes, to each reader. I've thought of writing a story about it, even if it's unworkable. To invent the plot would be impossible but the idea appeals to me. We know that Dante, after writing *Divina Commedia*, went to Venice and that he was essentially a literary man. Why not suppose that he had glimpsed another plot for another poem? Or, better, that it had occurred to him or that he had discovered it? If we could establish that idea, we would have done something . . . we would almost have become Dante. Because, what more could be written after *Divina Commedia*? It seems that everything is in that book. I am astonished that there are Italian writers who have dared to write after Dante. But, to cite one example, we have Ariosto, whose *Orlando* is no less pleasing or meaningful than *Divina Commedia*, and yet it has nothing in common with it. That is, no writer exhausts literature. But what could Dante, the individual Dante Alighieri, have written after such a book as complete as *Divina Commedia*? If we could merely describe the plot, we would have a very, very attractive story. But only Dante could have written it. After writing *Divina Commedia*, Dante would have had to interest himself in something else.

FERRARI. In Venice.

BORGES. Well, Venice would have stimulated him.

FERRARI. Of course.

BORGES. And as Venice seems to be a place for artistic stimulation, that wouldn't be such a bad thing. Without a doubt, that city must have surprised Dante. Moreover, it's not hard to suppose that he had never seen it—perhaps he speaks of Venice somewhere in *Divina Commedia* but I cannot recall it, though my memory is less perfect than the rhyming dictionary that has its flaws. So we can suppose that he had not heard of anyone talk of Venice, that he discovers Venice, that he reaches that city where the streets are, as Blaise Pascal would say much later, 'roads that move', that is, the canals. Well, that must have suggested something to Dante, yes, but what idea would be worthy of him? That's seems very difficult, even impossible.

FERRARI. It might emerge at some time, in a moment of inspiration.

BORGES. Yes.

FERRARI. You have recently written a book of essays on Dante.

BORGES. Yes. I'm told it's a collection of erratas and has a prologue I would rather forget for many reasons. I have also been told that it's an edition where paragraphs have been omitted—perhaps justifiably, for I couldn't, indeed cannot, correct the proofs. In the end, that book only contains a part of that infinite reading offered by Dante. At home I have 10 or 11 or 12 editions of *Divina Commedia*. I like rereading the poem and have sought out different editions so that I can read the text and the commentaries. I managed to read both nineteenth-century commentaries and contemporary ones. I also still have Longfellow's English edition, with its lengthy notes taken from Italian commentators whose works have not been reprinted. The Longfellow edition reveal novelties for those commentaries have been forgotten. It's curious that the earliest commentators were of a theological slant and that it was Boccaccio who thought of naming it *Divina Commedia*, a title he author didn't think of. So the first were theological, then historical, then, to cite Reyes, commentaries seeking 'sympathies and differences' between Dante and Virgil. Then, attempted in this century, we have the aesthetic commentaries. Paying heed to the sound and connotations of words, something not done before. So the history of Dantean commentary is interesting and makes for a good theme. Each different reading of a book may be understood by the four readings that Dante suggested. Above all, he thought about meaning, the fact that it could be read as a true version of Hell, Purgatory and Paradise; and, if not, I believe it was Dante's son who said that Dante had decided to describe the life of the just, which corresponds with Paradise, the life of penitents, which corresponds with Purgatory and the life of the wicked and the damned, which corresponds with Hell. I mean, Dante's proposition wasn't a description of those places but . . .

FERRARI. An ethical proposition.

BORGES. Yes, an ethical proposition and then an allegorical one. To talk of allegory today seems rather artificial, but it was the natural way of thinking in what we call the Middle Ages. By the way, that term Middle Ages is absurd. It was Horn, a Dutch historian, who invented this division in history and who was then criticized by Spengler in the early pages of *The Decline of the West*. How to divide history into the Ancient Age, the Middle Age and the Modern Age? The Ancient Age extends infinitely backwards, while the Middle Age cannot be justified and the Modern Age is growing and growing. One must also add to it contemporary history. The whole world has accepted this division and yet it is evidently illogical. Before, it was assumed that the Middle Ages was a period in which history had deteriorated, just as the Renaissance implies that everything had died and was reborn. However, we owe to the so-called Middle Ages a style of architecture that later went on to be called Gothic, which is far from negligible, and then the great heroic poems, the *Chanson de Roland*, *Beowulf* . . .

FERRARI. You mean the epic?

BORGES. The epic, yes, and also *Divina Commedia*, so you can tell it wasn't such a dead epoch. Then philosophy changed its vocabulary, but there are many schools. To suppose that the Middle Ages were a kind of long dogmatic sleep is a mistake, an obvious one. For example, up until recently, in histories of philosophy, even in Paul Deussen's, only one volume was devoted to philosophy of the Middle Ages and three to India. What happened later, from the Renaissance onward, fills volumes and volumes. One whole volume, among others, was devoted to Schopenhauer. I have no idea why the Middle Ages have been so underrated and rediscovered only later by the Romantics.

FERRARI. Borges, this evocation of Dante reminds me that we have been talking of your stories and poems but not about your essays. You have written essays throughout your life.

BORGES. Yes, but I have now put them aside because I think that the essay corresponds to opinions and opinions seem changeable and slight to me now . . . I do not know if I will write essays again, possibly not, or perhaps in an indirect fashion in the way the two of us are doing now. In fact, I see my future—I hope a brief one—devoted to short stories, fantastic ones of course, and to poetry for I have succumbed to the bad habit of writing verse.

FERRARI. But you know that when a poet reflects in essays, he practices a lucidity different from that of a philosopher or a theologian, and that can be as useful for it opens up new fields.

BORGES. Ah, yes. Moreover, I am certain that criticism enriches works, as you mentioned with reference to Girri.

FERRARI. Yes.

BORGES. It can be that way. Surely Shakespeare's work is richer now than when he was writing, for Coleridge and Bradley and other critics have read through his works and have enriched them. The same goes for Dante—so many readings have been attempted and they must have enriched it. The fact that Miguel de Unamuno wrote about the life of Don Quixote has modified for many *Don Quixote*, a work that is renewed with every reading. Especially readings by very inventive critics.

FERRARI. Dante is also, perhaps, a milestone in a vision of love that begins with Plato and continues, among others, with Dante's romantic vision of love.

BORGES. Yes, love 'that moves the sun and the other stars'. Well, he gives love a theological meaning as well.

FERRARI. Exactly so, the possibility of transcendence through love, the possibility of elevation, isn't it?

BORGES. Yes, also aesthetic beauty which for me is the essence of *Divina Commedia* for I cannot believe in its mythology, in its idea of punishment and reward. These are quite alien to me. I even think that as ideas they are immoral. However, as we read *Divina Commedia*, our imagination accepts without the slightest doubt the concepts of punishment and reward. We also forget that later there will come Swedenborg who too will believe in each individual choosing Heaven or Hell. That is, it's not something imposed by a judge but a tendency in every one of us. Swedenborg thought that when we die, we find ourselves a little lost, then we meet strangers and those strangers—we are unaware—may be angels or devils. And talking to some of them gives us pleasure while talking to others gives us displeasure. That's how we consciously choose Heaven or Hell.

FERRARI. We are free to choose.

BORGES. Yes, we have free choice, not only during our lifetime but also after dying. He often imagined the case of a damned person who reaches Paradise or Heaven—he finds himself in Heaven's gardens, hears heavenly music, talks with the angels but it all seems foul and horrible to him. Moreover, he suffers. For example, light wounds him.

FERRARI. His Heaven turns out to be Hell.

BORGES. Yes, and then he returns to Hell. I have just remembered Milton's Satan who says that wherever he finds himself, that's where hell is. Then he says, 'I myself am hell.' That is, he conceives of hell not as a place but as a state of mind or state of the soul. In Swedenborg's case, the devils, of course, live in a world rather like that of the politicians, and they are always plotting one against the other. It can be assumed that the devil is not always the same individual for they are constantly plotting against one another, replacing one another . . .

FERRARI. Are you making a political analogy in this case?

BORGES. I think that it is more than believable, isn't it? It's so exactly a world of personal ambitions and hierarchies.

FERRARI. Of power.

BORGES. Yes, of tyrants. What's more or less called 'The Trial' seems more like Hell than Heaven.

Realist and Fantasy Literature

●

OSVALDO FERRARI. Borges, one feels that you are inevitably associated with fantasy literature. Apart from writing fantasy literature, you have also reflected on its value.

JORGE LUIS BORGES. Well, I would say that all literature is essentially fantastic—the idea of realist literature is false because the reader knows that what he reads is fiction. Moreover, literature began as fantastic or, as Valéry said, the most ancient genre is cosmogony which is the same thing. That is, the idea of realist literature perhaps begins with the picaresque novel; it's been a disastrous invention because everyone, especially on our continent, has become devoted to novels of customs which happen to derive from the picaresque novel. Or, if not, the so-called 'social indictments' that are also a form of realism. But luckily for our America and for the Spanish language, Lugones published *Las fuerzas extrañas* (Strange Forces) in 1905, a book of deliberately fantastic stories. Lugones tends to be forgotten; it's taken for granted that our generation, I mean Casares, Silvina Ocampo and

I, initiated this kind of literature and that it spread and led to writers as famous as Márquez and Cortázar. But no, it was really . . .

FERRARI. Lugones—he came first.

BORGES. Yes. There's a tendency to be unjust with Lugones, to always judge him by his last political position as a fascist. It's forgotten that before he was an anarchist he was a socialist, that he backed the allies, that is, democracy. I don't know why he let himself be dazzled by Mussolini. Well, Hitler was dazzled by Mussolini too . . .

FERRARI. Now, your *Antología de la literatura fantástica*, compiled with Casares and Silvina Ocampo . . .

BORGES. I think that our book did a lot of good, that it was worthwhile work. We published a second volume later which must have had an influence on other South American literatures. On Spanish literature too. We also have that other great fantasy writer: Ramón Gómez de la Serna. He too is essentially a writer of fantasy literature.

FERRARI. In your reflections, fantasy literature is not escapist but something that helps us understand reality in a deeper, more complex way.

BORGES. I would say that fantasy literature is part of reality for reality must include everything. It's absurd to suppose that this everything is revealed by the morning newspapers. Or what others read in the papers—personally, I don't read newspapers. I've never read one in my life.

FERRARI (*laughs*). Well, that explains why you do not seem partial to realist literature.

BORGES. Realist literature is a very recent genre and may even vanish. Now it's a common prejudice that a writer has to write for a specific audience, that audience has to be his compatriots, that it is forbidden to imagine going beyond what is personally familiar. That each writer should talk of his country, of a certain class in his country . . . Such ideas are quite alien to literature because literature, as you know, began with poetry. And poetry is definitely not contemporary. After all, no one assumes that Homer was living at the time of the siege of Troy.

FERRARI. Of course. The opposite would imply a sort of totally negative, literary determinism.

BORGES. Yes, but that's very common. For example, it's very common that journalists, when they come to see me, ask, 'And what's your message?' I tell them that I do not have one. Messages are peculiar to angels for angel means messenger in Greek. And I'm certainly not an angel. Kipling said a writer can be allowed to invent a fable but is not allowed to divulge its moral. That is, a writer writes with an end in mind but the end he seeks is the fable. I imagine that even Aesop— or whom the Greeks call Aesop—was more interested in little animals talking like humans than the fable's moral. Moreover, it would be very odd for someone to start with something as abstract as a moral and then try and turn it into a fable. Literature began as fantasy. We do not reason in dreams and dreams are a very ancient form of art. We create little dramatic works.

FERRARI. Earliest literature not only was not realist but it was also religious and sacred.

BORGES. And magical. For example, whoever dreamt *The Arabian Nights*, one of the works most important to me, had no morality in mind. They dreamt and let themselves dream and thus gave birth to that splendid book.

FERRARI. Realist literature corresponds more to the twentieth century than any other.

BORGES. Well, there was naturalism in the nineteenth century.

FERRARI. Yes, but it was consolidated in the twentieth century.

BORGES. Yes. But already in the nineteenth you find Zola's curious idea that each one of his novels was a scientific experiment which, fortunately, isn't the case for Zola was more a man of hallucinations, wasn't he? His novels read like pleasant hallucinations today, not like scientific works on the French during the Second Empire, which is what he intended.

FERRARI. Borges, I am reminded that you have compiled another anthology of fantasty literature, *Libro de sueños* (Book of Dreams).

BORGES. You're probably right. I made the selections with Roy Bartholomew. It's an attractive book, isn't it?

FERRARI. Very.

BORGES. Although we took too many dreams from the Old Testament, didn't we?

FERRARI. But they're among the best. Also, you have some of your own compositions there. The one I prefer is 'Sueña Alonso Quijano' (Alonso Quijano Dreams). I don't know if you remember it.

BORGES. No, I do not remember it. I try to forget what I have written. I must. If not, I would lose heart. Because I want to continue to write. It's convenient to forget the fallible past and think of the future that, perhaps, never arrives but which I think is more generous than the past.

FERRARI. Over time, there have been meetings or missed meetings with Alonso Quijano or Cervantes.

BORGES. That's true. Someone published a thesis on my relationship with *Quixote*. Somehow, he found many compositions or passages in which I return to the *Quixote* theme. It was Macedonio who was devoted to the *Quixote*. He didn't like Spanishness in general but he did like the *Quixote*. And Macedonio proposed, demagogically, that we South Americans and Spaniards should call ourselves 'Cervantes' Family'—Cervantes was the link reaching across the Atlantic. It's a lovely idea. 'Cervantes' Family' sounds so apt.

FERRARI. It does.

29

Silvina Ocampo, Bioy Casares and Juan R. Wilcock

●

OSVALDO FERRARI. Borges, something has caught my attention and I fully agree with it for it seems like an act of justice—I'm talking of the special place you have allocated in our literature to Silvina Ocampo.

JORGE LUIS BORGES. Yes, her surname has prejudiced her, hasn't it? She is seen in relation to her elder sister Victoria Ocampo and that exhausts her definition but that is completely false. Of course, Victoria wrote about her but she did so in the tone of an elder sister speaking of a younger one. It's better to forget about that relationship for they are such different people, each one equally beneficial for this country. Victoria, above all, has written works of opinion; her work is very important but has little importance in a poetic sense. On the other hand, I see an extremely fine sensibility in Silvina who sees everything poetically.

FERRARI. That's true.

BORGES. Now, as far as I'm concerned, I prefer Silvina's poetry to her prose—there's an element of cruelty in the prose which I cannot share in. On the other hand, her poems, for example, 'Enumeración de la patria' (Enumeration of the Fatherland)—there's not a hint of cruelty. She has splendid poems, like 'Oda escolar' (School Ode). One finds a kind of universal sensibility in her. The fact that she is sensitive to English poetry, Italian poetry, even Spanish poetry, that she experiences them with equal intensity and can, moreover, feel these different modes within the Spanish language . . .

FERRARI. That's true. She was discovered in Italy and France some time back and is constantly being re-evaluated.

BORGES. Yes, that's right. Definitely in France. I didn't know about Italy but it's possible.

FERRARI. She received prizes in both countries and a few weeks ago was decorated in France.

BORGES. In France, of course.

FERRARI. Do you recall writing that book with Silvina Ocampo and Adolfo Bioy Casares?

BORGES. No, that book was compiled by Bioy and me; Silvina hardly participated. Are you referring to that anthology? No, I have the impression the Bioy and I put it together but I am not certain—my personal memories are so blurred.

FERRARI. There was also an anthology of Argentine poetry compiled in collaboration.

BORGES. Yes, then the *Antología de la literatura fantástica* which was so important, I would say, for the Spanish language, wasn't it? Literature then was conceived of as realist whereas our anthology of fantasy literature allowed readers the freedom to dream. I think that *Antología* *de la literatura fantástica* is, perhaps, the most important book we published together. Then we published a second volume, no less important, which also opened up vast potentialities that were later exploited. So I believe, if only on the basis of the *Antología de la literatura fantástica*, that we have had an influence across diverse literatures based on the Spanish language. That is, we have had a positive effect.

FERRARI. But there's not a shadow of doubt about that!

BORGES. We have opened up possibilities. Now, in Silvina Ocampo's case, we are not only dealing with an excellent poet but also an excellent painter, sculptor and musician. She was interested in diverse forms of beauty and in areas where I cannot follow her, of course. I haven't a clue, really, nor a sense of painting and I don't know if I am capable of feeling music beyond the 'blues' or 'spirituals' and perhaps milongas. I am moved by Brahms but I can't explain why.

FERRARI. You share that emotion for Brahms with her.

BORGES. Yes, perhaps. Bioy and I discovered that fact for Silvina used to play the records. We realized, after some time, that some of the records that she played allowed us to work well. When she played some other ones, we were not as stimulated. Then we checked the names and it turned out that Debussy was not suitable, or was even harmful, but that Brahms worked well for us. That's all I can say. It's obvious that I know nothing about music—I cannot even tell one composer from another. I knew I was moved and that's it. I was receptive to Brahms but Debussy, perhaps unfairly, had no effect on me.

FERRARI. In Silvina Ocampo's case, you have pointed out something that seems important to me. You said that her prose acquires its richness by the irruption of poetry in it. She applies her sense of the poetic in her prose.

BORGES. I do not know if there is an essential difference between prose and poetry. Except that, according to Stevenson, what we call prose is the most difficult form of poetry. There is no literature without poetry. Even in the literature, let's say, of the redskins or the Eskimos or the barbarous tribes there's always poetry. On the other hand, there are literatures that have never achieved prose status. For example, at university in 1955, we started to study ancient English or Anglo-Saxon. I quickly discovered that the Saxons had written admirable epic and elegiac poetry in Anglo-Saxon. But during the five centuries that they dominated England, they didn't write a single page of prose. Prose thus came as a late and complex form of poetry. Now, many people think the opposite and suppose that prose is easier; those people clearly have no ear and have not grasped that what they call prose is merely cacophony. Stevenson's explanation is the following: If you have achieved a metrical unity, for example, let's say, a line of hendecasyllables or octosyllables as written by the popular poets known as *payadores*, or an alexandrine or a line with alliterations, such as in Germanic poetry, or a line counting long and short syllables, such as in the Greek and Roman hexameter . . . you merely have to repeat that unity and you have a poem. That is, if you have a hendecasyllable and write 13 more and they rhyme as they should, you have achieved a sonnet. On the other hand, with prose, you have to continuously invent variations, variations that must be pleasing as well as unexpected. That is, if you have written 'In a place in the Mancha whose name I wish to forget' you do not have any method to follow for you cannot repeat the line. On the other hand, if you write 'Corrientes, pure, crystalline waters' then you already have a unity and it's enough to repeat it. You cannot do that in prose. In prose you have to keep altering the unities and make sure they are constantly both pleasing and surprising. So prose becomes, as I said, the most difficult form of poetry.

Now, the words 'poetic' and 'prosaic' have another meaning. It's understood that prosaic is what's common, everyday, whereas poetic is what's extraordinary, sensuous. But perhaps it's an error, for I have said elsewhere that a poet may say that every moment be poetic, that nothing be prosaic (in the derogatory sense of the word), that nothing have to do with the art of prose.

FERRARI. That's true. But you say that Silvina Ocampo can feel every moment poetically.

BORGES. I think she can.

FERRARI. Yet, she speaks . . .

BORGES. Of many things. For example, I've noticed that in her work she talks of insects.

FERRARI. And magic.

BORGES. Yes. Insects to me are just a nuisance. But that could be my mistake, given that there are so many insects. Perhaps they please God, if God exists that is. If not, why are there so many insects? I do not need millions and millions of ants but it seems that God does (*laughs*) and his necessities are very different from mine. I would rather that not one ant existed—I could live happily without ants. I would even prefer mosquitoes. But not God. For God, a mosquito is no less precious or unique than, let's say, Shakespeare.

FERRARI. You'd like a de-insected world? (*Both laugh.*)

BORGES. Yes, I think so. But that's my impoverished sensibility. Perhaps for God every insect is as individual as Shakespeare, if at all an insect has an individual consciousness. That's something we do not know. Perhaps they have a collective consciousness. Perhaps a bee does not feel like a bee but like a member of a beehive. That could explain why animals do not invent. A beehive or an ant's nest have been repeated through the centuries. On the other hand, man tries out slight variations, from a cabin to an igloo to Manhattan, for example.

FERRARI. And attempts this as an individual.

BORGES. And attempts this as an individual, yes.

FERRARI. Silvina Ocampo said, 'I have the intelligence that comes from sensibility.' I find that a magnificent expression of how a female artist feels.

BORGES. I'm not sure that applies only to women. I do not think that there can be poetry without sensibility. I believe not. That many people think that poetry is wordplay is to me a mistake. If it wasn't backed or modified by emotion, poetry would be worthless. Then it would simply be wordplay.

FERRARI. But you would recognize that, in general, in a man, intelligence precedes movement. Whereas in a woman, sensibility seems to be the first.

BORGES. Yes. I believe that better, that sensibility be more important than intelligence. But that could be one of my personal heresies.

Poe believed that writing a poem was an intellectual operation. I do not agree. I am sure that he was wrong or that it was one of his jokes—after all, he didn't write 'The Raven' for intellectual reasons. I do not believe that a poem is written for intellectual reasons—it's written for something more intimate or more mysterious than a series of syllogisms.

FERRARI. What do you think of what Baudelaire said about the best poem being the one that's written for the pure joy of writing?

BORGES. I think that he was right. I believe that the act of writing has to be gratifying. I think that if there is difficulty, it implies a certain awkwardness. Clearly, writing should be as spontaneous as reading; two different kinds of felicity. Although it might be rash to write. It certainly might be rash to read (*laughs*).

FERRARI. There's a strange case of an Argentine writer, a friend in common with Silvina Ocampo and Adolfo Bioy Casares called Juan Rodolfo Wilcock who left for Italy and now writes in Italian . . .

BORGES. He was fluent in those languages. His father was English and his mother Italian. I guess that at home they mixed both languages. What I know about him is that he abstained from Spanish and managed to become a famous poet in Italy. That's where I last saw him.

FERRARI. Italy seemed to have become a second exile for him. I was with him there . . .

BORGES. I didn't know that. I thought that he was at ease in Italy.

FERRARI. He was very lonely and constantly recalled Buenos Aires.

BORGES. Perhaps to be in a place, perhaps the best way of being in a place, is to be far away and miss it? Not being in a place is a form of being in it, wouldn't you agree?

FERRARI. It's true.

BORGES. I didn't know that Wilcock missed Buenos Aires.

FERRARI. At least that's what he said.

BORGES. When did you see him?

FERRARI. 1975.

BORGES. Oh, not so recently.

FERRARI. Just before he died.

BORGES. Yes, I'd met him at Silvina Ocampo's. He lived in Barracas, on Avenida Montes de Oca . . . which was called the Long Road of Barracas before. And the Long Road of the Recoleta was Quintana. It was longer and more important than the Barracas one.

FERRARI. I ask you about this because Wilcock was recognized and is still well considered in Buenos Aires. Yet he left Buenos Aires for ever.

BORGES. I know nothing about his intimate reasons for travelling. What were they?

FERRARI. Well, we could say that there is no literary explanation for leaving Buenos Aires for he had found success here. To go and write in a foreign language in another country is odd for a writer, don't you think?

BORGES. Yes, but maybe it was not a foreign language for him.

FERRARI. Well, till that time he had always written in Spanish.

BORGES. Yes, but if he had been reading continuously in Italian . . . although, I don't know if he read in English or wrote in English . . . Well, Wilcock is of course an English surname.

FERRARI. Once again we have reached the end of this talk. In case you wish to add anything, we have one more minute.

BORGES. Well, I am very pleased that you have mentioned those two dearly beloved names: Silvina Ocampo and Juan R. Wilcock. I would like to thank you.

FERRARI. And Adolfo Bioy Casares.

BORGES. Adolfo Bioy Casares too, of course.

FERRARI. For me it was also a pleasure, Borges. See you next week.

BORGES. See you next week.

30

On History

●

OSVALDO FERRARI. Borges, with reference to a certain book, you have mentioned that going through it is like getting lost in an adventure novel whose protagonists are generations of humans, whose theatre is the world and whose time span is measured by dynasties, by conquests, by discoveries, by changing languages and idols. Have you guessed which book I'm referring to?

JORGE LUIS BORGES. Could it be Gibbon?

FERRARI. Gibbon, just so. You have recalled him many times during our conversations.

BORGES. Well, Gibbon had the luck to live in a period of censorship, I say luck because it forced him into irony, into saying things indirectly which is the strongest and most efficient way of saying things. We could say the same about Voltaire. All this could end in a curious praise for censorship; if complete freedom was allowed, everything would be said directly, or weakly. Censorship, on the other hand, can force people into euphemism, metaphor and irony. I am unhappy to praise censorship. Anyhow, and what follows is absurd: Why should I allow someone else to make decisions for me? For example, if a film is shown, I—and not some official—should judge whether or not I want to see it. This lends itself to all kinds of obscenities. At the present moment we are witnessing a kind of apotheosis of pornography, but that may be better than leaving it in the hands of others, especially in the hands of the state. The state for me now is the common enemy. I have said many times: A minimum of state and a maximum of individuality. Perhaps, it's best to wait a decade or two, or even a century or two, which historically is nothing. I certainly will not see this world without states. For that, we will need an ethical humanity as well as a humanity that's tougher intellectually, tougher than how we are now. There's not a shadow of doubt that we are very immoral and that we have a limited intelligence compared with men of the future. That's why I agree with the sentence: 'I believe dogmatically in the future.' I think that belief is necessary, that we should believe in progress even though progress may not exist. There's Goethe's idea of a spiral, a lovely metaphor about what is more probable than progress, that is, progress as a spiral, turning but not in a straight line. If we do not believe in progress, we cannot believe in action.

My belief in progress is another way of stating my belief in free will. That is, if I'm told that all my past has been fated, has been compulsory, it won't affect me, but if I'm told that I cannot, at this moment, act freely, then I despair. I think it's the same—the concept of progress is to history what the concept of free will is to man, to an individual. In a certain way, hypocrisy is also progress, because if there is hypocrisy it means that there's awareness about evil. That's something. Those who act in an evil way are aware of it, and that's an advancement. It used to be said that hypocrisy is a tribute that evil pays to goodness or vice to virtue.

FERRARI. So hypocrisy is immoral and not amoral.

BORGES. That could be so . . .

FERRARI. It would be the consciousness of good and evil.

BORGES. Of course. From the moment I hide myself it's because I know my action is evil. But that I know that my action is evil implies a minimal intellectual progress, if not an ethical one, doesn't it?

FERRARI. Now, returning to history. I thought of Edward Gibbon because I associated him with you. You say that Gibbon, when he narrates, appears to abandon himself to the facts that he's narrating as well as to reflect on them with, let's say, a divine consciousness, for he makes them identical to destiny which is the real flow of history.

BORGES. I said that?

FERRARI. Yes.

BORGES. How odd. If that is the case, I was right to say so. Thus the historian would become an impartial god, wouldn't he?

FERRARI (*laughs*). In the best of cases.

BORGES. Like a god he would surrender himself to the facts and would refer to them without praise or blame.

FERRARI. An interpreter of destiny without his own will.

BORGES. Yes, he would have the impartiality of destiny or the impartiality of chance—we don't know if there is a destiny or chance. Perhaps these two words name the same thing.

FERRARI. We don't know.

BORGES. No and possibly will never know, although some say that after death we will know. The best argument I've read against the soul's immortality is in Gustav Spiller's psychology, in his *The Mind of Man*. In it he has a paragraph dedicated to the soul's immortality where he says that if a person breaks a leg or an arm he suffers a mutilation which implies not advantage but accident. But unlike a partial accident, death, the complete accident, is usually supposed to benefit the soul, is usually supposed to be an advantage for the soul. But that's an absurd argument for death would become . . . well, a dead man is still a person whether he was paralytic or blind or had lost his memory or his reasoning. Why suppose that this leads him immediately to another world of wisdom and justice? That's logically unsustainable.

FERRARI. Although you could also say, why not suppose so?

BORGES. We can suppose anything in a literary sense. Literature is based on that—on the freedom of dreams.

FERRARI. A little of the same applies to religions too.

BORGES. Yes, except that religions impose those imaginations. When I said that religion and metaphysics are branches of fantasy literature, I didn't say so in a hostile or adverse way. On the contrary, what more did St Thomas Aquinas want than to be the greatest poet in the world? (*Both laugh.*) Of course, if we take Spinoza's concept that 'God is an infinite substance, made of infinite attributes,' it's more odd than Wells' idea about the first men on the moon or the time machine or Poe's 'The Masque of the Red Death' or Kafka's nightmares. Spinoza is far more odd.

FERRARI. That is, literary fantasy is easier than the mystical kind.

BORGES. Yes, but that means that I want to carry everything over to literature which is my discipline.

FERRARI. Or your religion.

BORGES. Or that it's my religion, yes (*both laugh*). Well, it comes to one of my vain affirmations but it's certainly not hostile. Indeed, I rather admire the imagination of the theologians as much as I admire the imagination of the poets, except that the poet's imagination is far poorer than the theologian's and that of the mythologist who is, in reality, another kind of theologian.

FERRARI. Well, you have admired Swedenborg's imagination, for example.

BORGES. Yes, of course, in him you have both things.

FERRARI. Now, returning to the book I mentioned at the start of our conversation, *The History of the Decline and Fall of the Roman Empire* . . .

BORGES. Yes, I recall reading that Gibbon wrote and rewrote the first chapter three times. Only then, according to Lytton Strachey, he thought he'd found the right tone. Then, of course, he continued documenting himself and wrote, for example, a chapter on Islam. It's possible when he wrote the first chapter he knew nothing about his theme but he had found his style, his meaning, his intonation. And once he had found it, he continued. The same happens to me in my capacity as short-story teller. Once I start a story or a poem and find the exact intonation, the rest is a question of time, of patience, of waiting, till certain things reveal themselves to me. But I have found what's important which means that if I have a page, that page dictates the others or tells me how the others should be written.

FERRARI. That reminds me of Mallea quoting Julien Green: 'If the tone is there, it's nearly all there.'

BORGES. Ah, did he say that?

FERRARI. Yes, and you refer to intonation.

BORGES. Well, it coincides exactly with what I said. I had no idea Green had said that. But what a strange case his is! He chose another language and wrote in French and was an American.

FERRARI. That's right.

BORGES. I was talking to a friend who told me that it was a pity that Conrad wrote in English, that he rejected becoming a great novelist in Polish. But the important point is that those novels were written. And that they were written in an accessible language rather than a secret one is an advantage, not to put down Polish literature, of course (*laughs*). More or less until the seventeenth century what was important was written in Latin. How odd that Francis Bacon wrote in English but that when a Latin edition of his work was wanted—because he sought to disseminate his ideas—he suppressed everything that could offend his, say, Catholic, readers. He did so in order not to upset or estrange people but to win them over to his cause. So, using a universal language made him universal.

FERRARI. Of course, it depends on the intention. We have mentioned the links, or lack of links, between the literary imagination and the theological one. But history and literature meet in Gibbon, that is, he is the nexus between history and literature.

BORGES. Between the study of the documents which seems to have been exhaustive—he showed the responsibility of his age—and the writing down of all that.

FERRARI. Precisely why you said that his book is a crowded novel.

BORGES. Well, it's a fact that history is a novel. It's a story, as the English implies, and it's a form of history. It comes down to the same thing.

FERRARI. And you speculate on the moment when Gibbon reaches Rome, knows Rome and somehow anticipates what will happen.

BORGES. Yes, he says that the idea of his book occurred to him in Rome; he gives the precise circumstances. He wanted to be a historian and wanted his work to be famous and he first thought of a history of England. Then he thought that such a history would be interesting only in England. But he wanted to leave the island and reach the continent and then the world, so he took our common past—Imperial Rome—as his theme. That's the past of all European nations, including England because Britain was a Roman colony for five centuries—the furthest west in the Empire . . . Hadrian's Wall what divides England from Scotland. And Kipling set some stories on that wall of which now little remains. It was very important. Gibbon comments on the fact that the Romans didn't conquer Scotland and that Scotland's freedom is due not only to the bravery of the Scots but also to the 'Lords of the World', the Romans who scorned conquering such a poor and barbarous country where the wild tribes hunted deer (*laughs*).

FERRARI. Borges, I have always thought that your greatest concern was with time, but when you talk of time I do not sense that you refer to historical time. One of your sayings is 'Reality is always anachronistic'.

BORGES. I was referring to the fact that historical reality is based on theories or on dreams of previous generations. For example, let's say, Thomas Carlyle or Johann Gottlieb Fichte imagine something about the German race and then that's used by Hitler, but much later, so we can say that reality is always posthumous. But I'm not sure that always applies. Now, we are living a very ancient idea of democracy and living it politically. That is, in some ways we want to be what Thomas Jefferson and Walt Whitman dreamt (*laughs*).

FERRARI. And Plato and Aristotle.

BORGES. And Plato and Aristotle, going further back, although I do not know if their democracy would be the same. I don't think so, a democracy with slaves . . .

FERRARI. Like the Greek one.

BORGES. Yes, slightly different to ours, but the idea is the same and the word also, of course.

31

The Affinity with Domingo Faustino Sarmiento

●

OSVALDO FERRARI. Borges, you have dealt with Domingo Faustino Sarmiento many times.

JORGE LUIS BORGES. Yes, I have written about Sarmiento, I have written a prologue to an edition of *Recuerdos de Provincia* (Memories of a Province) and I have referred to him many times. I believe that Sarmiento and Almafuerte are the two men of genius that our country has given us. I can talk enthusiastically but not impartially about Sarmiento, especially as there is no political link between my family and his. On the contrary, my grandfather Francisco Borges got himself killed after Mitre's surrender and defeat in the battle of La Verde by Arias, or maybe the skirmish of La Verde. Anyhow, whether a skirmish or little battle, one dies just as others in great battles. The battle of La Verde was in 1874. The revolutionaries or 'Mitristas' were numerically superior but the other side had the advantage of superior technology—Remington rifles were used for the first time in this country. They had been imported from the United States and had been used, no doubt, in the Civil War. The revolutionaries were many more in number; it seems they had travelled the country recruiting men, workers on the estancias or great farms. The farm owners had no reason to risk their lives but they sent their workers, just as the land owners had done during Aparicio Saravia's revolution. Like my uncle Francisco Haedo—he also sent many of his workers.

FERRARI. When you talk of Whitman, you compare him to Adam. I tend to remember Sarmiento in our country as someone who has acted like Adam.

BORGES. That's true. I hadn't thought of that but it's right. Whitman compares himself to Adam. In a poem he compares himself to Adam early in the morning. It gives a lovely image, perhaps not of the Whitman who wrote the book but of the Whitman who shared something with Adam, as he says . . .

FERRARI. Whitman would be a literary Adam, an Adam of words. And Sarmiento, yes, of words but also of concrete deeds in his political and democratic life. You told me that the eucalyptus and certain birds were brought here by him?

BORGES. Sparrows and eucalyptus trees, now part of Argentine landscape, were brought from Australia, their land of origin. I have a memory about a eucalyptus. When an epidemic of Spanish Flu broke out after the First World War, eucalyptus leaves were burnt in great pots. I guess they were supposed to be curative. That was in Geneva; I smelt the eucalyptus which I hadn't smelt for ages, and thought: Goodness, I am in the Hotel Las Delicias in Adrogué or in our quinta or country house La Rosalinda. I felt I was back in Adrogué thanks to the smell of those supposedly curative eucalyptus leaves in 1918 in Geneva.

FERRARI. I return to Sarmiento to remember that he identified his own life with his country's. I mean, as if it was a matter of growing together, at that time.

BORGES. That's right, and nostalgia for all that found its expression in *Facundo*. I think that what has been written against *Facundo* is false. Because, for us, Facundo is less the historic Facundo Quiroga whom Rosas had doubtless killed in Barranca Yaco than the Facundo of Sarmiento's imagination. So it doesn't matter if facts are found contrary to that dream—it's the dream that lasts. If we remember, Facundo was very lucky to have been assassinated in such a dramatic way, in a covered wagon driven by Santos Pérez, and this was uniquely narrated by Sarmiento. So that when I wrote my poem 'El general Sarmiento va en coche al muere' (General Sarmiento goes in his coach to his death), and then, when I wrote another poem—'Barranco Yaco'—to correct the first one, it was absurd because that story had been told that way for ever, resonating for ever in our imagination, just as Sarmiento had told it in his *Facundo*. In that sense, the historical Facundo doesn't matter. What matters is the book's influence.

FERRARI. In that sense, Sarmiento says that Facundo was what he was not by accident of his character but by inevitable happenings beyond his will.

BORGES. Of course, that could be said about everyone, especially by fatalists.

FERRARI. You have said it about Wilde.

BORGES. Yes, as I do not believe in free will and I think that could be said about everyone in the world through universal history.

FERRARI. However, Sarmiento added that Facundo was a mirror in which certain social movements of that period were reflected.

BORGES. Well, he saw Facundo as a precursor to Rosas. And had him assassinated, but that doesn't matter. I had started to tell you that as far as I know, my ancestors were not followers of Sarmiento but his enemies. Proof of this is that my grandfather died in that Mitrista revolution, in La Verde. There's an error that I would like to correct here. There's a plaque there with an inscription saying that the revolutionary forces commanded by Colonel Borges, who died in action, were routed by Colonel or General Arias. But no, it wasn't like that. Moreover, it's absurd because if Mitre led the action, he wouldn't have delegated leadership to one of his colonels. Also, there were Colonel Machado, Benito Machado, my grandfather, Colonel Francisco Borges and two other colonels. But in order to not state that Mitre was routed, because that would be viewed badly by his newspaper *La Nación*, it was said that the troops were commanded by my grandfather, which is clearly false, and that he died in action. No— he got himself killed later, after the action, and he wasn't able to command the forces because a general commands a revolution and does not delegate the control of forces to a colonel. There are hierarchical reasons too. So on that plaque my grandfather is made commander of the battle and a man who was routed. Well, he was routed like all the rest who formed the revolutionary forces—it wasn't he specifically but Mitre who was routed. But it was not convenient to have Mitre routed. Hence, my grandfather commanded the action and was routed. It's totally false.

FERRARI. Once and for all that historical incident has been completely clarified.

BORGES. Yes.

FERRARI. It has been suggested that the pen that was once Sarmiento's is now yours.

BORGES. That's just absurd (*both laugh*). What could be said is that the pen, in that case, is more than the sword for Sarmiento's writing is more telling than his military actions, isn't it?

FERRARI. It's strange that in those days a great writer could become president of the Republic, don't you agree?

BORGES. Yes, I believe that Sarmiento's genius hasn't been begrudged by anyone except Groussac. According to an epigraph in Groussac's article on him, it seems that Sarmiento handed over his manuscripts so that Groussac could give them a literary polish. But when Sarmiento died, Groussac published an article that began 'Sarmiento is half a genius,' which, as Gerchunoff told me once, doesn't mean anything. What does it mean to be half a genius? Can genius be divided? Does it mean anything to say 'half of' when referring to the mind, as 'half' seems to refer to quantity and not quality? So 'half a genius' means nothing. Gerchunoff was perhaps Lugones' sole friend.

FERRARI. But Borges, there's another important aspect to Sarmiento, and it's the way he resolves that permanent dichotomy, that meeting and not meeting between . . .

BORGES. Civilization and barbarism . . .

FERRARI. No, between . . .

BORGES. Yes, but now it's more complex. Before barbarism corresponded to the countryside and civilization, as its etymology confirms, to the city. Today, it doesn't seem so for we have barbarism in the city, of course, with its industries.

FERRARI. I was referring to the dichotomy between Europeanism and Americanism because Sarmiento resolved it in a universalist way. And that marks a step in a universalist direction in our culture . . .

BORGES. I would resolve it that way too.

FERRARI. Of course, that's why I say he was followed with dignity.

BORGES. Because in his day, barbarism was what was rural. Now, industrialization has created an urban barbarism as factories represent the city more than the country.

FERRARI. But that's all over the world.

BORGES. Yes.

FERRARI. Technocratic barbarism?

BORGES. Yes, of course, and we sadly continue to suffer it. At least in Maipú Street (*laughs*) which is certainly not rural. Although my mother remembers it from before it was paved. Well, all cities grow from the countryside. I recall that joke where someone asked: Why aren't cities built in the country? And that's exactly where they are built—a city does not begin as a city but as wasteland or just plain country.

FERRARI. But we continue to cultivate that universality that was Sarmiento's and you know that it's part of the Argentine spirit.

BORGES. I think it is and hope that it's also mine, although I am just a minuscule part of that spirit.

FERRARI. Allow me to confirm that.

BORGES. Many thanks.

32

The Detective Story

●

OSVALDO FERRARI. Borges, there's a genre for which you and Casares have shown a fondness, given that in 1943 and in 1951 you compiled two anthologies of that genre. I'm referring, of course, to the detective story.

JORGE LUIS BORGES. That has been unfairly slandered. However, it's a genre invented by a man of undoubted genius—Edgar Allan Poe—who inspired later writers like Charles Dickens, Robert Louis Stevenson, Wilkie Collins and G. K. Chesterton, names sufficient to scare off any criticism. Of course, you could say that there are awful detective stories, just as there are awful sonnets and awful historical novels. Indeed, any genre we could cite has given bitter fruit. But I believe that the works of the writers I have just mentioned are sufficient although they are not the only ones. Why not think of Nicholas Blake or Ellery Queen or Eden Phillpotts, who are good enough to justify the genre? I recall once cheekily asking Pedro Henríquez Ureña if he liked fables. He answered with a lesson on how to be sensible: 'I am not an enemy of genres.' A text can be a fable or a detective story but that doesn't let you know whether it's execrable or excellent.

FERRARI. What counts is whether it's good or bad.

BORGES. Of course, and Boileau has already said that. All genres are good except the genre of boredom. In Poe's case, it's odd how he fixed certain rules within the detective story, rules which have been followed by all his famous successors, including Arthur Conan Doyle. The idea of a detective as an individual who solves mysteries, whose deeds are always narrated by a friend and that the friend is always rather stupid and full of admiration for the detective. This was sketched out with Poe's Auguste Dupin. Conan Doyle took it up and tried to make it more intimate—which of course, it cannot be. Poe's detective stories can be terrifying in the literal sense of the word, such as 'The Murders in the Rue Morgue'. Or they can be mere intellectual games, such as 'The Purloined Letter'. You certainly won't find in them the intimacy that exists in the stories of Sherlock Holmes and Dr Watson. I was rereading the Holmes stories with my sister Norah—our way of returning to the past when we had once read them together, many years ago, in different latitudes . . . Anyway, we can confirm that the plots in Conan Doyle's stories hardly matter. What does matter is the friendship between the two characters, the relationship between a person who is supposedly very intelligent (Sherlock Holmes) and another who is almost professionally stupid (Dr Watson). That they are friends and like each other . . . one feels that their friendship is more important than what happens.

How strange, at this very moment, as I speak, I recall a famous Argentine book, Estanislao del Campo's *Fausto*. When one rereads

Fausto, one always says the same thing to oneself: What counts is not the story about the opera but the friendship between the two comrades. I'd say the same happens in the Sherlock Holmes stories, even in the best one—'The Red-Headed League'. What's important is the friendship and the story openings which are almost more important than what happens later. There's always a little surprise. You expect to find Holmes and Watson by the fireside, for example. But at times it's not like that—at times there's a change which the reader appreciates. There are diverse ways of entering the tales, small variations on the well-known theme of the friendship between these unequal characters.

Then there are other themes, one of them being 'the locked-room' mystery in which something that seems impossible happens—someone is assassinated in a locked room. This has been resolved in a number of ways. John Dickson Carr wrote many novels that were a pleasure to read; though, when you reach the end, the solution is invariably pathetic. For example, in one such locked-room story, there's a barred window and a fire burning in the fireplace. And there's a man killed by a dagger. But you don't know how the assassin could have got into or out of the room. Then there's the trivial solution: he has been wounded by an arrow of ice. The arrow has melted, thanks to the fire in the fireplace. But that's pathetic, although reading the book isn't.

FERRARI. An arrow of ice? Like a stalactite?

BORGES. Yes, a stalactite. Above it all, one must guess what kind of weapon shot it . . . maybe a bow, maybe not.

FERRARI. Maybe it fell from a cornice although I don't know how it got into the room.

BORGES. Well, the solution is impossible but the mystery is pleasing. There's a story by Israel Zangwill where the solution, which was repeated later, is thus: the person who discovers the crime, or one of those who discover the crime, is also the perpetrator. Moreover, to add to the surprise, he's a police inspector. He enters the room with a lady and announces, 'He's been killed.' She is naturally horrified; he takes advantage of this and kills the man to whom he had given a sleeping pill the night before. And later, in *The Mystery of the Yellow Room*, a title that is a real find—any other colour would have been a mistake, don't you agree? If you had 'The Mystery of the Black Room', it wouldn't do, or 'the Red Room', that's worse, or 'the Green Room' would be ridiculous. But 'the Yellow Room' is just the right colour, isn't it?

FERRARI. I think . . .

BORGES. Yes, slightly terrible.

FERRARI. Then we have Chesterton's detective stories.

BORGES. With Chesterton, I would say we have the genre's master-pieces. His detective stories are also supernatural stories—every title suggests a supernatural solution. But when he arrives at a solution, we have to admit it is a rational one, offered by Father Brown or by any of Chesterton's other detectives. And, anyhow, his stories, as Xul Solar pointed out to me, are like plays and paintings. I don't know if you remember that Chesterton tried to be a painter before he turned to literature. Though he turned away from painting and drawing, I think that through his literature he continued to be a painter.

FERRARI. That's why he's so descriptive.

BORGES. Very descriptive, and it is all combined in a special way. His characters appear as if walking onto the stage. There's always a red-headed woman and this redhead is seen against, for instance, an orange twilight.

FERRARI. Chesterton's descriptions of skies are memorable.

BORGES. Skies, woods, landscapes, architecture . . . and in each story it's different. Some stories are set in a Gothic cathedral. And the mystery takes on that form. Others are set in the Scottish Highlands, yet others in the outskirts of London. Some take place in Paris, 'The Duel of Doctor Hirsch', for example, and everything fits in well.

Another curious trait of Chesterton's stories is that no one is ever punished. Obviously, Father Brown is a priest and cannot hand anyone over to the police. So an assassin can die or be arrested but Father Brown is never an inquisitor nor an executor nor a hangman. He's an indulgent man. Sometimes, like in 'The Invisible Man', Father Brown discovers the assassin and they then converse. We realize that the assassin has confessed his crime and that Father Brown has given him absolution—because he doesn't talk about him any more. His later destiny doesn't concern him. And Father Brown is not stained.

FERRARI. It could be presumed that your penchant for the detective story is due to it being a partially epic genre.

BORGES. A partially epic but also partially logical genre. Note that everything is admitted in the psychological novel, every extravagant character trait. Yet, in a rather chaotic period of literature, logical rigour was saved by the detective story. A detective story is an intellectual story, that is, it's a story that has a beginning, middle and end and in which everything is explicable. Thus there's a logical satisfaction in detective stories.

FERRARI. Perhaps there's a balance in detective stories between fantasy literature and realist literature.

BORGES. Yes, it's fantasy literature trying to be realist. But all literature is in the end fantastic.

FERRARI. Naturally.

BORGES. The rules of the game change according to each period, just as the value or power of words change. If one says, for example, that Darío seems a little antiquated today, it means that the magic in his words has been worn thin by us. In the case of the words 'swan', or 'princess' or 'lake', words that no doubt have their magic, Darío wore them out. Or we have worn out the magic by reading and rereading Darío. This inevitably happens with all poets who depend on certain words. Those words lose their prestige. Yet any word can be magical. It's best that poets do not get too fixed on certain words because then they begin to abuse them and make them sound mechanical.

FERRARI. Of course. But we could say that the magic or suggestions in detective stories have found their destiny in your work too—you have recently written a poem titled 'Sherlock Holmes'.

BORGES. Yes, but that has been in recollection of my childhood and adolescent reading. Also, the thought that Sherlock Holmes is a kind of affectionate myth, a part of human memory. Sherlock Holmes is in everyone's memories, his name is immediately recognized. We could even think that the stories are bad, yet there is something there. Something that the author didn't grasp which is why he tried to kill off Sherlock Holmes. But people demanded that he be brought back to life. So he had to write about the return of Sherlock Holmes.

33

On Friendship with Pedro Henríquez Ureña

●

OSVALDO FERRARI. Borges, a while ago we talked about Alfonso Reyes—although I spent more time listening for I feel it only right that I do so when you evoke writers. Today I would like to recall another of Argentina's illustrious neighbours, Pedro Henríquez Ureña.

JORGE LUIS BORGES. In the first instance, I remember the last conversation I had with him. It was around one in the morning, on the corner of Córdoba and Riobamba. And we were talking about that line in 'La epístola' (The Epistle), one of the greatest poems of the Spanish language written by an anonymous poet from Seville. Ureña remembered later that he was a Spanish captain who died in Mexico. I think his name was Andrade. But he wished to remain anonymous, as he says in the poem:

> I possess a life that's average
> A common style and moderate
> Not noted by anyone who sees it.

Well, I remembered those lines. (The first one is padding but all rhymed poems have padding. What's essential is not to notice the padding for the rhyme itself is padding.) Then I remembered the next six:

Without restraint, have you seen anything
As perfect? O Death, come stealthily
As you usually do on an arrow!
Not in the thunderous pregnant machine
Of fire and rumours, for my door
Is not made of folded metals.

And then at the end, that very mysterious line that Lanuza and I admired:

Come and you'll see the high end to which I aspire
Before time dies in our arms.

Well, I don't exactly know what it means or if it wants to mean something, for what does meaning have to do with poetry? the important point is magic, that almost inexplicable magic in the lines. Well, it was with Ureña that I spoke about that line:

. . . Oh Death, come stealthily
As you usually do on an arrow!

And I remember saying to Ureña that the image of 'arrow', *saeta* or *sagitta* in Spanish, seemed to be written by a Latin poet. And he said to me that he would find out if it had been. Indeed, it seemed to him too that the metaphor was very probably translated from the Latin. Unlike today, no one in the seventeenth century considered carrying a line over from Latin into a modern language as plagiarism. On the contrary, it was seen as proof that Spanish was not unworthy of lofty Latin examples. Well, that's the time I saw Ureña. I never saw him again. Later, after many years—I can't remember how many for dates are vague to me—I was told that he had died, that he had died teaching. He had a chair at the University of La Plata and was rushing along a platform at Consititución Station to catch a train. He was with Dr Cortina, I think that's his name, and both caught the train as it was about to move. Ureña had run a little; he placed his file in the net above him and sat down opposite Cortina. Cortina spoke to him but Ureña didn't answer. Cortina then realized that he had died. They took his corpse away at Barracas, the first station after Constitución. We remembered '. . . Oh Death, come stealthily /as you usually do on an arrow!' And death took him as stealthily as in a heart attack.

FERRARI. Very odd.

BORGES. I wrote a story about this but cannot recall it. Perhaps it's best forgotten. Its called 'Perdo Henríquez Ureña's Dream'. I learnt later that his brother had died in a similar way. The brother, Max Henríquez Ureña, wrote the excellent *History of Modernismo* where he pointed out that Modernismo was born in America though obviously under the guidance of France, Hugo and Verlaine. America was closer to France than to Spain; Spain was only geographically closer, separated as it was by a long history of wars, et cetera. Well, Ureña's brother was due to give a class at the University of Las Piedras in Puerto Rico. He arrived late; he too had run up the marble staircase in the department I would later become familiar with. He too suffered a heart attack. Really, the same kind of death as his brother Pedro.

FERRARI. That's right.

BORGES. I don't know if Ureña ever found the original Latin for that line. I have searched for it but not found it. He possibly knew it and then forgot it. I hold the best memories of Ureña, the man and his style. He was a shy man and I believe that many countries treated him unfairly. In Spain, of course, he was considered a mere Indian or Central American. And here, in Buenos Aires, no one forgave the fact that he was from Dominica and of mixed blood, certainly Jewish blood, as his surname, like mine, is Judaeo-Portuguese. Here, he was assistant to a professor whose name I do not wish to recall. The professor knew nothing about his subject while Ureña knew an awful lot. But Ureña had to remain his assistant because, in the end, he was just a foreigner. The other man had the inestimable virtue of being Argentine and so could hold a chair in a subject he knew little about while Ureña could not, despite his profound knowledge of Spanish literature.

I have the highest possible regard for Ureña and not a day passes when I do not recall him. I remember his goodness, his irony. It was a resigned goodness. He was a man ill-treated by everyone—the Argentine Republic did not treat him well nor did Spain. He always lived in exile and was not completely accepted. Also, he did not try to create a collection of his work. He published a book called *Plentidud de España* (Plenitude of Spain), I think. And then a book that I wrote a commentary for, titled *Seis ensayos en busca de nuestro porvenir* (Six Essays in Search of Our Future).

I have no idea why he parodied 'Six Characters in Search of an Author' but in the end he was resigned about the title. I remember his prose style as being, as George Moore used to say, almost anonymous, that is, he avoided any kind of surprise. But it was his style and one can tell there was a kind of hidden smile in all that he wrote. At that time rhyme was under attack and I published an article, the first one I published for *La Prensa*, titled 'Milton and his Condemnation of Rhyme'. Marechal said that if one compared Verlaine's poems to prose translations by Enrique Díez Canedo and Ureña, the translations appeared far superior to the originals. That would have scandalized the translator and everyone else too. Then Ureña published a note on Marechal's article about the advantages of turning Verlaine's verse into prose, verse which above all else is musical. Ureña simply transcribed the note and wrote 'Really', followed by three dots (*laughs*), and thus perfectly expressed his amazement. I have the impression, and its obviously absurd to say this, but I have the impression that Ureña had read everything and knew everything. At the same time, he did not employ this to overwhelm us in a conversation. He was a very polite man and, like the Japanese, preferred that the person he was addressing always be right—a rare virtue, especially in our country where an argument is seen more in terms of winning or losing when, in truth, a dialogue should be an investigation into truth. And if one reaches a conclusion, it doesn't matter who states it as long as one has reached some truth.

FERRARI. Well, Macedonio Fernández was also able to see this in terms of whoever spoke to him.

BORGES. Yes, Macedonio could too. But Macedonio did more—he gifted his opinions to whoever was conversing with him. He would say, 'You must have noticed *che* that you said . . .' and then say something that the speaker had not even thought of. Especially when that speaker was me (*laughs*), because I had never thought those things but Macedonio generously attributed them to me. I collaborated with Henríquez Ureña on a book titled *Antología clásica de la literatura argentina*, or *Antología de la literatura argentina clásica*, I can't exactly recall which. I do remember that I was lazy and inefficient, that Ureña did all the work but insisted I was paid. That was evidently unfair and I told him so. I met him in La Plata where he taught with someone whom I consider one of our best poets, Ezequiel Martínez Estrada, to whom I owe a lot. I had met Ureña, Estrada and Alejandro Korn there.

FERRARI. The philosopher?

BORGES. Well, we could call him that, why not? Also his son, Villafañe, María de Villarino—a writer from La Plata—Sánchez Roblé and Amado Alonso. But I had the impression that Ureña knew more than Alonso but Alonso was easily assertive as all Spaniards are and Ureña wasn't. I do not know if Ureña did justice to his gifts through what he wrote. It's possible that he gave his best in conversations. I would say the same about Assens.

FERRARI. And once again, Macedonio Fernández.

BORGES. Yes, Macedonio too. There are people who give their all in conversations. If Plato is a dramatic author, as Shaw believed, then Socrates also gave his best in conversations.

FERRARI. Naturally.

BORGES. Although there's always the suspicion that Plato invented Socrates. Yet, that cannot be so. Because there's Xenophon's text, although it reveals a slightly different Socrates.

FERRARI. Now, you state in the prologue to Ureña's *Obra crítica* (Critical Work) that he found true and secret affinities between the republics of this continent.

BORGES. I haven't found them but it seems that he did. I haven't sensed it. I have spent pleasant moments in Peru, Colombia and Mexico, but have sensed more the differences than the affinities.

FERRARI. But Borges, why are they true and secret? How do you know if they are true and secret?

BORGES. The truth is that I don't know. Possibly it's about the demands of style . . . (*laughs*).

FERRARI (*laughs*). . . . the demands of style.

BORGES. In any case, I accept 'secret' but not 'true'—who knows? (*Laughs.*) I only recognize one of those adjectives, and that's enough. Statistically, it's 50 per cent.

FERRARI. Later generations do not know how to interpret Ureña. For example, it's said that he was a cosmopolitan, a humanist.

BORGES. There's no doubt about that.

FERRARI. But how was he all that?

BORGES. That's not pejorative.

FERRARI. On the contrary.

BORGES. I think that our duty is to be cosmopolitan. Our duty is, as far as possible, to make that ancient Greek dream come true. To be 'cosmo-politan'—citizens of the world. And that must have been a paradox when it was first stated for the Greeks defined themselves through their cities: Thales of Miletus, Heraclitus of Ephesus, Zeno of Elea. It is paradoxical to pass from being a mere citizen (belonging to a city means even less than belonging to a country) to being a citizen of the world, a cosmopolitan. Today, to say cosmopolitan is to think, for example, of a tourist or guests in a hotel. But that wasn't the idea. It's the idea that Goethe translated into German as *Weltbürger* to mean citizen of the world. This refers to a sense that all cities are home to us and I believe that I feel that. In any case, I have at least five or six fatherlands scattered across diverse continents. I think of Geneva, Austin, Montevideo, Adrogué and Buenos Aires with similar affection. As each of these cities is linked to my memories, so many intimate memories, that the fact of having been born in one or the other . . . well, no one remembers their birth, do they? (*Both laugh.*)

FERRARI. We could almost think of cosmopolitanism as a vocation in some cases.

BORGES. Yes, I think so.

FERRARI. Now, how about Ureña as a humanist?

BORGES. Well, he worshipped Rome, as all men should, which is in reality the same as worshipping Greece. Rome, to me, is a Hellenistic extension. One cannot conceive of, say, *De Rerum Natura* without the Greek philosophers, nor *The Aeneid*, which has its own values, of course, without the Homeric poems. Except that *The Aeneid* is more rare because it is an epic as well as an exquisite poem. It's an epic but also, one could say, a baroque one. Every line has been worked on, which, as I have been told by those who know Greek, is not the case with Homer who is more like a great sea or great river. It's not like that with *The Aeneid*. One does feel it's like a great sea but that each line is memorable and that every line has been polished. Or as Virgil said about bees, 'In tenue labor,' that is, they're working with what's tenuous, minimalist. A laborious process. When one reads Virgil, one does not only think of a sea but also of a cabinet-maker or a jeweller. It's a very rare combination which hasn't happened since.

FERRARI. He's like an artisan.

BORGES. Like an artisan. But it's a very rare combination, not present in other writers.

FERRARI. At the end of this talk, we should remember that it is Pedro Henríquez Ureña's centenary.

BORGES. Well, I feel that it's absurd to wait a hundred years to celebrate Ureña (*both laugh*). Let's suppose that we pay tribute before and after. That we continue to pay tribute. I thank him for pleasurable hours of friendship and arguments about literature. As I have a love for English literature and he did too, we have talked so much about English writers and, of course, classical Latin ones because he professed that slightly onerous love for Latin which I try to share, despite my failing memory.

FERRARI. He probably showed us, in his own way, that in Latin America we are all fellow citizens.

BORGES. Yes, I'm sure of that. I am sure that we are fellow citizens, that we are Europeans in exile but an exile that allows us to deserve not only a region or a language but all the regions and all the languages that we can learn or should learn.

34

Memories of Libraries, Cockpits and Strange Poems

●

OSVALDO FERRARI. Borges, in many of our conversations, unknow-ingly, we approach the topic of the National Library on México Street where you were the director for many years.

JORGE LUIS BORGES. Yes.

FERRARI. For a long time I have wanted to know about the journey that brought you to that library, that is, the libraries you worked in for a long time before reaching the National Library.

BORGES. I worked for nine years in the Miguel Cané library on Carlos Calvo and Muñiz. I began as a second assistant. Then someone insisted, perhaps too strongly, that I be named first assistant. There was a difference of 30 pesos, barely a difference today, but then it was quite something. I think that Honorio Pueyrredón was the mayor and he said, fine, he would name me first assistant as long as he didn't have to hear my name again. But I think perhaps he ended up having to hear it a few more times (*both laugh*). In any case, I was promoted and started to earn—*incredibili dictum*—240 pesos a month. Two hundred and forty pesos a month was far from negligible. Now, I should have left that library—the atmosphere was extremely mediocre. But I went on working, although I'm not sure the word 'work' is correct here. We were, I believe, some 50 employees and the work handed out had to be done slowly. I remember that I was given books to classify on my first day following the Brussels manual that uses the decimal system, the same way as it's done in the Library of Congress in the United States. I worked and classified nearly 80 books. Every day one had to pretend that one was working. Word got around that I classified books. The next day I was rebuked by one of my colleagues—he said that I was hurting them because they had decided to classify an average of 40 books a day. In reality, the number was not even 40—it could be 39, 38, 41, so that things would seem more credible, as in a naturalist novel. I thought to myself that I could not continue that way. The next day I classified 38 so as not to seem presumptuous. As a result, the work was completed in, let's say, half an hour or three quarters of an hour. The next six hours were free and we dedicated them to talking about football, something I am deeply ignorant of, or gossip and if not, dirty stories. I hid myself because I had found a strange occupation— reading the books in the library. To those nine years I owe my knowledge of the works of Leon Bloy and Paul Claudel. I also reread the six volumes of Gibbon's *History of the Decline and Fall of the Roman Empire*, and I discovered books I'd never heard of. That's how I made use of my free time.

FERRARI. In that atmosphere, you decided to read more difficult works than you did at home.

BORGES. That's true, yes (*laughs*). But that I was reading books was not met with approval. So I have a bittersweet memory, although I do recall some excellent friendships, for example, with Alfredo Doblas, a great colleague. Then there were others who were less likeable. There was one, whose name I do not wish to recall, who boasted of coming from Villa Crespo. One day he was washing himself and I got a glimpse of his chest—a map of knife scars. Once I asked him if he danced tangos and he proudly answered, 'What a question! I'm from Villa Crespo!' I remember being asked which 'square' I preferred. I thought they were referring to a canvas or an oil painting. But no, 'square' meant football team. So I said I knew absolutely nothing about football. They told me that because we worked in the Boedo and San Juan area, I should say that I supported San Lorenzo de Almagro. I memorized that and thereafter always said that I supported San Lorenzo so as not to offend my colleagues. But I noticed that San Lorenzo de Almagro almost never won. But my colleagues said, no, the fact of winning or losing was secondary—and they were right—and that San Lorenzo was the most 'scientific' team of all.

FERRARI. They told you that?

BORGES. Yes, that they were scientific.

FERRARI. That they lost scientifically?

BORGES. Yes, that they didn't know how to win but that when they lost, they lost methodically (*both laugh*).

FERRARI. So that was then the Miguel Cané library.

BORGES. Yes, the Miguel Cané library, with its director Francisco Luis Bernárdez. I also have very pleasant memories of Horacio Schiavo who worked there. But just because I recall those two names, Doblas and Schiavo, I am not implying that I don't have good memories of the others I haven't named. As you know, memory has its ups and downs and at this moment I especially remember Doblas and Schiavo.

FERRARI. Of course.

BORGES. Schiavo wrote a book titled *La catedral* (The Cathedral), a long poem devoted to Chartres Cathedral. Later, I wrote a poem about Schiavo. Schiavo's poem corresponded, in spatial terms, with Chartres Cathedral. For example, one section of the poem concerned the naves, another the portico and the apse and so on. He employed the same amount of lines as the length of the cathedral in metres or yards. You could say that it was a symmetrical poem. I don't know if this was a logical idea because when you look at a cathedral you can appreciate the correlations. But in the case of a poem, which is read continuously, I don't know if one can exactly realize which part of the poem corresponds with which part of the building. It's an odd idea. Doblas took Casares and me to see a cockfight. I had seen many in Montevideo but Casares had never seen one.

FERRARI. And where was that?

BORGES. It was in the Saavedra quarter where the Saavedra Museum is today. My mother contributed something to the museum for we are relatives of that nebulous leader Cornelio Saavedra. There was an estancia there before, a run-down one. It was in a poor quarter and we went there one Sunday to see a cockfight. It was an excellent event for a myopic man like me—it's as if one is at the ringside, as if the cocks are only metres away. They gave us newspapers, to cover

252

our knees with, so that the blood from the cocks didn't splatter us. The cock owners entered the ring, their fighting cocks under their arms. Then they were placed down, face to face. At first absolutely nothing happened. Then they were made to touch each other's beaks. Then they were possessed by a warlike frenzy and destroyed each other. I have seen cocks that were no longer cocks but a sort of scarlet bird without feathers.

FERRARI. Survivors?

BORGES. Yes, survivors. They were blind but they fought on. They are simple animals—I don't know what frenzy possesses them.

FERRARI. It seems that the Dogo Argentino shares that characteristic.

BORGES. Yes, true.

FERRARI. They fight to the end. But Borges, you always speak about the happiness in libraries. Did you feel that then?

BORGES. Yes, but what I didn't like was the idea that the happiness lay in those six hours (*laughs*), that it was a measured happiness. Also, when I worked it was difficult to be alone—one had to chat, listen to the latest gossip . . .

FERRARI. You had to fulfil a ritual.

BORGES. Yes. But I read countless books. I do try to retain good memories of that library in Almagro Sur. And then when he whom we know came to power, the town council appointed me inspector for the sale of chicken and eggs. I, of course, knew absolutely nothing about that matter. So sent in my resignation which was expected. In reality, that did me a lot of good for I was immediately called by the

Colegio Libre de Estudios Superiores where I began to give lectures. I had to do something and that earned me enough money. It also gave me the chance to travel around Argentina, to go to Montevideo a few times to give lectures. Otherwise, I would have vegetated in that library for ever. I don't know why but each year I would say, 'This is my last year here.' I was too much of a coward to leave. I had been offered another chair but I was too shy. I thought: No, I cannot utter one word in public, and thus, incredibly, ended up staying for nine years in that library. I remember that I travelled to San Juan and Boedo every day of the week and bought the same lottery ticket. Now, I can't remember what that lottery ticket was, except that it ended in '74. I thought: My grandfather got himself killed in the La Verde battle in the revolution of '74, after Mitre's surrender—the year '74 owes me something. I was loyal to that number and won once, I think. But when I resigned that post, that number won me the big prize.

FERRARI. It has struck me that in your *Personal Anthology* and in your *New Personal Anthology* you excluded 'The Library of Babel' but included, on the other hand, your story 'The Wall and the Book'.

BORGES. It's just that 'The Library of Babel' seems to me to be merely an attempt, a vain attempt, to be Kafka. Although I'm told the result is different—luckily for Kafka it's different but sadly not for me. Of course, when I wrote 'The Library of Babel' I was employed in that small and almost secret Almagro library. I thought that it was infinite, that it included and was part of the universe.

FERRARI. Then we have your poem 'Lectores' (Readers).

BORGES. I do not remember that one.

FERRARI. In it you feel closer to Alonso Quijano than to Cervantes.

BORGES. Ah, yes, Alonso Quijano.

FERRARI. And you say of *Quixote* that . . .

BORGES. Yes, I believe I say that Alonso Quijano decides to become Don Quixote and leave his library. On the other hand, I am a shy Alonso Quijano who did not leave his library.

FERRARI. You say 'On the perpetual verge of adventure'?

BORGES. That's true. How strange! 'On the verge' is very important both in terms of unpleasant events and pleasant ones. Being on the verge is terrible.

FERRARI. Now, Dumas proposes the opposite. He says that the true man of action is the one who prefers, above all, the memory of actions he took part in and to linger in that memory.

BORGES. Ah, that's good. But I do not know if men of action linger in their memories.

FERRARI. According to Dumas they do.

BORGES. I suspect not. I think they're rather superficial. Possibly. I'll pick a deliberately false example—the siege of Troy meant more for Homer than it did for Hector or Ajax or Achilles.

FERRARI. Ah, of course.

BORGES. I think that the life of a man of action is rather superficial. It is a series of intense moments that perhaps are not remembered. Well, I think of the greyish memoires that Colonel Suárez, my great grandfather, left behind. One of the most boring books I've ever read. Yet there he speaks of the battle of Ayacucho and the battle of Junín.

FERRARI. Where he is a protagonist.

BORGES. Yes, and all that reading is tedious and I guess that his memories were also tedious for him. Or, better put, we can suppose that he had no literary talent, that he simply recorded facts as if he was someone else. If you remember something many times, it's converted into a kind of formula, isn't it? There are people who recount their own lives and always in the same way. I have heard my grandmother tell stories that must have been important to her but she told them always in the same words. This means that the memory had already vanished. What remained is something simply memorized . . .

FERRARI. Mechanical . . .

BORGES. Yes, just like we repeat a sonnet or the Lord's Prayer.

35

An Evocation of Kipling

●

OSVALDO FERRARI. In some of our latest radio talks we have travelled for a brief time to India, we have talked about Buddhism and Indian culture and religion.

JORGE LUIS BORGES. Yes, of course, an unending theme.

FERRARI. And while thinking about India, I remembered a writer whose stories you've read and reread over time and who seems to be one of your permanent favourites—Rudyard Kipling.

BORGES. Of course, do you want me to talk about Kipling?

FERRARI. Well, I thought I had only to name him and . . .

BORGES. When Kipling died, he was talked about with a rather tepid enthusiasm. This was because he was judged for his political opinions. Perhaps it would be best for writers not to make their political opinions public. Kipling's concept of the empire was, of course, a noble one. That's to say, he saw the empire as 'the white man's burden'. And I have no idea if this corresponds with reality. As Lope de Vega said, talking about another empire:

Under the colour of religion
they go off to seek silver and gold
as covered treasure.

That is, there's always an economic explanation for things which is
what communists want and which is the most melancholic one. Doubtless, there are others. Kipling thought of the empire as England's debt
and called it 'the white man's burden'. Beyond this judgement, this ethical and religious meaning to empire, is Kipling's work. It is curious
that Kipling began writing admirable stories. A few days ago I was
rereading the stories from *Plain Tales from the Hills* and three or four of
them are short, secret masterpieces. I'm thinking of 'Beyond the Pale',
'The Gate of the Hundred Sorrows' and others such as these.

FERRARI. I think that the ones you mentioned are the most perfect.

BORGES. Yes, but then, at the end of his life, he did something completely different. His first stories are very brief and relatively straightforward, if such a thing is possible in this complex universe. But at
the end of his life Kipling began changing his themes. He moved, as
someone said, from soldiers and sailors to doctors. This perhaps corresponds to other reasons, such as his cancer. I don't know if you
know that Kipling was twice operated on for cancer and that he died
after the last one. There's a story called 'The Wish House' and its
theme is cancer. I'll narrate it in brief. There are two women from a
village in Sussex, in the south of England. They talk. One comments
to the other that she is fond of doing favours, so to speak. The other
woman tells a story. It's about a woman abandoned by her lover. She
finds out later that there's a house in a new quarter of the village.

This house is a 'wish house', a house where desires are granted. But this magic gift imposes its conditions. She finds out or is told that her lover has a new lover and that he's ill and knows he has cancer. So she goes to that new house on a new street and knocks on the door. She hears footsteps approaching and then a grunting that's not human. She knows that someone is behind the door, waiting. Then she asks this magical someone that she be given the pain experienced by her lover who is suffering from cancer.

FERRARI. That the man's suffering be given to her?

BORGES. Then she hears the steps receding and returns home. She has prepared her bed; she gets into it and begins to feel the pain of cancer. Terrible, isn't it?

FERRARI. It's terrible and noble.

BORGES. Yes, and noble. Then her pain increases and she tells this story to her friend and they understand they won't see each other again because she's dying. Then the woman takes the last bus after having tea and cakes and biscuits . . . well that's the story.

FERRARI. It's a fine story.

BORGES. Yes, a very fine one. And she bumps into the lover and notices that he's getting better. But he doesn't speak to her and cannot know that she has absorbed his diminishing pain.

FERRARI. He never finds out?

BORGES. No, he doesn't. She gives him her life and he gives her death but will never know. But you and I know and so do millions of Kipling's readers. It's a very strange, magical story. It begins as a trivial tale. He makes the two village women ignorant. They talk of trivialities. One highly praises her tea, they exchange gossip and then we get this dreadful story. It's one of the last stories Kipling wrote and then the cancer got to him. Also, Kipling's son died in the First World War; he was among the first hundred thousand that England sent to France. Kipling never directly mentions this death, but there's a story in which a Roman soldier dies, a very carefully written story and it's there that Kipling indirectly explains this loss. That's the most expressive way to convey his pain at the death of his son. Kipling doesn't mention a father but an uncle, as he was a very modest and shy man as well. I think, once when he was introduced to Shaw, Kipling ran off. I mean, he ran like a rabbit because he knew Shaw was a witty, eloquent man who would tie him up in knots. He had his convictions but didn't like arguing. So their conversation lasted no time at all.

FERRARI. Moreover, Kipling came from a completely different world.

BORGES. Yes, completely different. He had all that past in India. I don't know if you realize that Kipling knew Hindi before English. In a poem he refers to pagan talk but in Hindi. He has a story where one can guess that it's a Sikh talking and that's written in English. I lent it to a Sikh friend of mine, who gave it back and said, 'This story is admirable. I noticed that Kipling definitely thought it in Hindi and as I read it I was retranslating each of his sentences back into Hindi.' So, Kipling always felt tied to India. I have several Indian friends and every time we talk about literature in India, they nearly always mention Kipling first, that is, they consider him to . . .

FERRARI. Belong . . .

BORGES. Yes, we could say 'belong'. That India is now an independent country has nothing to do with it, because they understand Kipling's love for India. One of his poems is titled 'A Song of Fifty Horses' which were the 50 horses for his carriage. He tells his 50 horses that they are to travel to France. There are three or four stanzas and each one ends, 'It is enough, it is France.'

FERRARI. He won the Nobel Prize at the start of the century . . .

BORGES. Yes, he was famous then, having published *Kim* in 1901. That book was illustrated with photographs taken by his father, Lockwood Kipling. Strangely, just this morning I was showing Indian-type illustrations from the 11th edition of the *Encyclopaedia Britannica* to a lady from *La Prensa*, Mrs Barili, and they were all by Kipling's father. Kipling was born in India because his father was sent to India on a government post to defend Indian crafts from British commercial art. I believe Kipling was William Morris' nephew, the translator of Scandinavian sagas. The English government needed someone to defend Indian arts and crafts, and that someone was Kipling's father. He begot his son near a lake called Rudyard somewhere in England, which explains his son's name. But he had no Indian blood as many people have imagined. It's just that he was born in India, in Bombay, and his first book of poems, *The Seven Seas*, was dedicated to the city of Bombay. Every now and then he would speak scornfully of the English in England and call them 'the islanders'.

FERRARI. Of course, he's from that continent.

BORGES. In a poem he says 'And what should they know of England who only England know.' That is, he knew the empire. He wrote another book called *The Five Nations*—England, India, Canada, South Africa and Australia. He travelled to all those lands and wrote about them with greater or lesser enthusiasm.

FERRARI. Do you associate him with a generation of writers or see him as a solitary figure in literary history?

BORGES. I think that any writer worth anything is a solitary figure.

FERRARI. Naturally.

BORGES. Also, in his particular case, as Novalis said, 'Every Englishman is an island.' Now, it's odd to think that Kipling returned to England a little before 1890 and was contemporaneous with Wilde and what's called 'the Yellow Nineties', all that decorative literature and painting. Well, Wells, Shaw and Kipling are contemporaries along with decorative writers like Wilde.

FERRARI. Yet, they are not linked together.

BORGES. No, they are not but they are contemporaries.

FERRARI. Of course.

BORGES. Wilde wrote, somewhat scornfully, about Kipling, 'A genius who drops his aspirates', because common people drop the *h* in English. Wilde also said that when one reads Kipling's *Plain Tales of the Hills*, as one turns the pages, one is reading life itself, illuminated by splendid sparks of vulgarity (*both laugh*). So Wilde spoke with some scorn about those 'splendid sparks of vulgarity' at the same time as he realized that Kipling was a genius.

FERRARI. A mistaken scorn in this case.

BORGES. And now as I travel, I have the impression that Kipling is more appreciated in France than in England where, I'm not sure, but thanks to other writers, he's rather forgotten. Not in France. As a French critic said, he was an Englishman of a certain efficient kind, very energetic and very new. Kipling's great contemporaries were socialists like Shaw, Wells or Bennett who judged him as an imperial bureaucrat for he didn't interest them. But it seems that a recurring motif in Europe is the discovery of the East, that vague entity called the East which people who actually live in the East do not imagine or feel. I mean, I don't know if a Persian feels close to a Chinaman. I don't think they have any affinities; I don't believe that an Arab and a Japanese have any either. But for us they do. We compose that thing, that heterogeneous and magnificent thing called the East. And every now and then, through the centuries, that East is discovered by Europe. And now that East is discovering the West, that's a fact.

FERRARI. Of course.

BORGES. Well, there are stages . . . For example, there's no doubt that the Greeks perceived India as they also perceived Egypt, which is the East, or nearly. Then Marco Polo's journeys, *The Arabian Nights*. One of the latest discoverers of the East was, without a doubt, Kipling. Of course, the East that he knew was, above all, India, but that East is Hindu and Islamic and many other things—India, like the United States, even more than the United States, is not one country but many, with many religions, many races and a very complex history of hostility between the regions . . .

We must also mention Kipling's poetry, and a trait that no one has pointed out is that Kipling, who managed difficult metrical forms with such ease, never tried to write a sonnet. Maybe he didn't because he thought that the sonnet was thought of as intellectual, something that corresponded to a certain kind of poetry, and he didn't wish to betray the idea of being a popular writer by trying to write a sonnet. Which is a shame, because he would have honoured the sonnet.

FERRARI. Without a doubt. I think that, along with Kipling, we will have to return to the East another time.

FERRARI. Very well.

36

Borges and Memory

●

OSVALDO FERRARI. Not long ago we talked about Funes and memory and recalled that word 'memorious', which has, at times, been applied to you, you who invented it in Buenos Aires.

JORGE LUIS BORGES. It's unfair, because my memory is now a memory of quotations from pages of poetry I have read. As far as my personal history is concerned, it could be that I have transformed it into a fable or have tried to plot fables with it, but if you ask me something about my life then I make mistakes. Especially regarding journeys and the chronology of those journeys. As for dates—I remember 1955, which is linked, of course, with the revolution we had so awaited and which granted us many things and which is also related to my loss of sight and my appointment as director of the National Library. So 1955 marks serious events, especially about myself. Apart from that, my memory is more a memory of quotations. I think that I have sometimes recalled Emerson's melancholic occupation, referring to a text that is called *Quotations*, where he says, 'And life itself becomes a quotation.'

It's rather sad when one begins to see one's life, and sufferings and unhappiness as between quotation marks. It's terrible, isn't it? Well, my life is a bit like a series of quotations thanks to my fallible memory. But perhaps, given that I have never studied anything by heart, these quotations are from texts that have imposed themselves on my memory; they have moved me to such a point that they have become unforgettable. And I can also remember lines from poems that are so bad that they are unforgettable.

FERRARI (*laughs*). There must be some possible conjectures related to your memory, what we might call your literary memory.

BORGES. I think that we shouldn't forget what French philosopher Henri Bergson said about memory being selective, that is, it's memory that chooses. It's natural that people who are temperamentally sad tend to remember unhappiness, as unhappiness serves to make their pathos eloquent. But as I am not one of those I forget my misfortunes and my unhappiness. I'll quote, inevitably, from *Martín Fierro*:

You should know that forgetting misfortune

Is also having a memory.

Now, I think that memory requires forgetting. The justification of this thought can be found in my story 'Funes the Memorious'. Of course, Funes' case, that of a man overwhelmed by an infinite memory, is hypothetical. He remembers every moment. He doesn't recall a person but each moment that he saw him, whether full face or in profile. He recalls the hour of the day when he saw him . . . he recalls so many circumstances that he cannot generalize. He cannot think for thinking requires abstractions and those abstractions can be made by forgetting the small differences and linking things according to the ideas they contain. And my poor Funes cannot do all this so he dies overwhelmed by that infinite memory. I seem to remember that he dies very young.

FERRARI. Yes, conjectures about memory develop along those lines. You state that memory somehow demands forgetting. So I can ask you now: Does Borges' literary memory feel it too is overwhelmed, like Funes', and needs conversation to mitigate its weight?

BORGES. Well, I really enjoy talking. Of course, I also enjoy remembering. Now I have reached a stage of forgetting and—I've said this before—I repeat the same concept in differing ways, without realizing it. Some of my stories, in any case, can be judged as variations of others.

FERRARI. Creative forgetting and creative memory.

BORGES. Yes, creative memory and forgetting. I don't know if I talked to you about two sonnets on chess or about the story 'The Circular Ruins' or about a poem where each link is a tiger. Well, they all correspond to the same idea. That's how I realized this. Then there's another theme which I repeat with variations, with such varied variations that I don't realize I'm repeating it . . . it's about something lovely that turns out to be terrible, intolerable. Just a moment ago we were recalling Funes' infinite memory. An infinite memory seems like a gift, yet kills he who possesses it or who is possessed by it. That's the same idea as 'The Aleph', the point where all points in space converge, a point that can overwhelm a man. There's another story 'The Zahir', about an unforgettable object that, because it is unforgettable, and the protagonist continuously remembers it, stops him from thinking about other things, thus driving him mad, or to the point of becoming mad, as he is writing the story. It's the same idea in 'The Book of Sand', an infinite book that turns out to be atrocious for its owner. So, variations on the same theme—a precious object or gift that becomes terrible. And I will doubtless write more stories with the same plot or, actually, I have already written one for my next book, *Shakespeare's Memory*, which is about a German scholar who possesses or is possessed by Shakespeare's memory, his memory of a few days before his death which, in the end, is somehow flooded by that infinite memory and he has to transfer it to someone else before going mad. I mean that it's the same story and I try out its variations. But perhaps universal literature is a series of variations on the same theme. For instance, the theme of separated lovers or lovers who meet and are driven apart—that's one universal theme.

FERRARI. Those variations can lead to a story being perfect, but what I wish to ask you is whether you have ever, like Funes, felt fear when faced with your memory?

BORGES. No, because my memory is selective. I choose some facts and try to forget negative ones.

FERRARI. And literary memory, to put it like that, has it sometimes overwhelmed you? Have you felt that it has?

BORGES. No, I have to spend a lot of my time alone; I lie on my bed and recite stanzas. Especially stanzas from Verlaine and Swinburne, from Almafuerte, sonnets by Francisco de Quevedo . . . I don't know if I like them but for me they are unforgettable. There's a sonnet by

Enrique Banchs I always repeat, the sonnet about a mirror, as well as some poems by Juan Ramón Jiménez. Then, there are the Latin poets, anonymous Anglo-Saxon ones . . .

FERRARI. So in that sense your memory is your permanent company.

BORGES. Yes, and an anthology.

FERRARI. Of course.

BORGES. Although I know that the best anthologies are those compiled by time. Let's consider an anthology, say *The Hundred Best Lyrical Poems in the Spanish Language* by Menéndez y Pelayo. To start with that's fine, because they're poems chosen by time, although time can make mistakes, for I do not believe that the best poems in the Spanish language should include Quevedo's 'Érase un hombre a una nariz pegado' (There Was a Man Stuck to a Nose) or the Marqués de Santillana's 'La vaquera de la Finojosa' (The Cow Girl from Finojosa) which are more suited to forgetting and forgiving. Anyhow, the anthology is more or less good until you reach the present. Then, Pelayo naturally has to consider his colleagues and contemporaries and we find that the poets of today have been happily forgotten (*both laugh*). It's curious but Pelayo wrote better verse than his contemporary Spanish friends but didn't include them in his anthology. Another aspect of Pelayo is that no one remembers him as a poet. Well, Homero Guglielmini knew his long epistle to Horace by heart. I do not know it by heart but remember some felicitous lines and some mysteriously happy ones too . . . literary excellence is always mysterious, always inexplicable. I recall two passages. One is very brief, a line, 'La náyade en el agua de la fuente' (The water nymph in the fountain's water).

That's very pleasing and without a metaphor. It's an image, of course, but the idea of the visual image of the nymph in a fountain's water seems trivial—what really counts are the words, don't they?

FERRARI. It's simple and direct.

BORGES. The other one talks of Jupiter's rape of Europa; he had taken the shape of a bull and carried her off swimming:

That the snow-white bull of the hundred cities,

Crete, leads the stolen nymph.

Now, 'snow-white' (*níveo*) is trivial and, doubtless, 'Crete, of the hundred cities' is a translation of the Greek name Crete. But what remains is the inversion, the hyperbaton. The word 'leads' is not apt but it doesn't matter for the current of the lines draws one along . . .

People remember Pelayo as a literary historian and as a very arbitrary critic, especially because he negated what came from abroad and praised only what was Spanish. Rather like Ricardo Rojas in his *History of Argentinian Literature*, except that Argentinian literature was more a supposition. In the end, it occurs to me that Pelayo's work was more serious. Despite this, I remember Groussac's joke about Pelayo. He had published his *History of Spanish Philosophy* and Groussac said, 'Bit of an overwhelming title, but it corrects the severity of the noun philosophy with the smile of the adjective Spanish' (*laughs*). That's from one of Groussac's best books, *Un enigme littéraire* which I do not think has been translated into Spanish. It's about what's known as the false *Quixote* or the continuation of the *Quixote* that someone wrote and drove Cervantes to write, luckily for him and for us, the second part of his *Quixote*. As far as I know, this book hasn't been translated from French into Spanish though it's one of Grous-sac's best. Groussac felt his destiny had been frustrated—he would have liked to have been a great French writer. He did become famous here but, for him, 'To be famous in South America still means remaining an unknown.' Now, being from South America is to be famous, isn't it (*both laugh*), after what's been called the Latin American 'boom'.

FERRARI. In one way.

BORGES. But Groussac in his day could still feel . . .

FERRARI. The opposite.

BORGES. Yes, he felt that South America was a forgotten corner of the planet. Now it's remembered too much for we are given virtues which I am not sure are true and, in my case, I do not deserve.

FERRARI (*laughs*). So, Borges, memory is a pleasant companion that also allows us to create.

BORGES. And gives us the chance to have a conversation lasting a quarter of an hour (*laughs*), which, I believe, is hardly less valuable, given our times.

FERRARI (*laughs*). Yes, more or less that, more or less 15 minutes.

37

The Florida and Boedo Groups and the Sur *Magazine*

•

OSVALDO FERRARI. Borges, I would like you to tell me how in 1930 or 1931 the magazine *Sur* and the group around it began.

JORGE LUIS BORGES. I know very little about *Sur*. I know we were in Victoria Ocampo's house and that she created an editorial board. On it were people who couldn't be consulted, like Waldo Frank and José Ortega y Gasset. I don't know if Reyes was in Buenos Aires then. All the people present were made part of the board, perhaps not to offend anyone. People like Alfredo González Garaño, like María Rosa Oliver who had nothing to do with the magazine later. But Victoria wanted to be generous. The person who can tell you about this is José Bianco, the magazine's real editor. Before him, for a short time, it was Carlos Reyles, the son of the Uruguayan writer Reyles. I replaced Bianco for a few months. Isn't it odd that though Victoria was a dictatorial person she didn't get involved in the magazine? She didn't know what was being published from one volume to the next. I'm not sure if the title *Sur* was suggested by Eugenio d'Ors or by Ortega y Gasset. Maybe

Ortega. *Sur* is a lovely name. I teased Victoria once by saying what right did she have to give the name *Sur* to her magazine when she lived in San Isidro. Had she lived in Lomas or Adrogué, it would have been understandable. Then Pierre Drieu La Rochelle sent in a very odd article, I do not know why it was published. An excellent writer, it seems that he wrote it scornfully because he signed it as 'Pierre Drieu La Rochelle, dreamer from the banks of the Seine'. Isn't that odd? In that article he pointed out that though the magazine was called *Sur*, why hadn't Australia or New Zealand or South Africa been taken into account, because the South was not limited only to what's called the Southern Cone. I don't know why he sent that article, perhaps as a joke or perhaps because a magazine from Buenos Aires didn't seem serious enough to him. He saw the magazine as lost in the very South with which it shared a name.

It was a lovely group. And though my name appears in the board of collaborators, I never voiced my opinion about what was published. It was Bianco who ran the magazine, something not recognized today because it's thought that the director was Victoria Ocampo and its secretary was Bianco, though Reyles was the first one and my name appeared there for a couple of months while Bianco travelled in Europe. So Bianco decided *Sur*'s destiny, apart from certain regular correspondents like Count Keyserling, Waldo Frank and Ortega y Gasset. People have been very unfair with Bianco. Once he was asked why he never published anything by Roberto Arlt and he answered, completely logically, that Arlt hadn't sent anything—he couldn't publish work by non-existent collaborators, could he? (*Laughs.*) He ran the magazine with impeccable standards.

FERRARI. In that same article or letter from Drieu La Rochelle, the one you mentioned, he suggests that Argentine writers should not hurry to say 'this is our South', 'this is Argentinian' . . .

BORGES. He was right, and since then we have said nothing but that. We have been tied to geography, even to topography. You remember those two illusory groups—now studied in universities—called the Florida group and the Boedo group? They never existed. The whole thing was organized by Roberto Mariani and Ernesto Palacio. According to them, Paris had literary groups which were controversial, so we should have some here too. So they invented those two groups and warned me about them the following day. I said to them, 'I know Florida too well. So I would like to belong to Boedo which I am unfamiliar with.' But they said I couldn't decide for the selection had already been made (*laughs*). So it was my lot to belong to the Florida group. Some writers like Nicolás Olivari or Roberto Arlt belonged to both groups, because the groups were fake, mere self-promotion. Now all this is studied, like the epitaphs published in *Martín Fierro* which specialized in epitaphs. They were written by the same people because no one wanted to attack anyone, and then a writer from the other group would sign it. Thus they created a sham of a war that was the least cruel, the most friendly one ever. That's for the best, because what advantages are there in writers disliking each other or in people disliking each other?

FERRARI. Borges, what you have just said will shock those who compile anthologies and who classify and write literary histories.

BORGES. But literary history is made of these kinds of shams, isn't it? Perhaps France is partially to blame because many writers in France write for literary history. They classify themselves. For example, they are right-wing writers and left-wings ones, they're from such-and-such a region, they are from Normandy or from the South. All this is done professionally, with the right emphasis. On the other hand, Novalis said, 'Every Englishman is an island,' that is, the English are individualists which is why there have been fewer literary movements there. Although, of course, the great Romantic movement officially began in England with Coleridge and Wordsworth's *Lyrical Ballads*. But, really, all that was happening on its own. There was a Pre-Raphaelite group as well. After that, nothing . . . Ezra Pound tried something with the Imagists but I do not think anyone remembers it or gives it any importance. Also, the theory was false, the idea of reducing poetry to an image. Perhaps a little less false than our theory based on Lugones who reduced poetry to metaphor which is nothing more than one of many rhetorical figures and is certainly not essential. I think a few days ago I told you that Japanese poetry, from what I have known of it through English, German and especially North American translations, lacks metaphor—one feels as if everything is unique, that it cannot metamorphose into something else. On the other hand, they use contrast a lot. I don't know if I have already recalled that famous haiku:

On the great bronze bell
Lands a butterfly.

There's the contrast between the solid bell and the fragile butterfly. But one thing is not compared with another—they're simply contrasted. I think that you can imagine poetry without metaphors. In my example, cadence is perhaps most important. But if it is like that, my quotation is false for I have not employed the five–seven–five syllabic structure of a haiku. I have quoted it literally. Perhaps that is to falsify it. In any case, I believe it can serve as proof that in those lines there's not one metaphor.

FERRARI. That's right. Now, returning to *Sur*. I've noticed your generous enthusiam for the young Mallea. Victoria Ocampo often cites Mallea when she remembers the origins . . .

BORGES. Now I'm told that he has been forgotten although I don't think that is due to people not liking his work. I think its due to the fact that today people prefer another kind of literature. That what's called the psychological novel has become obsolete as has the novel of customs. Mallea wrote psychological novels about a certain class in Buenos Aires and that kind of novel no longer interests readers. But that doesn't imply that Mallea's work has no merit. Something that everyone admits is his discovering splendid titles for novels, such as *La ciudad junto al río inmóvil* (The City by the Motionless River). And a writer, whose name I do not wish to recall, though he is an excellent one, said that it was a mistake, that it should have been 'The Motionless City by the River'. I tell you it was Mallea's mistake (*laughs*). Evidently, its effect lies in the contrast and, of course, the river Plate is not motionless but it appears so to the eyes. The image one has is of a muddy almost motionless river. And I think that the 'motionless river' is more apt than Lugones' 'the great lion-coloured river' as no one associates lions with the river Plate. Not even in poems. Mallea has other attractive titles. Which ones can you remember now?

FERRARI. Well, *La barca de hielo* (The Ship of Ice) is one.

BORGES. I don't know if that's so good. Let's hear another . . .

FERRARI. *El sayal y la púrpura* (Coarse Cloth and Purple Cloth).

BORGES. That's a fine title. Also *La bahía de silencio* (The Bay of Silence).

FERRARI. Or *Fiesta en noviembre* (Fiesta in November).

BORGES. *Fiesta en noviembre* was translated into English. It should have been translated as 'Party in November' but they used 'fiesta' because that word 'fiesta' in English immediately suggests something Mexican or Spanish, doesn't it? In Spanish, 'fiesta' is a calm word. In English, though, 'Fiesta in November' suggests guitars, cowboys, women in black and who knows what else. And all that is completely alien to Mallea's image. I remember his first book of stories, it was called *Cuentos para una inglesa desesperada* (Stories for a Desperate English Woman).

FERRARI. Yes, he had published only that when *Sur* was founded. But I also wanted to ask you about the group around *Sur*.

BORGES. I do not have an idea about that group. Of course, I was among the earliest and collaborated perhaps much too frequently on the magazine. And Victoria was a very indulgent person and very kind with me. I owe her, as I have often repeated, my appointment as director of the National Library. I owe it to a clever move by Esther Zemborain de Torres and Victoria Ocampo and I always thank them. I was very honoured by that post especially when I recalled that Groussac had died in that building. I thought of him continually and even wrote a poem about both of us being directors of that library and of both of us being blind. And after I had written the poem I discovered that three of us directors had indeed been blind. One of the first directors of the National Library was José Mármol, also blind. If I had known that, I couldn't have written the poem because it is hard to deal with three people—two are more amenable, aren't they?

FERRARI. You could feel the presence of those two predecessors in the National Library?

BORGES. Yes, although I learnt about Mármol much later. At home we had read and reread his novel *Amalia*. I think that when one speaks about Rosas' times, the image that we all have is not from his contemporaries but an image from *Amalia*. To have created an image of a period is not a minor feat and Mármol did just that.

FERRARI. Borges, are there any other magazines that you remember with such enthusiasm?

BORGES. Well, there was a mural magazine,which I edited with Lanuza, called *Prisma*, I think. Then the magazine *Proa* which had exactly six pages on three sheets, each one folding into the other. It imitated the Spanish magazine *Ultra*. We had another plan, along with Lanuza, which we couldn't carry out but maybe it could now be done with someone else. We thought that people talked too much about promoting themselves, so we thought up an anonymous magazine—no one would sign their pieces and we would not name the editors or the secretaries. Everything would be published but no one would know who was writing, or maybe only some friends would know. But apart from Francisco Piñero, who died in the South and González Lanuza and me, no one showed much enthusiasm for anonymity. It was useless to suppose that in the end everything is anonymous. That didn't count, no one wanted to go ahead with it . . .

38

About Dialogues

●

OSVALDO FERRARI. Borges, our dialogues have become a kind of special journey as they travel from radio to newspaper and end up in a book. To start with, this contradicts our idea of ephemerality concerning radio waves and newspapers.

JORGE LUIS BORGES. Yes, a book seems more permanent. In any case, that destiny is expected for one reads a book in another way, doesn't one? The newspaper is read in order to be forgotten, the radio is listened to fleetingly but a book is read with some respect.

FERRARI. Yes, that's still a fact.

BORGES. And typeset letters have a prestige that handwriting doesn't.

FERRARI. In our case, radio waves and the weekly page have spread as far as becoming a book.

BORGES. Yes.

FERRARI. And this diffusion has helped our dialogue to be understood.

BORGES. Yes, and I'm astounded that we signed 181 copies the day the book was launched.

FERRARI. Yes, but the good news is that this understanding has taken place among those who frequent literature and those who do not.

BORGES. Among those who abstain ascetically from literature, masochists who punish themselves without knowing why (*both laugh*), abstaining from that happiness that is so close to hand for all of us. Nevertheless, people give it up. It's as if . . . they give up water or breathing or the taste of fruit or love or friendship. Well, shunning reading is a kind of asceticism practised unconsciously—no one can justify it. No one says, 'Let's gain some points and give up reading and thus win something in the next world.' No, it's carried out spontaneously, innocently. And if we continue to do this, what I saw many years ago in a German house might happen. That man had, I think, many volumes of an atlas or a dictionary. I wanted to consult one of them but it turned out that they were only the backs of books—there was nothing behind them (*laughs*).

FERRARI. A fake library.

BORGES. Yes, a fake library and typical of some homes.

FERRARI. The validity of our dialogue reminds me, for example, that according to Karl Jaspers, Socrates was in charge of dialogues with all Athenian citizens—not just philosophers. That means that dialogue reaches everyone.

BORGES. Well, that's how Christ acted five centuries later. As Gibbon noted ironically, God did not reveal his truths to learned men or to philosophers but to fishermen and ignorant people. Then Nietzsche translated this by saying that Christianity was a religion of slaves which means the same thing with perhaps less vigour.

FERRARI. Not long ago we said that Nietzsche failed in his work . . .

BORGES. Of writing a sacred book.

FERRARI. No, in his attempt to replace a God who according to him had died.

BORGES. Yes, he failed abysmally with Zarathustra, with his lion who laughed, with his eagle. All that seems so stiff and so old compared with the Gospels which are alive today or, better still, are the future.

FERRARI. Let's say they were ephemeral antichrists.

BORGES. Yes (*laughs*).

FERRARI. That valuing of each citizen, which we agreed Socrates had achieved when he addressed each individual, seems to me to correspond with the notion of what we could authentically call the people. That is, all the citizens or all the individuals.

BORGES. Yes, because today the people means the masses.

FERRARI. It's a mistake.

BORGES. Yes, it's a mistake . . .

FERRARI. Made by politicians?

BORGES. Demagogues. It's not so much a mistake as it is sophistry which can, of course, be a kind of mistake. It's political cunning. It's understood that the people are . . . what my grandmother used to say, 'The sovereign people, bursting with savagery'. That is in effect what the word 'people' means today, and not each individual who makes it up. We are all part of the people. But that is not accepted—it's understood that they have to be poor or professionally poor, doesn't it?

FERRARI. The meaning of the word has been degraded.

BORGES. Yes.

FERRARI. I believe that dialogue, from Greece onwards, reveals an exceptional virtue in that it creates, let's say, civilized communication between men and women.

BORGES. And it allows the possibility of countering dogma. Let's say, when Plato invented the dialogue, it's as if he branched into diverse people like Gorgias and not only Socrates. His thought branched out and diverse opinions became possible and somehow replaced dogma and prayer. That means the topics created the thoughts and interjections were abandoned.

FERRARI. One participated.

BORGES. One also participated.

FERRARI. In Argentina, I've thought that perhaps one of the ways of saving our rare predisposition to be communal or to act for the common good . . .

BORGES. Would be dialogue.

FERRARI. Could be deciding to start a dialogue.

BORGES. It seems so hard. I believe we've talked about one of the differences between the Spanish of Spain and our South American Spanish or the Spanish of this region. The Spanish of Spain tends to be dogmatic, with exclamations, facilely grumpy and indignant. While we, on the other hand, speak as if in doubt, knowing what we say is fallible. Spaniards talk with the gravity of those who ignore doubt. We happily know it, as doubt is one of humanity's most precious possessions. Uncertainty is a possession, insecurity also.

FERRARI. And now that I'm thinking of it, it's perhaps what started the dialogues in Greece.

BORGES. Yes, humanity started to disagree but disagree in polite ways, without the urge to kill one another.

FERRARI. Just refuting one another.

BORGES. Something I've noticed many times is that only Judaeo-Christianity has produced religious wars. On the other hand, you have Ashoka, Emperor of India, who declared tolerance. And closer to us, the Emperor of Japan and disciple of Buddha practised that vague pantheism called Shinto. The idea of religious war would have been completely incomprehensible. But in the West religious wars have been very cruel for they have been based on intolerance, on the supposition that the adversary has to be converted or annihilated.

FERRARI. There has been no dialogue.

BORGES. No, none. As Estrada says in an admirable line, 'Fire was more merciful.' Or, in a variant, 'steel'.

FERRARI. They are forms of the monologue.

BORGES. Forms of the monologue, yes (*laughs*).

FERRARI. Something that seems to me to be indispensable for that eventual dialogue between the Argentines would be a dialogue without prejudices, one of the virtues I sense while conversing with you.

BORGES. I try to forget my many prejudices. I learnt in Japan that admirable habit of supposing that the other speaker is always right.

One may be wrong, as wrong as the other speaker, but just to suppose that the other speaker is right is a good prelude for dialogue. The fact of being hospitable with other people's opinions though they may be opposed to our own. That's not possible here, even less in Spain. María Kodama made me realize one of the virtues of the French. Say, one is listening to a conversation in their language. Although one may not follow it well, one can grasp that the words are pointing to nuances, slight differences, admitting something, rejecting something else, but politely. Well, French is a . . . thinking language, not a language that begins with a presupposed truth but one that studies the diverse nuances and possibilities of a topic. And one can hear that in the way the French speak.

FERRARI. All that prevents a dialogue from being killed off before it starts.

BORGES. Yes, we should reach a dialogue, we should return to that ancient Greek, perhaps Platonic, invention.

FERRARI. Especially here in Argentina. And we are conversing about this principle in May 1985 when you're about to start a new journey.

BORGES. Yes, I'll soon be a Californian and then a New Yorker and then I could say like Paul of Tarsus, *Civis Romanum sum*, I will be a Roman citizen. I remember for the umpteenth time what Chesterton said, that if someone goes to Rome and doesn't have the urge or conviction to return to Rome, the journey has been worthless. Rome is our starting point. Of course, we have been born out on a limb in a continent ignored by Rome and in a hemisphere not even guessed at by the Romans but, in whatever way, I am a Roman—even better, a Greek—in exile.

FERRARI. So your journey begins this time in California.

BORGES. Yes, I believe I have to give three lectures—I'm not sure if two are in Spanish and one in English or two in English and one in Spanish—at the University of Santa Barbara which is situated, I think—my sense of geography is rather vague—in southern California. Then there's something with a group of psychiatrists or psychologists or astrologists and, finally, sociologists.

FERRARI. One of those modern disciplines.

BORGES. One of those imaginary disciplines, in New York. Then something of a discursive nature and, in my case, a hesitant one, is to happen in Rome. Then I come home and await an oral future of the same kind here. But that's much later—it's best not to think of it now. I know that the worst of all events is the eve before. A lecture itself cannot be terrible. Tomorrow I will talk in Morón about my dear friend Santiago Dabove, Macedonio's disciple, whom I met at a gathering at Macedonio's. But it's better not to think of that— tomorrow will arrange everything, doubtless it all has been fixed earlier, even my hesitation . . .

FERRARI. The eve becomes oppressive.

BORGES. The eve, yes, but we can pretend to forget that there are eves and they stop being so. Of course, very soon, I have to talk in Morón.

FERRARI. Naturally. Now I recall that in one of our earliest dialogues, I think it was last March, you found yourself, as you do now, faced with a journey that began or ended in Rome.

BORGES. Yes, I think so. 'Ended' sounds better for Rome, doesn't it?

FERRARI. All roads lead to . . .

BORGES. Yes, and Rome is not only the hills we know about but the city itself. It's an apex.

FERRARI. Let's hope, then, that a future path leads again to a dialogue like this one.

BORGES. Doubtless it will have to be so.

FERRARI. Not only between us but also between all Argentinians.

BORGES. Well, about time, right? High time as the English say. We've lost . . . well, the whole of Argentine history is a kind of quest for that dialogue which never happens, does it?

FERRARI. That's true.

BORGES. I was brought up in the Unitarian tradition, despite a vague relationship with Rosas. A bit like in the Russian films and the first American films—good on one side and evil on the other. Now I think that there's some good in the others and some evil in me.

FERRARI. That sounds great to me.

BORGES. Yes, we should all reach that conviction, shouldn't we?

FERRARI. It won't be easy, but you are a good example.

BORGES. No, it's a question of waiting about a hundred years, more or less, which is nothing historically. I won't see it but others will.

39

On Gauchesque Poetry

●

OSVALDO FERRARI. I believe that among the Gauchesque poets your favourite is Hilario Ascasubi. I remember that you wondered about the Argentinians choosing between *Facundo* and *Martín Fierro*. But you also wondered that, if José Hernández hadn't existed, whether Ascasubi would have been the archetypal Gauchesque poet.

JORGE LUIS BORGES. Well, the types of gaucho that both writers show us are completely different. In *Martín Fierro*'s case, we have what long before, in Chile, Sarmiento had called 'the bad gaucho'. Curiously, he would later be called a delinquent in Ascasubi's *Los mellizos de la Flor* (The Twins of La Flor). But I think we should judge Ascasubi, above all else, by *Paulino Lucero*. The title is already a kind of poem— it reads *Paulino Lucero o los gauchos de la República Argentina y de la República Oriental del Uruguay, cantando y combatiendo hasta derribar al tirano Don Juan Manuel de Rosas y a sus satélites* (Paulino Lucero or the Gauchos of the Argentine Republic and the Eastern Republic of Uruguay, Singing and Fighting until they Knock down the Tyrant Rosas and his Satellites). 'Singing and fighting' is already a poem. Courage is one of *Martín Fierro*'s themes but Martín Fierro's courage is sad and rancorous. On the other hand, there's what we could call a celebration of courage or a happiness about courage. For example:

Let there be a rabid sky
Lovely thing in certain cases
Where walks a man with an urge
To have fun with bullets

Or these lines celebrating Rivera's victory over Echagüe at Cagancha which open:

Love them, my life, the Uruguayans,
Horse tamers without problems.
Long live Rivera, long live Lavalle;
Hold Rosas so he doesn't faint
Those at Cagancha would animate the devil
On any pitch.

Or the celebration of an ephemeral victory of the Unitarians from Corrientes over the Federals from Entre Ríos—that has wordplay that's also a poetic success. That's difficult because usually wordplay is unfortunate, based as it is on the mere chance of similar sounds.

Once again with victory
The strong current rose up.
Ah faithful and patriotic people
Who never surrender.

The Spanish *correntinada* suggests or is justified by *correntada*, meaning 'strong current' and 'Corrientes'. These are followed by lines that are, of course, erotic, about the dance *cielito* which is described in a way as if the words follow the dance. The dancer is Colonel Lucero:

> He took his partner
> Juana Rosa out to dance
> And they begin to mix
> Half a drink with a full rum.

(which suggests intimacy, doesn't it?)

> Ah woman, if your hip
> On your body breaks
> Well, you'd miss it so much
> In every wiggle you made

(meaning, as he courted her)

> that she half lost it
> when Lucero began to swing.

They are mischevious lines (*laughs*) but honest too and reveal that tone of joy, that happiness that Ascasubi felt, an epic happiness. As is evident by the fact that he signed his work in the dance songs as *Aniceto the Cock*. During the Siege of Montevideo, there was a cock on the Argentine flag that he justified, as in this stanza:

> See the mark of the cock
> On the flag
> Of our true fatherland
> Of the 25th of May.

Even this, which is just an epigraph, sounds good.

Ascasubi had seen wars in Uruguay, in Salta and many other regions but what came out best was something that he hadn't seen, something that he had imagined or, even better, dreamt for it doesn't match any historical truth. It's all too vast, and yet there are lines that are more important than what could have been an Indian attack, an attack Ascasubi had never seen. Then he says:

> But when the Indians invaded
> You feel, that's for sure,
> Country bugs and insects
> Fleeing with the horses
> As well as wild dogs,
> Foxes, ostriches, pumas,
> Does, hares and deer
> And rush in panic
> Through the villages

Something that never happened. Then:

> But then, the first
> To announce the novelty
> With utter certainty
> As the Indians advance
> Are the chajá birds
> Hooting chajá chajá in the air.

And the stanza ends admirably with the hooting of the chajá, the southern-crested screamer which its scream is its name in Spanish.

> Then behind the lairs
> That the savage Indians scared

> Far out in the land rises
> Like clouds, the dust
> Pregnant with the uncombed pampas
> As on their strained nags
> Rushing in a hurry
> Charge as they yell
> In crescent moon formations

An epic picture.

FERRARI. It's wonderful.

BORGES. It's wonderful and it has power. Lugones in his *El payador* thought that he had to sacrifice all the other Gauchesque poets in order to exalt Hernández. That was a mistake, because why can't we suppose that there are an indefinite number of good poets which is what really happens. Why should we suppose that supporting Hernández mean sacrificing Ascasubi? It's absurd!

FERRARI. And there's Ascasubi's personality too, full of noble traits.

BORGES. Of course. Ascasubi knew what to write. He saw the gauchos as soldiers, as Unitarian soldiers. That was natural because he too was a Unitarian. Hernández, on the other hand, shows the soldiers as deserters, deserting the Desert Conquest. And, of course, those who speak with such respect for the Desert Conquest believe that our history is best represented by a deserter from that campaign. Curiously, the great battle of the Desert Conquest, the San Carlos battle, was fought in 1872, the year that *Martín Fierro* appeared. Which means that it's absurd to think that it deals with the gaucho— if all the gauchos had deserted, the battle wouldn't have been fought.

There were few gauchos like Martín Fierro in those troops who gave their lives for the cause.

FERRARI. You say, elsewhere, that Ascasubi's love for his country made him risk his life.

BORGES. Yes, it did. I recall that Lugones hadn't read *Paulino Lucero* because he said that Ascasubi's gaucho appears in *Aniceto el gallo*. That book came later and corresponds not to that war but to later ones between Buenos Aires and the Confederation. I have no idea if Lugones read *Paulino Lucero* because he sought out Ascasubi's weaknesses from *Aniceto el gallo* and he did that on purpose. If not, it would be very strange for he hadn't read *Paulino Lucero* or *Santos Vega* from which come those stanzas describing the Indian raids.

FERRARI. Among the details of Ascasubi's life, we remember that he was a soldier . . .

BORGES. He was a soldier, a baker and a printer. He brought the Foundlings' printing press from Córdoba to Salta. He lived a life . . . well, in those times a man had to be many men, as was the case in the United States with Mark Twain who wasn't only Mark Twain the writer but also a river pilot on the Mississippi, a gold-digger in California and a traveller across his country during the Civil War.

FERRARI. Like all the great men from our last century, all of them were many men.

BORGES. Yes, the times demanded this. It's a shame that Ascasubi had to be sacrificed to Hernández's *ad majorem gloriam*. Why not suppose that both could live together, even if they wouldn't have got on politically? Because Ascasubi, like Estanislao del Campo, was a Unitarian and Hernández a Federal. That can be seen in the two references to Rosas in *Martín Fierro*, references that seem to be written by a Federal. He speaks of the stocks and adds:

> The very same in Palermo
> Where they kept men in stocks
> Until they got ill.

'The very same in Palermo', where Rosas had his mansions and his regiments. Then when Martín Fierro isn't paid, an officer says:

> These are not Rosas' times
> Now all are paid.

Then they do not pay him! So Hernández wants to point out that either before the battle of Caseros or after, the gaucho's sad fate is the same. That's the meaning behind the two allusions to Rosas in *Martín Fierro* and both written by a Federal.

FERRARI. As for the descriptions or cruel details of that period, you say that Ascasubi, in his *La refalosa*, was as capable as Echeverría.

BORGES. I think that's true. In *La refalosa*, a thug from the Mazorca in Oribe's troops, that is, the White Party, was sent to threaten Ascasubi. And this wasn't an unreal threat because the Mazorqueros assassinated Florencio Varela during the siege of Montevideo in what's called in Uruguay the 'Great War' or the 'Campaign of the Great War'.

40

Sonnets, Revelations, Travels and Countries

●

OSVALDO FERRARI. Every now and then, as I know you work incessantly, I am keen to ask you what you are doing at the moment, what you are working on at present.

JORGE LUIS BORGES. I am doing too many things as usual. Firstly, a book of verse—I can't say poems—which will be published in Spain and whose title hasn't revealed itself to me yet.

FERRARI. Hasn't revealed itself to you?

BORGES. Yes, because I think that a poet's work is rather passive—one receives mysterious gifts and then tries to give them shape. But it always begins as something alien, as something the ancients called the Muse, the Hebrews, the spirit and Yeats, the Great Memory. Our contemporary mythology prefers less lovely nouns, like the subconscious, the collective subconscious and so on, but it's the same idea—of something outside us. So I have this book and Alianza Editorial in Madrid will probably publish it. Then, I have a book of fantasy stories to be titled *La memoria de Shakespeare* (*Shakespeare's Memory*). I don't know if we have talked about this book—the title story was revealed to me in a sentence from a character in a dream. I lost the rest of the dream but recalled this sentence: 'I will sell you Shakespeare's memory.' The idea of selling is too commercial for me, and 'donate' was a bit pompous, so it was reduced to 'I'll give you Shakespeare's memory.' That is, Shakespeare's personal memory. There'll be other stories in that book, like 'Blue Tigers' which doesn't refer to blue tigers but to something stranger, much stranger, and more stories I'm currently writing.

FERRARI. Won't you tell us more about 'Blue Tigers'?

BORGES. No, I won't. Then, before the year ends, there's *Atlas*, written in collaboration with María and made out of 'collages' or photos taken by María in the most heterogeneous countries across the world—Japan, Iceland, Edinburgh, the United States, South America, Egypt, Italy . . . a deliberately miscellaneous book. These, then, are more or less my projects.

FERRARI. But there's also something about sonnets, I believe?

BORGES. Yes, I'm also compiling an anthology of sonnets. I was rereading the classics when, naturally, I thought of the Argentine poets. For the moment, I dare say, the best sonnets in the Spanish language have been written by Lope de Vega and Enrique Banchs (*laughs*).

FERRARI. It's a risky thesis.

BORGES. It is a rather risky thesis, because one would first think of Quevedo, and Lugones who sounds like Quevedo, and Góngora. It has been almost impossible to find a sonnet by these writers which is free of flaws. In De Vega's or in Banchs' case, though, the sonnet flows from beginning to end, the 14 lines flow and no flaws stall the reader. But in even the famous sonnets by Quevedo, one suddenly finds atrocious lines. For example,

> In his funeral rites, he lighted Vesuvius,
> Partenope and Mongibello Trinacria.

It's hard to find anything uglier, except perhaps in Lugones:

> The curved sky filled with bats
> in the manner of a Chinese screen

It's just as flawed, it even seems to be competing with Quevedo's. Góngora, even in his best sonnets, also has flaws but they are decorative flaws. And he constantly appeals to a mythology that he doesn't seem to believe in—I'm not even sure if it's right to use that term. For example, it's fine that a Greek poem mentions Phoebus instead of the 'sun' because they could believe in Phoebus; but in Góngora's case, it's purely decorative—he decidedly wasn't a devotee of pagan gods; he referred to them as an inheritance from the classics though I'm not sure if he had the right to receive that inheritance. Thus, I am compiling that anthology and lines from Etchbarne, whose name has been forgotten, fill my memory. One of his sonnets opens thus:

> Who knows what will become of the farmhouse
> in the parish of Magdalena
> rough country with the sea in the distance.

It's written with great emotion.

FERRARI. It's lovely. You often remember it?

BORGES. Yes, and the parish of Magdalena . . . because if he'd said 'the parish of Vicente López' it would sound ridiculous, wouldn't it? (*Laughs.*)

FERRARI. It would have no feeling, yet 'of Magdalena' does. Now, as ever, apart from your literary works, there are your travels.

BORGES. Yes, there are my travels, but travelling must stimulate, especially if you are not looking for it, that is, if you do not think 'I am in Rome and must seek Rome in Rome,' according to the famous translation that Quevedo made of Joachim du Bellay's sonnet which in turn was inspired by some lines in Latin by Ianus Vitalis. Well, it's one of poetry's traditional themes. Quevedo also says, 'And only what's fugitive lasts,' that is, the Tiber river lasts and Rome's monuments do not.

FERRARI. Of course.

BORGES. I believe that Vitalis was the first to state this and then Du Bellay in a sonnet admirably turned into Spanish by Quevedo and then admirably turned into English by Ezra Pound. Quevedo says, 'You look for Rome in Rome, oh pilgrim / and Rome in Rome you do not find' and then, 'Corpse was what boasted walls / and tomb of itself the Aventine.' I'm not sure 'corpse' is apt, but in the end one resigns oneself to it, doesn't one?

FERRARI. You have, coincidentally, talked of Rome just before receiving the doctorate honoris causa which you will be given on 12 October by Rome University .

BORGES. Yes, I have in fact written a sonnet about the honours given to me by universities as diverse as those I can mention—I have been awarded a doctorate in Crete, both from a new university and an ancient one; a doctorate from the famous mediaeval University of Cambridge in England; one from the University of San Juan where, of course, one can sense Sarmiento's great shadow, for me the greatest Argentine of all. And now I am to receive this distinction in Rome, which needs no commentary or explanation, does it? It's obviously the world's most famous city.

FERRARI. There's another prize, I believe?

BORGES. Yes, in Miami. Yes, how odd, Miami in Florida. Well, that's fine, the Deep South.

FERRARI. And you have something in Spain before you go to Rome?

BORGES. Yes, in Seville. Of course, I lived for a year in Mallorca and felt in some way Andalusian, there in the country of my distant ancestors. Curiously, in Madrid they thought I was Andalusian for I spoke with a slight Andalusian accent there, among the poets of the happily forgotten Ultraist group in Seville, which, in the end, was one of Assens' jokes. So, in my 85th year, I still have projected journeys and books. Although, in my case, the two go together—journeys are stimulants for writing, especially if you do not seek them but let them seek you.

FERRARI. The journeys in this case are not only projected but a fact.

BORGES. Yes, they are a fact too. I have just written a sonnet—I have to polish it—which will be published in Montevideo, I think. It's a version of a theme which deals with happiness. Despite my slight shame at reaching my 85th year and my blindness, I feel happier or more serene than when I was young. I mean, than when I tried uninterestingly to be unhappy. Now, unhappiness finds us—we do not have to look for it.

FERRARI. It's very interesting what you say about feeling happier than when you were young. It's paradoxical.

BORGES. Well, no. I believe that the young are easily unhappy. Of course, passions run high and among them there's despair too, isn't there? (*Laughs.*) To repeat the sentence from *Julius Caesar*: 'Caesar despairs' and the Caesar of literature, not history, answers 'He who never has hoped cannot despair.' Well, I go on hoping.

FERRARI. That is precisely what I think serenity is.

BORGES. Yes, I think so, to hope with too much impatience, of course.

FERRARI. Clearly, this is a late passion. Perhaps you had it when you were young but now it's more obvious. I mean, a passion for travel which goes beyond numbers—there's no 85 or birthdays, no limits. A passion for travel is very important.

BORGES. Yes, for a long time I resisted travelling, even during my summer holidays. I stayed in Buenos Aires all December, January and February, during that time when everyone escapes the city. I stayed in Buenos Aires despite the summer which I hate. But, at that time, I had sight, I could read and write. Now these activities have been banned, except when someone is there to dictate to or to read to me. But, in the end, I have to accept that the fact of living implies accepting conditions and that condition is obligatory. I cannot act in any other way. It would be sad to forego the pleasures of reading and writing because I am blind.

FERRARI. There's no reason to do that.

BORGES. No, no reason as I now have young friends like you who generously help me.

FERRARI. Well, it's you who is generous, as always. But you have confirmed what I was saying about your passion for travel increasing in your later years.

BORGES. I know that I cannot see countries but I can sense them. So I travel. Also, people are so good, so indulgent, abroad. I have been translated into many languages and those who have read these translations can think, 'Well, this is not so good but maybe the original is acceptable.' So it's convenient that I am read in translation for people are more indulgent with me. All the mistakes are attributed to the translator and all the best passages to the author. Perhaps, in fact, the best parts are due to the translator and the mistakes due to the author, but it doesn't matter. That unhappy Italian pun '*Traduttore, traditore*' makes people think poorly of all translators and well of the original (*both laugh*).

FERRARI. In Spanish there wouldn't be a rhyme.

BORGES. '*Traductor, traidor*', no. However, it's usually quoted in Italian. '*Traduttore, traditore*', yes, it's nice in Italian because the two words are almost identical.

FERRARI. That's true. Now, I have always said that you created the genre of conjecture. But with your life you have created yet another genre—paradox. Because, for example, to travel and not see the countries is a magnificent paradox. Although when we read the poems that reflect your travels we come to realize that you do 'see', just in another way.

BORGES. Inevitably I see them in an incorrect way for I have them described to me and then I imagine them and that imagination persists in my memory. I'm sure it's wrong because it would be very rare that a landscape or a place could be conveyed through the medium of words. In fact, it's impossible. And it's a mistake made by many writers. Groussac spends four or five pages describing the Niagara Falls but I do not think that one actually sees anything in those pages for vision is something complete and instantaneous. On the other hand, description is necessarily a sequence, given that language is successive. Even a memory conveyed by pages in sequence would certainly not be similar to an instantaneous image.

FERRARI. However, there are poets and writers who have spoken of the sea without seeing it and done so in a marvellous way.

BORGES. Yes, Coleridge is a case in point. Clearly the sea of Coleridge's imagination is far more vast than the actual sea. I recall that Assens— it's always a pleasure recalling him—wrote an ode to the sea. I read it and at the end conveyed my admiration for that poem dedicated to the sea. He told me, 'I hope to see it sometime'—he had never seen the sea.

FERRARI. That confirms it then.

BORGES. Yes, that could also be proof of Plato's archetypes, that he in some way had seen the sea or knew the sea as a concept, of course, without ever having seen it.

41

Ethics and Culture

●

OSVALDO FERRARI. Throughout your life, your admiration for Sarmiento's *Facundo* has been a form of faith in culture, or so it seems to me.

JORGE LUIS BORGES. Yes, culture, it seems to me, is our sole salvation. I wrote my story 'Brodie's Report' around the theme of a rudimentary culture needing to be saved from barbarity. At the start one comes across a minimal culture; then at the end, the Yahoos, men like monkeys, from Book Four of Swift's famous parable *Gulliver's Travels*. Of course, all culture is more or less rudimentary but we must try to save it. That's the thesis of *Facundo—Civilización y barbarie*. It's not that Sarmiento thought that civilization was perfect. He believed in progress; but he also believed that civilization, that imperfect culture of the Unitarians, had to be saved from barbarity or the Federal's inclination to barbarity. Unfortunately, *Facundo* hasn't been chosen as a classic that corresponds to *Martín Fierro* and its gaucho cult of what's primitive and uncultured. We made that decision and perhaps it's too late to change our minds. But had we chosen Sarmiento's *Facundo* as our book, given that the Holy Scriptures have disappeared—it's understood that every country has to have its book—our history would have, doubtless, been different. Although *Martín Fierro* may be superior in a literary sense to *Facundo*.

FERRARI. You always talk of ethics, you've told me that having ethics is even more crucial—as Kant saw it—than having a religion.

BORGES. Religion can only be justified on the basis of ethics. On the other hand, ethics, as Stevenson said, is an instinct. It's not necessary to define ethics—ethics is not the Ten Commandments. It's something we feel every time we act. At the end of the day, we will, doubtless, have made many ethical decisions. And we will have had to choose—I am simplifying the theme—between good and evil. And when we have chosen good, we know we have chosen good; when we have chosen evil, we know that too. What's crucial is to judge each act for itself and not for its consequences. The consequences of any act are infinite, they branch into the future and, in the end, become equivalent or complimentary. Thus, to judge an act for its consequences seems to me to be immoral.

FERRARI. Now, in the month of your 85th year . . .

BORGES. Don't remind me of such sad things. I have let myself live—I am idle and a daydreamer and 85 years have passed. When I was young I thought about suicide, but not now—it's too late. At any moment . . . history will decide it.

FERRARI. To me, it seems more happy than sad . . .

BORGES. Yes, I am sure I am happier now than when I was young. When I was young, I sought to be unhappy for aesthetic and dramatic reasons. I wanted to be Prince Hamlet or Raskolnikov or Byron or Poe or Baudelaire, but not now. Today, I am resigned to being who I am. And, to summarize: I do not know if I have attained happiness—no one does—but I have sometimes attained a kind of serenity and that's a lot. Also, seeking serenity seems to me to be a more reasonable ambition than seeking happiness. Perhaps serenity is a kind of happiness. Now, I am resigned to life, to blindness. I have ended up resigning myself to longevity which is another evil. I do not think there's a day in my life without at least a moment of serenity—that is enough. Although the dreams that visit me at night leave me in a state of panic rather than happiness.

FERRARI. Borges, in your serenity, you can possibly enlighten me, given that we have talked about ethics and culture, about the importance of an ethical attitude to culture.

BORGES. I do not believe that culture can be understood without ethics. It seems to me that an educated person has to be ethical. For example, it's commonly supposed that good people are fools and intelligent ones are wicked. But I do not believe that—indeed, I believe the opposite. Wicked people are usually also naive. Someone acts in an evil way because he cannot imagine how his behaviour might affect another. So I think that there's some innocence in evil and some intelligence in goodness. Further, goodness, to be perfect—though I do not believe that anyone attains perfect goodness—has to be intelligent. For example, a good and not-too-intelligent person can say disagreeable things to others because he realizes that they are disagreeable. On the other hand, a person, in order to be good, must be intelligent—if not, his intelligence would be . . .

imperfect, he would be saying disagreeable things to others without realizing it.

FERRARI. You have said that before and it seems very important to me.

BORGES. Yes, I identify wickedness with stupidity and goodness with intelligence. But people do not often do this. They always suppose that good people are simple-minded. No, a person can be good and complex and a person can be evil and extremely simple, as is the case with criminals.

FERRARI. Your vision of all this already existed with the Greeks. They too held this idea.

BORGES. Everything is already there with the Greeks. In English you say, 'The Greeks had a word for it.' That implies that the Greeks have thought of it all, in the West, of course. In the West, those who began to think, and perhaps thought everything, were the Greeks. And we have Rome, but Rome is a Hellenistic extension—Rome cannot be conceived without Greece though one can easily conceive of Greece without Rome. Greece came before and the Greeks were cultured at a time when the Romans were barbarians, when the rest of the West was barbarous.

FERRARI. Borges, it seems important to me to highlight what we mentioned earlier, because the identification of culture with ethics could be a definite way for us.

BORGES. Or with intelligence, yes.

FERRARI. A culture with an ethical basis.

BORGES. It's indispensable, because if it's not like that then what use is it? For cruelty?

FERRARI. For confusion, perhaps.

BORGES. Yes, for confusion.

FERRARI. You know that one of the fashions of our time is confusion, and it's often intentional.

BORGES. Yes, it seems that today chaos has become very successful, hasn't it? In literature it has been deliberately sought out. Dadaism, for example and, in some ways, Expressionism too. And Surrealism. Yes, confusion has been sought out. Also, everywhere there's a cult of evil and crime. But that has illustrious precedents, doesn't it? It's enough to think of Shakespeare or Dostoyevsky. We can see how assassination attracted them.

FERRARI. Well, there's an authentic way to live evil and good. I mean, if it is lived authentically then it's authentic evil and authentic good. But in our confusion and inauthenticity, our lived evil and lived good have grown confused and inauthentic too.

BORGES. It's chaos, in its most confused sense—disorder and nothing else.

FERRARI. We will continue with your serenity helping us see clearly in our confused times.

BORGES. Yes, of course.

42

Two Trips to Japan

●

OSVALDO FERRARI. Ulises Petit de Murat comments that when you returned from Japan, you described to him places you visited and people you met with the same fidelity as a specialist of that country. That reveals that you, in some way, made an initial discovery *in situ* and then continued to discover Japan on another trip.

JORGE LUIS BORGES. I made two journeys to Japan and I owe this to chance, if chance exists. María teaches Spanish to Japanese business-men. We went to Ezeiza to bid farewell to one of them. The plane was delayed as usual, and we had to somehow pass an hour. We drank coffee and this gentleman asked me if I would be interested in getting to know Japan. I answered that I wasn't completely mad, that naturally I had a great interest in Japan. We also talked about Buddhism. And he said, 'Well, I'll see what I can do.' After a few months, an invitation arrived from the Japan Foundation, asking me to spend a month in Japan. It seemed, and still seems, incredible. The month turned into five weeks, we visited seven cities, we got to know holy places, gardens, lakes, mountains and all this was because of a book I wrote with Alicia

Jurado, *What is Buddhism?*, which was translated into Japanese. Perhaps to prove that Westerners knew nothing about Buddhism (*laughs*). That book was written from second- and third-hand knowledge, but with integrity. I had the curious sensation that I'd never had before, despite being educated in Switzerland: How odd, I thought, I am in a civilized country. You can sleep there with your street door open . . . then there's the politeness of the people where it's taken for granted that the other is always right. Now I am trying to find my way into that curious, but perhaps not lovely, labyrinth that is the Japanese language. What I have learnt up to now is more than alarming. For example, Japanese adjectives are conjugated. In Spanish, one says *alto* (high) and that can refer to the Colossus of Rhodes or perhaps to a future observatory. In Japanese, on the other hand, the adjective is conjugated. There's a root and that root varies according to whether one refers to things in the past, in the future or in the present, with another form for conjecture—the subjunctive—which makes everything very hard. Then, there are nine ways of counting, there are words for long things and cylindrical ones. For example, this walking stick, a spade, an arrow. There's another system to count animals but that system splits into two—for one cannot count mice with the same word used for counting bulls— and yet another for abstractions.

FERRARI. There's a code for everything.

BORGES. Yes, and the word varies according to what is being counted. For example, *ichi* is one but that is used in mathematical operations. To say 'one minute' you do not say *ichi* but *ippun*, and 'three minutes' returns to the first form *pun* (*sanpun*). That's repeated for four but four is *yon*. Then it changes for 'five minutes' and is *gofun*. That is, plurals change according to the number of objects and the numbers for objects change according to the objects. All this tells me that, as I study Japanese, I am entering into an infinite adventure. I felt something similar when I was studying Anglo-Saxon. I thought: Well, I will never learn it but there's something enchanting in the fact that I'm involved in an infinite adventure. That is, in the fact of knowing that that adventure is doomed to failure, like Milton's Satan who knew he was fighting the All Powerful and that made his war heroic because he was doomed to fail. But it's more heroic if you know it beforehand. So I will continue to study Japanese, knowing that I will never know it. I wrote a poem when I began to study Anglo-Saxon, with a title that shocked many people, 'On Starting to Study Anglo-Saxon Grammar'. I was told that couldn't be a title of a poem—but why not? Why not suppose that that circumstance isn't also poetic? So I sought another solution. I said to myself that the soul, in a secret way, knows that it's immortal and for that reason we can undertake any enterprise. If we do not finish it in this life, we will do so in another one or in many others. Well, I don't really believe that. I hope to be deleted but, if death doesn't do so, I will take up another adventure that could be just as interesting as the one in this life.

FERRARI. Apart from the Japanese language, can we look at Japanese literature chronologically or historically like we do with Western literatures?

BORGES. Well, the best has been done, in that sense. But I think that the historical idea of literature is a recent idea and that it could disappear. In any case, histories of literature are interesting. I don't know if this has been done in Japan. The historicist tendency is one of many Western tendencies. Japanese poetry is interested, above all, in stopping the moment, fixing it.

FERRARI. Is it then Faustian?

BORGES. No, just a moment and nothing more. And that moment is saved for ever if the poem is felicitous. Worrying about time exists only in the sense of every haiku, made up of seven, five and seven syllables, somehow indicating the seasons of the year. I've been told that there are thick volumes in which one can find, for example, 500 ways of indicating autumn, 500 ways of indicating summer, et cetera. And the reader accepts those 500 ways, with the seven–five–seven syllables of Japanese poetry. The fact of using them, these commonplaces, is not thought of as a mistake—they feel that originality corresponds to vanity and so it's better that a poem is not original. It's enough that it is eternal—that is crucial. So that one can take any of those ways of indicating the seasons or take any line that one wants from another poet—it doesn't matter; they believe that poetry is eternal.

This is close to the Hebrew concept which consists of taking four very different books that presuppose different worlds and correspond to different periods and to suppose that the spirit has written them all. Although, of course, what can the Book of Job have in common with Genesis? Or the Song of Song with the Book of Judges? Absolutely nothing. But it's supposed that the same spirit dictated them to different scribes. Japanese poetry has the same idea—that it doesn't matter if the poet is original. What counts is whether what he writes is beautiful. That is far more important.

FERRARI. The Muse or the spirit continues to preside over Japanese inspiration.

BORGES. Yes. On the other hand, Wilde said, 'If it was not for classical forms, we would all be at the mercy of geniuses.' Which is what happens now (*both laugh*). Everyone is a genius—but they are mere geniuses, merely extravagant.

FERRARI. The classicism in their works hasn't been replaced.

BORGES. No, I do not think so. At the same time, it's taken for granted that every writer wants his place in literary history, so that what counts is to innovate and found a school. And that's what we see in this country. For example, the poets who have founded a school are remembered. On the other hand, poets who have simply been perfect, like Enrique Banchs in *La urna* or Arturo Capdevila in *Aulo Gelio*, have been forgotten because they are not leaders of a school and have not influenced anyone. It doesn't matter that their compositions are simply perfect or very beautiful. No, that doesn't count. What's important is to figure as chief of any old sect, even if it's nonsensical. For example, if I write a novel about postmen, that novel could be awful but, who knows, that novel could be the start of a school and may lead to many people becoming postmen and then I would feature in literary history. Which is what happened to Bartolomé Hidalgo. His work is rather weak, but out of it arose Hilario Ascasubi, Estanislao del Campo and José Hernández. And Mitre pointed this out in a letter to Hernández when he said, 'Hidalgo will always be your Homer.' But he said it against Hernández and I think that was a mistake—because what's to stop a poet from being influenced by another? We talked about this when we discussed Poe and his influence.

FERRARI. Yes, but returning to Japan, we have always been told that the most crucial wisdom comes from the East, now, in Japan . . .

BORGES. And with the lovely metaphor *Ex Oriente Lux*?

FERRARI. Yes, but in Japan's case it's very particular because it seems to have chosen the most modern line in Western development and then given it back to us as wisdom.

BORGES. Yes, and at the same time they embody Western culture better that any Westerners.

FERRARI. Precisely.

BORGES. For example, all the instruments made in Japan are not only better but also aesthetic. For instance, a camera, a telescope, a tape recorder, a Japanese computer—they are all superior.

FERRARI. They are perfecting Western ideas.

BORGES. Yes, they are perfecting Western ideas and I hope that this positive influence continues. I went to this completely civilized country very late but I am looking forward to returning. Also because it's, of course, pleasing to be surrounded by people who are never aggressive. That is ethically irreproachable. Also, though I cannot see them I do not believe that I am unworthy of Japan's gardens, holy shrines and seas. I feel them which is more intimate than seeing them.

FERRARI. Borges, we will continue to get your news from that advanced civilization and hope that it can be helpful to us.

BORGES. Well, I hope so too.

43

Evaristo Carriego, Milonga *and Tango*

●

OSVALDO FERRARI. You have said that our writers, our men of culture, our intellectuals of the early nineteenth century, tended to think of themselves as honorary Frenchmen.

JORGE LUIS BORGES. Yes, that's true. Of course, everyone knew French—not perhaps to converse in but, more crucially, to read. To enjoy French literature in French. Although they may have failed to hold a conversation, they wouldn't fail while reading it which seems to me a more essential activity.

FERRARI. You particularly refer to a significant person among us— Evaristo Carriego.

BORGES. Yes, Evaristo Carriego. The last time I saw him he had started studying French but, of course, it was very basic because when we said goodbye, he kissed my mother's hand and said, 'Au revoir, Madame' and it was taken for granted that this was a linguistic feat (*laughs*). He had always felt a love for France, he had read Dumas' novels in translation and wanted, like everyone, to get closer to

France. Now, it's a pity that French has been replaced, or studying French, has been replaced by English, studying English. I love English a lot and perhaps owe more to England than to France, but I think that this fact is deplorable because when French was studied it was done so in terms of its culture and literature. On the other hand, the English now being studied is not studied in relation to Emerson or De Quincey but in terms of business—it's studied for commercial purposes. In that sense, I do not know how far we have moved from one language to another. Some people have assured me that we have moved from French to English and now from English to ignorance, which could be the nadir, couldn't it? (*Laughs*)

FERRARI. The Buddhist nadir, for example, which tends towards emptiness or nothingness as its aim (*both laugh*). But there's another characteristic to Carriego that seems important to me. He was also, as you have said, the first observer of our suburbs, the outskirts.

BORGES. Yes, but it was perhaps unfair to say that because I think that popular theatre came first. It could have been good or bad but it did try. You would have to consult, perhaps in the shape of a thesis, Vacarezza of Villa Crespo's dates with Carriego of Palermo's dates, to know how many blocks we would have to cover to discover the literary outskirts. But Carriego did it deliberately because, as Marcelo de Mazo told me, he owed it to his barrio, his patch, and that can be seen in some of his compositions. And he was Almafuerte's disciple. How odd that Almafuerte, a man of genius and perhaps the most local of our writers . . . but when he deliberately tried to be local, it didn't work. For example, *El Misionero*, *Confiteor Deo*, *Paralelas* are splendid pages. On the other hand, when he deliberately tried to write *milongas*, they came out badly. I recall that deplorable song:

> Here I sit down to sing with whoever sits with me,
> the best, the great *milonga*
> the one that will last.

It's not very memorable, is it? Now, he has some lines which may not be beautiful but they are true:

> There's no job less exquisite
> than the job of living.

FERRARI. That's better.

BORGES. That is better but, unfortunately, there are two lines before it that say, 'Much mud has to be beaten up' (which is decidedly ugly) 'on the way to the cemetery', but this is padding for what follows: 'There's no job less exquisite / than the job of living.' And that's true. I mean, we have all more or less stained ourselves . . .

Well, Carriego decided to sing about his barrio, but he moved to Palermo around 1902 and I think that the Palermo that Carriego sang belonged to the century before. When he wrote 'El alma del suburbio' (The soul of the suburbs), which is included in *Misas herejes* (Heretical Masses), his first book, Palermo was no longer that barrio. He wrote from memories of his childhood in Palermo. So his Palermo was tinged with nostalgia and melancholy; it wasn't exactly as it had been. On the other hand, in his other book, he describes a middle-class Palermo which I knew—not the merely poor Palermo although no doubt poverty existed. I remember that my father asked Carriego why he spoke so much abut tenements when the tenements belonged more to the centre than the outskirts. It's natural, for land is worth more in the centre and, anyhow, the centre is full of tenements. Upto 15 years ago there was one opposite my house: Maipú and Charcas, that was painted yellow. And Barletta, for example, was born in the tenement called Five Corners. He used to say, 'I am a petty thug from Five Corners,' which was Libertad and Juncal where Quintana avenue begins. I remember another one, clearly not in the outskirts, opposite the house where Casares was born on Quintana Avenue 174. There were tenements all over the city. Now, in La Boca, they have been far cleverer—instead of making poverty vanish, they have exploited it. So now it's a prosperous barrio thanks to its publicized poverty, perhaps.

FERRARI. On the other hand, there was something in Carriego that you compare with what happened to tango.

BORGES. Yes, that's true.

FERRARI. A way that poetry has of getting close to daily unhappiness, illness, disappointment.

BORGES. Well, that means that he was following the city or country's evolution because the *milonga* was somewhat happier, more valiant. The first tango is also called 'From the Old Guard'. Then, Carlos Gardel came along with that melancholic tendency. And, curiously, in France they think that tango came to be a middle-class dance, not a popular one. Here it wasn't seen that way either, it was seen as belonging to brothels, as sentimental. Proof of this is that, in the tenements, they never danced the tango because people knew where tango was born. Lugones, in *El Payador*, from around 1915, talks of tango as 'that reptile from the brothels'—a fine phrase that reveals everything, from the origin of tango to its sinuous steps. Buenos Aires came to be seen as a sinister zone, that is, Junín and Lavalle, which I think is now Jewish. That was the brothel centre of Buenos Aires. But in Rosario, where prostitution was far more visible than in Buenos Aires, it's supposed that tango was born in the quarter known as Sunchales, today known as North Rosario. And in Montevideo, according to Vicente Rossi, tango was born around 1880 in the academies (as dance halls were then called) in Yerbal Street, the south of the old city but close to the centre. That was the brothel quarter. But, in the end, what's important about this? Everyone agrees about the date, 1880, and about the instruments, a piano, a flute and a violin, which confirms that it wasn't popular. When I was a boy, you would see someone tuning a guitar on every corner. But Carriego always talks of the guitar and not those other instruments.

FERRARI. Not even of the *bandoneón*?

BORGES. No, the *bandoneón* came much later and arrived in a quarter that was a bit foreign. I think someone told me it was Almagro but it would more likely have been La Boca because there was nothing different about Almagro. The instrument was German and in German it's called *Schiffklavier*, a piano on a ship, not exactly an accordion.

FERRARI. No, it's far less melancholic than an accordion.

BORGES. Yes, I know little about those things but I do know that the popular instrument was the guitar. And now that I've mentioned the guitar, I'm going to tell you about a fact about the origin of the word 'guitar'—the origin of this humble and everyday guitar is *zither*. You can hear that they are assonants—*zither* and guitar sound almost the same, don't they? Well, stringed instruments come from central Asia and then spread around the world and led to such diverse ones as the harp, the guitar, the violin and the lyre.

FERRARI. But do you think it's important to differentiate two periods in tango, that of the *milonga* and the other?

BORGES. Yes, *milonga* would be what we call today old-guard tango, a phrase used then, of course. Well, because the quarter today called Palermo Viejo was Palermo Nuevo when I was a boy. It's located near Plaza Italia, that intermediary region between what continues to be called Palermo and Villa Crespo. I believe it was called Villa Malcolm then though I don't know why. There must have been some Scottish gentleman . . . I don't think it was named after Shakespeare's character. Yes, Villa Malcolm but that's no longer in use. Other quarters have vanished. For example, a rough quarter between Saavedra and Villa Urquiza was called 'Siberia'. Not long ago I spoke to a driver who said to me, 'Yes, I was born in Siberia but I never tell anyone'— because it wasn't seen as a proper place. But the name 'Siberia' is a good one for a place like that which is, of course, somewhat desolate. And between Urquiza and Saavedra there were many empty plots, a somewhat ambiguous zone.

FERRARI. Still, within that second period in which tango became sad or melancholic, we note that in the city there was a form of energy similar to tango but which is now lost. Like the city's very rhythm.

BORGES. I do not know. What I do know is that when I hear a tango I can or cannot like it but my body follows it. I was taken one night in Córdoba to hear a concert by that man Piazzolla. And there I said to my companion 'I want to hear tangos' because none had been played. Otherwise, I was going to return to my hotel. 'What do you mean?' I was told, 'they played tangos all evening!' But my body did not recognize them—they were not tangos. I think that he says the same, that he plays the music of Buenos Aires though I don't know what he means by that but they're not tangos. His titles do not derive from tangos. For example, one is called *Lunfardo*—tangos were not called *Lunfardo*, they were called *La garúa*, *El comisario*, those kinds of names. But *Lunfardo*—never.

FERRARI. It's more like a title from someone who is researching tango.

BORGES. *Lunfardo* referred earlier to delinquents and thieves and then it was applied to the slang that supposedly came from there.

FERRARI. Borges, we must inevitably come back another time to Carriego and tango.

BORGES. Yes, why not.

44

Scandinavian Mythology and Anglo-Saxon Epics

●

OSVALDO FERRARI. In a fragment, which may refer to you or to one of your characters, you speak of the cult of the North, a cult that led you to Iceland.

JORGE LUIS BORGES. Yes, when I say the North I am referring, above all, to the Scandinavian north. The story of this cult is straightforward. My father gifted me a copy of the *Volsunga Saga* translated into English by William Morris. I read that poem which has the same plot as the *Nibelungenlied* but which was written earlier and which retains thosee mythological characteristics that were lost in the later German version. Anyway, I read all that and was very moved by the stories of Sigurd, the Rhine gold, Brunhild and then Attila. How odd, Attila was a character added to the German tradition. And when Bede in his ecclesiastical history *Gentis Anglorum* meant to say that the Saxons were of German stock, he says, 'from the same stock as the Danes', that is, the Scandinavians, Prussians and Huns. Moreover, in the Elder Edda there's a song, Attli or Attila's song, which was written, amazingly, in Greenland. There were, then, Scandinavians who wrote a song about their traditions, heroic stories and Attila's song added from the German tradition. Well, my father gave me that book and I was duly amazed and asked him for more books on Scandinavian mythology. So he then gave me a book I still have, a manual of Scandinavian mythology taken from the Younger Edda. With María, we have translated the Younger Edda's first book, *Gylfaginning* (*Gylfi's Hallucination*), not long ago. It's the first manual of Scandinavian mythology that exists, written in the twelfth century.

FERRARI. And Snorri Sturluson accompanied you in that work?

BORGES. Yes, exactly. Then I read those two books and after, ah, yes, I read about the *Nibelungenlied* in an article by Carlyle. Then, I can't recall what took me to the Scandinavian north again.

FERRARI. Perhaps your father's English library?

BORGES. Yes, perhaps, but I'm not sure. I do know that I have returned to that theme and made not three journeys but, as Morris would say, three pilgrimages to Iceland. It's a beautiful island, lying very close to the pole. I had the chance to talk to a priest of the ancient pagan gods, a man María described as having a young face but a white beard, a giant, as they all are in Iceland, a shepherd with a flock of over a hundred sheep and who celebrates the summer solstice. The BBC filmed that celebration. Of course, the English also worshipped those gods once upon a time. I was moved to be with someone who worshipped the cult of those gods, gods once worshipped in England, in Holland, in Germany and across Scandinavia. Perhaps there are only some 300 faithful left, all very ignorant people who, doubtless, ignore the mythology and only retain the names of the gods. I was moved by all this and think that I cried. I cry easily—not about matters that make me sad but that fill me with emotion, a bit like that character in Lugones' story who said, 'And he cried over glory.'

FERRARI. That's a nice phrase. Your meeting with that pagan priest was completely unexpected?

BORGES. Yes, completely unexpected. I was talking to the vicar of Borgafiords when he asked me, 'Have you met the heathen priest?' I said, 'What do you mean?' And he said, 'Well, the one who still venerates the heathen gods.' So I went to visit him in a hut, a very simple place with sheep bones on shelves, many bones.

FERRARI. Instead of books.

BORGES. Yes, I do not believe that he could read. A very simple and ignorant man. I know he was celibate so his role cannot be hereditary. I guess he was picked by the faithful. The faithful come from all parts of the island . . . Iceland is quite vast. I suppose he was picked by the faithful who are all shepherds and fishermen, that is, humble people. Not learned men attempting a nationalist revival. They are simply people who have returned to that ancient past.

FERRARI. Your continuous speculations are infectious . . . now, even I am speculating . . .

BORGES. It's the most sure way—only speculation is certain (*both laugh*), all the rest is chance, isn't it?

FERRARI. Of course.

BORGES. All we have is chance and speculation.

FERRARI. In that case, my speculation is whether, besides your father's library, Geneva was another stage that favoured your cult of the North.

BORGES. Yes, it was precisely in Geneva that I read the other sagas, again in English in the Everyman's Library versions. I read *Egilskalla-grimsson*'s saga and *Njaal*'s saga, called 'the Njulla' by the Scandina-vians. And I was impressed by two things: one, it seems that it was the Icelanders who invented or discovered the circumstantial traits—because there are many—and I believe that they realized that these traits could be pathetic. And two, the epic spirit that animated the sagas. This epic spirit has always moved me. I have been more moved by the epic than by the lyric and the elegy.

FERRARI. Well, we see there your affinity with the North.

BORGES. Yes, that's true. The epic moves me greatly in all literature, in all languages. Sentimentality displeases me. Possibly because I am sentimental and not epic, I like the epic and do not like sentimen-tality (*both laugh*). I tend to be sentimental but have never been epic, have I? (*Laughs.*)

FERRARI. Another speculation.

BORGES. Another speculation, yes.

FERRARI. But your cult of the North seems to me to be mainly a cult of the literature of the North.

BORGES. Well, no. Writers as well as navigators and adventurers.

FERRARI. Of course.

BORGES. If you think that they discovered America a few centuries before the rest of Europe—I don't know how far they discovered it for they had no sense of nationality nor of religion. For example, they could worship Thor but there were no Thor missionaries. They were individualists and, as you know, the discovery of America was made in the name of Spain, Portugal and the Catholic faith. They were missionaries, officials and soldiers. That wasn't the case with the Vikings who were adventurers. For example, a Viking kingdom was founded in Dublin city and there was a Danish kingdom in Ireland and another Danish one in Yorkshire, but those kings never thought of themselves as, nor insisted on being, Danish.

FERRARI. And they didn't invoke Scandinavian mythology.

BORGES. No, not that either. They practised it. Now, that mythology has a curious trait. In Christianity or in Islam, for example, there are devotees of a god, a god is seen as ruling them. But among the Scandinavians no one said that so-and-so is a devotee of Thor or of Odin. They said, 'He's Odin's friend,' 'He's Thor's friend.' That is, they had a friendly relationship until things turned sour . . .

FERRARI. And I suppose they became enemies.

BORGES. Yes, they became that god's enemy, they could even damage their idols' images which I guess would have been very simple.

FERRARI. You ascribe a special ethic to the North in general, perhaps linked to Protestantism.

BORGES. I'm not sure that I would dare to say that there's something essentially immoral in the Catholic faith. I think the idea of confession and absolution is an immoral one because if I have committed a sin then no one else can absolve me—I should absolve myself. But if I commit a sin, if I am guilty and then I recite an x number of the Lord's Prayer or Hail Marys, I cannot undo what I have done. To me, the idea of the confession is essentially immoral. I'm not sure if that can be transmitted although I think all sorts of things are transmitted by radio, a small heresy of mine . . .

FERRARI. Do you think it transmits a kind of stupor?

BORGES. I don't think so but it could give rise to it without any qualms.

FERRARI. You always think that we reach truth through dialogue, so that could also be . . .

BORGES. Part of the dialogue, yes, of course, it can be part of the dialogue. But I don't usually believe it is. There's an ethic in Protestant countries that is missing in Catholic ones. This could be because Catholics perhaps do not take their faith seriously . . . it's rather more like a series of rituals, of ceremonies, of habits. On the other hand, of course, in the case of Protestants, it's taken for granted—each one has his Bible, and it's supposed that each one has his light, as Wycliffe said in the fourteenth century. Every reader of the Bible has a kind of light that allows him to interpret the Bible. It's the opposite of the Church's idea that it takes charge of interpretations.

FERRARI. However, over later years, this ethic that one attributes to the Protestants seems to have become impaired.

BORGES. Ah, unfortunately, yes. I am not religious, so there's no way I wish to become a Protestant missionary. My ancestors were—many of them—Methodist preachers. Methodism insists, above all else, on ethics and not on theology. On the other hand, Calvinism insists on theology, with predestination, for example. Calvinism's two capitals were Geneva where the Frenchman John Calvin preached and then Edinburgh where John Knox preached. Those two cities were similar, both very attractive, although, naturally, I prefer Geneva.

FERRARI. Thor of the North would be, according to your speculation, brother to Hector of the South. That might explain the necessity to merge the North with the South.

BORGES. There's something pathetic about the North's desire to link itself with the South—in the end, with the *Aeneid* for they did not know *The Iliad*. It's just that *The Iliad* beamed its light upon the North. We have that ancient Saxon epic of *Beowulf* but all speculations about *Beowulf* have changed ever since, in that intricate and tedious poem— the North's first epic, for Anglo-Saxon literature came before Scandinavian literature—in its 3,000-odd lines—I cannot recall exactly how many—someone discovered three lines from *The Aeneid*. Two are combinations and the other one is an almost literal translation. This changed everything. We can imagine that the author of Beowulf had read *The Aeneid* and then decided to write a Germanic *Aeneid* and so he wrote *Beowulf* in England. But the author took Scandinavian legends, and all his characters are Danes or Swedes. At the time, there was no idea that a writer had to write about contemporary events or local issues. On the contrary, what was distant was prestigious and perhaps there was a kind of nostalgia among the Saxons.

FERRARI. A hint of that distant world.

BORGES. Yes, so that changed everything. One can think of a Saxon reading *The Aeneid* in awe and then deciding to write a German *Aeneid*. That must have happened in the north of England and it employs, moreover, that deliberately artificial language of poetry. For example, not to say 'the sea' but 'the path of the whale' or 'the path of the swan'. Not to say 'battle' but the 'meeting of swords' or 'the battle of men'.

FERRARI. From epic to epic.

BORGES. Yes, from epic to epic. Well, it's just that literature begins with the epic, as you know. That's why in one of our earlier conversations, I pointed out that one of the merits of maligned Hollywood is that of having saved the epic in our time, because, without a doubt, the Westerns are essentially epic. Though this was done with commercial ends in mind, the fact is that the image of the cowboy is an epic one, although perhaps not related to historical reality.

FERRARI. That's an idea we owe to you, Borges. Thus, as a way of concluding this interview, we have a return to our South, to the chronological necessities of our South.

BORGES. Fine.

Borges and Alonso Quijano

●

OSVALDO FERRARI. In your poem 'Alonso Quijano Dreams', you propose or conjecture, I think, at least two dreams . . .

JORGE LUIS BORGES. Ah, if I'm not wrong it could become a dream at three removes for Cervantes dreams up Alonso Quijano and Quijano dreams up Don Quixote. Both dreams have a root, or one of their roots, in Cervantes' consciousness. I think that's what it's about. I wrote that poem so long ago that I cannot recall it but as I'm always writing the same poem, I should.

FERRARI. You say:

The knight was dreamt by Cervantes
And Don Quixote was the knight's dream.
The double dream confuses them.

And that reminds me of another of your stories 'Everything and Nothing'.

BORGES. Ah, that's right, yes.

FERRARI. In which there's a dream at three removes.

BORGES. What is it?

FERRARI. In that case, God dreams up Shakespeare.

BORGES. And Shakespeare dreams up his characters.

FERRARI. Yes, and in this case Cervantes could also be dreamt. Then we would have a dream at three removes.

BORGES. Well, no doubt that Cervantes was dreamt by God or by a universal consciousness, especially if we are pantheists. I have just written a poem titled 'What Did Time Dream?' which sees all history as time's dream—not as facts that happen in space as per the common interpretation . . .

FERRARI. This prompts me to think again that you often seem to see in dreams one of the most crucial realities, realities more solid than waking ones.

BORGES. I'm not sure about solid for the word solid suggests space. Perhaps 'intimate' would be more apt.

FERRARI. As well as durable.

BORGES. Yes, I have written a poem, or I will write a poem—in my case it's the same for I tend to repeat myself—on the theme of a dream before dawn: the dreamer or sleeper wakes up, tries to remember the dream but cannot. Now, what could we suppose? To suppose that the dream has fallen into universal history or out of time is false, for at one time it did exist. And we cannot say much more about anything than that at one time it did exist. I mean, that the lost dream is part of that plot we call universal history or the cosmic process.

And perhaps a no-less-precious part. I recall one of my poems titled 'The Plot'—it's not about a dream but about the dust that gathers on a bookshelf behind a row of books, behind volumes of De Quincey, to be precise, who dreamt so magnificently as we see in *Confessions of an Opium Eater*. I believe that the dust, which forms a kind of cobweb behind the row of books, is no less necessary to universal history or the plot than any other fact—than a battle, for example. Everything is part of that plot whose purpose we ignore—we do not even know if it has an end. Yes, if it has an end, it is, doubtless, inconceivable, given that there's no reason for the universe—a thing of such complexity—to be comprehensible for a man from our era, the twentieth century, on a lost project called Earth. There's no reason why we should understand why there's something as vast as history.

FERRARI. I agree, but the De Quincey anecdote, in any case, would be part of history or an anthology of the spirit, if we could conceive of such a thing. That is parallel but different to material history. And perhaps, again, more durable.

BORGES. Yes, it seems that words die out but what's written remains, what's oral passes but what's written stays. But what's written is also based on what's oral.

FERRARI. It's true, and, according to our conversations, we should try to conjecture that what's oral can also be part of what's spiritual.

BORGES. I think that is right. If not, then our conversations would be inexplicable and unjustifiable. We should try and avoid this. Moreover, in this case, what we say is being recorded, so it's oral and written at the same time. While we are talking we are also writing.

FERRARI. Moreover it's written because it's published.

BORGES. Yes, and that reminds me, not for the first time, of that terrible sentence of Carlyle's: 'Universal history is a text that we are reading and writing continuously and'—here comes the terrible part—'in which we are also written.' That means, not only are we writing symbols but also that we are symbols—we are symbols written by something or someone. We could think of those two words with capital letters so that they are more impressive—written by Something or Someone who we will not know or will perhaps partially know some time.

FERRARI. Coming back to Cervantes, I have often thought that Alonso Quijano's adventures, the dramatic experience of action of a man who, as you say, left his library to become Don Quixote, transmits something very noble, something very hard to express . . . before his encounter with action, after a lifetime of reading in his library.

BORGES. A worthy action, of course. An action for which I am unworthy for I have the impression of never having left the library. Deep down I am still in my father's library. The books have been dispersed, the house no longer exists, the library that looked onto a patio—in that patio there was a vine—all that has disappeared. But, deep down, I am still in that library. I have the impression that all I have done since is false—perhaps those first experiences were my sole ones. Now, something odd occurs to me about memory, something that should alarm me although I am not alarmed, and that is this—I tend to remember what I have read and to forget my actions and all that which has actually happened to me. This reminds me of another quotation, this time from Emerson—I enjoy remembering him—'Life itself becomes a quotation,' that is, in the end, all our past lies within quotation marks, if I can put it that way. So if I think of the past, I think of all the books I have read.

Similarly, but perhaps in a different way, I do the same with people. I was close to Ricardo Güiraldes; we ran a magazine together, *Proa*, founded by Brandán Caraffa, Ricardo Güiraldes, Pablo Rojas and me. And I try to recall Güiraldes, to whom I still feel very close despite the accident, let's call it that, of his death in 1929. I try to remember Güiraldes and what I remember are photos of him, as photographs are still and are more open to memory. On the other hand, a person's face is mobile and is hard to fix in a memory. That happens to me not only with Güiraldes but also if I think of my mother—I remember above all a photo of her, If I think of my father, I remember him in a photo. If I think of myself, I'm not sure if I remember the last time I saw myself in a mirror . . . no, I perhaps remember some photo of myself. Of course, I lost my sight in 1955 and now have no idea of my face. I do not know who looks back at me from a mirror . . . I have no idea.

FERRARI. I must remind you that Alonso Quijano, Cervantes' character, doesn't write in the novel. Thus there's one aspect of action that didn't take place. With you, we could say that the library sprung into action while writing, or, in this case, talking.

BORGES. Well, Alonso Quijano wrote in the sense that when he spoke he gave speeches, didn't he? I don't know if anyone has noticed—I believe that Assens observed it—that there is no dialogue in *Quixote* given that, as the text itself says, there are 'reasonings' between the knight and his page. But these reasonings do not try to be realistic. For example, in a real dialogue, one person interrupts the other; one doesn't finish a sentence because one realizes that the other has understood. Now, all this would have seemed unworthy to Cervantes—literature was something very serious—so, the characters converse. Unfortunately, I would say they converse too well. And I'm sure that they didn't converse that much. The same thing occurred to me as a boy when I read *Martín Fierro*, where after the fight following the posse, the sergeant of the posse, Cruz, and the criminal pursued by the police, Martín Fierro, become friends and Cruz immediately tells Fierro his story. I felt even as a boy that this was false and that doubtless what happened—I don't know where, not historically, but it's what should have happened—is that slowly each one learns about the other's past. I do not believe that Cruz would offer Fierro his biography straightaway, it's a literary convention—perhaps a necessary one for the work but quite unbelievable. No less unbelievable than the fact that they talk in octosyllabic six-line stanzas.

FERRARI. You say, in the poem on Alonso Quijano, 'The double dream confuses them'. And this confusion in the characters between action and dream can often be found in your stories. I'm not sure in the case of Cruz and Fierro . . .

BORGES. I'm sure they did not tell each other about their lives straightaway. We must remember that they were very rustic people, they were two gauchos. I don't think that they were accustomed to autobiographic tales. That would be bizarre.

FERRARI. That's why I say, confused in the very action, in the action faced with the posse in that case.

BORGES. Yes, of course, that episode is completely unbelievable. It's strange that a sergeant of the posse takes the side of the criminal he was meant to arrest and then kills his own men. Its odd that no one has noticed this—everyone just accepts that totally unbelievable act. I wrote that story to justify what seemed to me, even when I was a child, to be unbelievable. It's titled 'Biography of Tadeo Isidoro Cruz'. I called him Tadeo Isidoro after one of my great-grandfathers and so that they could cover, in some way, the brief surname Cruz. Because if one reads Tadeo Isidoro Cruz, the Cruz is hardly heard— Tadeo and Isidoro are two such long and ugly names that they are the ones that are remembered. I am called Isidoro, I must confess, I beg you not to spread this . . .

FERRARI (*laughs*). I didn't know that, it's a true revelation.

BORGES. I hope you do not drop me after knowing that I am called Isidoro (*both laugh*). There's also a San Isidoro of Seville, author of the *Etimologías*.

FERRARI. There's the prestige of saints in this case. But, after reading your story about Cruz and Fierro, that 'Biography of Tadeo Isidoro Cruz', what's hard to imagine is that the reality is different from how it appears in your story.

BORGES. Well, that's the aim of all stories. I remember when I read Capdevila's *Las vísperas de Caseros*, I thought, 'This book is perhaps false but I wish that events had happened as in that story.' It seemed so convincing to me. When I read Gibbon's *History of the Decline and*

Fall of the Roman Empire, the same happened. I said to myself, 'If only things had turned out like that.' The same again after reading Plutarch.

FERRARI. Suddenly literature is more real that a historical chronicle.

BORGES. In the long run, yes, and it's longer than history because events happen once while a text remains for ever.

FERRARI. We were not present during the historical event but we are present at the time of the literary anecdote.

BORGES. Yes, and we are continuously present in front of the text, whenever we turn to it. I don't recall how the poem on Alonso Quijano continues . . .

FERRARI. I just remember three lines:

> The knight was a dream by Cervantes
> And Don Quixote was the knight's dream.
> The double dream confuses them . . .

But I promise to remember the whole poem properly in a future dialogue.

BORGES. No, there's no obligation. I was just curious just as I am every time someone reads me one of my texts. I feel curious, but then lines that I have written come back too many times. Once I have received the revelation I feel cheated. The poem could be splendid, even if those lines are not. They are not splendid but they suggest a good poem which, doubtless, perhaps does not exist.

FERRARI. I would say that they are splendid.

BORGES. Well, they have the virtue of stating clearly what they mean, don't they? And in a way that's not baroque, I mean that is not vanity. It seems simply stated which, doubtless, caused me a lot of trouble. Here I recall something by Boileau who boasted of showing it to Molière, 'The art of making difficult lines easy.' You don't attain easy lines easily. It's a line that has to be pruned.